THE STUART PRINCESSES

ALISON PLOWDEN

SUTTON PUBLISHING

This book was first published in 1996 by
Sutton Publishing Limited · Phoenix Mill
Thrupp · Stroud · Gloucestershire · GL5 2BU

This new edition first published in 2003

British Library Cataloguing in Publication Data
A catalogue record for this book is available from the British
Library

ISBN 0 7509 3238 4

Typeset in 10/12pt Photina.
Typesetting and origination by
Sutton Publishing Limited.
Printed and bound in Great Britain by
J.H. Haynes & Co. Ltd, Sparkford.

CONTENTS

	Genealogical Table	vi
	Note on Dates	viii
ONE	The First Daughter	1
TWO	The Winter Queen	32
THREE	The Storms of War	61
FOUR	The Exile	94
FIVE	A Great Miracle	124
SIX	Madame de France	153
SEVEN	Princess of Orange, Daughter of York	191
EIGHT	The Two Queens	225
	Notes	247
	Select Bibliography	258
	Index	262

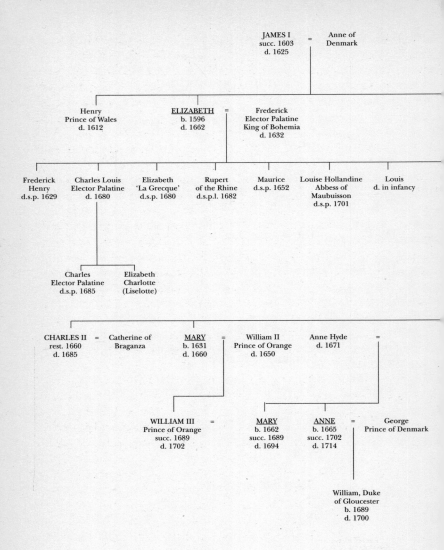

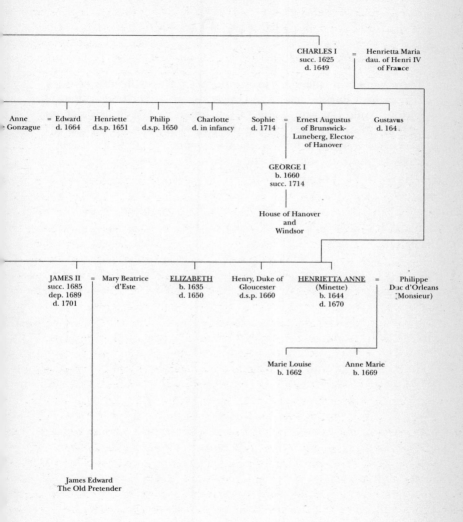

CHARLES I
succ. 1625
d. 1649
= Henrietta Maria
dau. of Henri IV
of France

Anne
Gonzague
= Edward
d. 1664
Henriette
d.s.p. 1651
Philip
d.s.p. 1650
Charlotte
d. in infancy
Sophie
d. 1714
= Ernest Augustus
of Brunswick-
Luneberg, Elector
of Hanover
Gustavus
d. 164_

GEORGE I
b. 1660
succ. 1714

House of Hanover
and
Windsor

JAMES II
succ. 1685
dep. 1689
d. 1701
= Mary Beatrice
d'Este
ELIZABETH
b. 1635
d. 1650
Henry, Duke of
Gloucester
d.s.p. 1660
HENRIETTA ANNE
(Minette)
b. 1644
d. 1670
= Philippe
Duc d'Orleans
(Monsieur)

Marie Louise
b. 1662
Anne Marie
b. 1669

James Edward
The Old Pretender

NOTE ON DATES

There were two calendars in use during the seventeenth century. Continental Europe used the Gregorian or New Style system of dating, while England clung to the Julian or Old Style calendar and was thus ten days behind the rest of Europe. In this book I have used New Style for Continental events, Old Style for those in England and Scotland, indicating when the two overlap.

ONE

THE FIRST DAUGHTER

> . . . that most princely maid, whose form might call
> The world to war, and make it hazard all
> Its valour for her beauty; she shall be
> Mother of nations.
>
> (Ben Jonson)

News of the birth of a princess, the second child and first daughter presented to James VI of Scotland by his wife Anne of Denmark, does not seem to have been received with any particular enthusiasm – in fact some doubt remains as to the exact date and place of the happy event. One source gives 15 August at Falkland Palace. Another records that the queen was delivered 'of a maid childe' on the nineteenth day of August at Dunfermline Abbey, a favourite residence of the royal family.[1]

The year, however, was unquestionably 1596. In England the old Queen Elizabeth, now approaching her sixty-third birthday and the thirty-eighth anniversary of her reign, continued to give every appearance of indestructibility. Indeed, her prestige had seldom stood higher, for the summer of that year had seen the brilliantly successful raid on the port of Cadiz by a large and well-equipped English fleet. From his lair in the Escorial, old Philip of Spain, ancient enemy of England and scourge of Protestants everywhere, swore to be revenged, but everywhere else there was only praise and respectful admiration for the great queen and her amazing seadogs.

In France, the Huguenot King Henri IV had already decided that Paris was worth a mass, but was still having a good deal of trouble securing his throne against the opposition of the ultra-Catholic and pro-Spanish Holy League, while in the Netherlands

1

the Calvinistic Dutch were stubbornly maintaining their resistance to the claims of Spanish imperialism.

In due course the new baby in Scotland would come to play her own part in the complicated cut-throat world of European power politics, but for the moment her parents were concerned only with the matter of her baptism and the choice of godparents. Not that there was any real choice when it came to godparents for this child. Queen Elizabeth might, in the not very distant past, have signed the warrant for the execution of the baby's grandmother, Mary Queen of Scots, but her father, with his nervously cherished expectations of inheriting his formidable kinswoman's throne, knew that he could not afford to miss any opportunity of currying favour in London and messengers were therefore despatched southwards to beg the Queen of England to stand gossip, or godmother, to the latest addition to the family.

This was by no means the first time such a request had been made. Thirty years before Sir James Melville had ridden the same road bringing the joyful news of James's own birth and asking the same favour. On that occasion Elizabeth had sent the Earl of Bedford to Edinburgh with the munificent christening gift of a gold font. Two years before she had performed a similar office for James's first-born, Prince Henry Frederick. Now, for the infant who was to be her namesake, royal generosity was noticeably lacking, for although she agreed, rather grudgingly, once more to stand sponsor, the queen does not appear to have sent any christening present at all – an embarrassing omission which her representative, Robert Bowes of Aske, Treasurer of Berwick, was obliged to gloss over 'in the fairest and most indifferent terms' he could.

The ceremony took place in the Chapel Royal at Holyroodhouse on 28 November. Mr Bowes, as proxy for the queen, held the baby and named her Elizabeth, after which 'she was cryed and called by the Lyon Herald Ladie Elizabeth, first dochtour of Scotland'. Few outsiders were present and it was noted that 'little or no triumph was made but in good fare and cheer, because that it was in winter season and ill weather'.[2] It was also the case that King James had spent more than he could afford on the christening of Prince Henry and was naturally hoping for more sons over which triumph would be made regardless of the season.

The newly baptized princess was now transferred to the custody of Lord Livingstone – Keeper of the Palace at Linlithgow – and his wife Lady Eleanor Hay, in accordance with the usual practice of handing over responsibility for the raising of royal children to some trustworthy member of the aristocracy. Trustworthy members of the aristocracy were few and far between in sixteenth-century Scotland, but the Livingstones had long-standing connections with the royal family – Alexander Livingstone was a nephew of one of Mary Queen of Scots' famous Maries – and they appear to have discharged their office as guardians with exemplary care.

Linlithgow, where Elizabeth Stuart spent most of the first six years of her life, was one of the grandest of Scotland's royal residences. Occupying a strategic position on the main road halfway between Stirling and Edinburgh, it stood in rich green countryside surrounded by parkland and gardens, with a picturesque little loch full of fish on its northern side. Among other amenities, Linlithgow possessed a fine chapel, a Great Hall a hundred feet long by thirty feet wide, with a minstrels' gallery and Long Gallery, and spacious living quarters in which, fifty-four years before, Mary Queen of Scots herself had been born. There was also a turret room known as Queen Margaret's Bower, where Margaret Tudor is said to have watched in vain for the return of James IV from the killing ground of Flodden; in the guard-room below James Stewart, the Regent Earl of Moray, had died of his wounds from an assassin's bullet.

The child in the palace would have been brought up on a rich diet of stories, tragic, romantic and bloodstained, about her more colourful forebears – stories told most probably by her mistress-nurse, Alison Hay, who had been with her from her earliest days. Alison's sister Elizabeth was 'keeper of the coffers', responsible for replenishing the princess's wardrobe, and entries in the Treasurer's Accounts record payments for fine woollen caps or 'mutchis' trimmed with pearling, for five and three-quarter ells of yellow satin 'to be a gown for Princess Elizabeth', and for another gown of fine Spanish woollen frieze, the sleeves to be lined with crimson satin.[3]

As soon as they could toddle, little girls were dressed as miniature adults and in September 1600, when Elizabeth was just four, seven ells of figured velvet, black upon red, were being ordered for another new gown. In March 1600 twenty Scottish pounds – about one-third the value of English currency – had been spent on two pairs of silk shanks or stockings, and in December 1601 a payment of £93 3s 2d was authorized for sixteen ounces of gold and silver lace for trimming two gowns. Another £26 8s went on eight ells of coloured ribands for the sleeves of the princess's nightgown and £11 6s for more trimmings of orange and green crape and for gold and silver fringes to be worn round the neck. Rather more modest items include 8s for a hairbrush, two 'babies' or dolls for 13s 4d, a velvet-covered comb-case and two pairs of embroidered gloves.[4]

Elizabeth remained the first and only daughter of Scotland. Another princess – Margaret – had been born in 1598 but lived for only two years. In November 1600 a second son arrived, so frail that he had to be baptized in a hurry, but against all expectations the infant Charles, Duke of Albany clung tenaciously to life.

Meanwhile, the children's father was having his own problems. Queen Elizabeth's obstinate refusal to nominate him officially as her successor was a long-standing source of grievance, but in recent months certain elements at the English court had been further unsettling James by hinting at the existence of a plot to deprive him of his inheritance. The instigator of this deliberate piece of mischief-making was the maverick Earl of Essex in pursuance of his campaign against Secretary of State Robert Cecil, whom he regarded as a deadly enemy and rival. In the autumn of 1600, a year after his ignominious return from Ireland, Essex sent another messenger north to warn James that unless he took immediate steps to insist on his right to be recognized as heir apparent, he might well find himself displaced by, of all unlikely people, the Spanish infanta, daughter of Philip II, who could claim remote descent from John of Gaunt. Essex, it appeared, had infallible proof that Robert Cecil was preparing to hand England over to the Spaniard and had been heard to say that he could prove the infanta's title to be better than that of any other competitor. The king was therefore urged to send representatives to London with whom Essex could safely confer and agree on a retaliatory plan of action. But by the time a deputation of Scottish diplomats arrived the following spring, they found that Essex had already paid the penalty of treason and instead of discussing with him how best to force the queen to give in to their just demands, they were in nice time to congratulate her on the successful suppression of his rebellion.

In fact, the removal of the Earl of Essex with his paranoia and wild whirling schemes led to a rapid improvement in Anglo-Scottish relations, for Robert Cecil seized the opportunity to assure James's ambassadors that their master had absolutely no need to worry about the future. The English succession had in the past been a major cause of public anxiety and political conflict, but in the years following the death of Mary Queen of Scots the problem had lost most of its urgency. It was now widely accepted that Mary's son, who was after all doubly descended from Henry VII, would eventually come to occupy his great-great-grandfather's throne and although she would never say so, there can be no doubt that Queen Elizabeth had always regarded him as her natural heir. Indeed, he had no serious competitor, with the possible exception of his first cousin, Lady Arbella Stuart. Her claim was dynastically inferior, but it could be argued in her favour that she had been born in the realm, while James was technically a foreigner. She might have attracted some support, for not everyone fancied the idea of a Scottish king. But Elizabeth had never given her any encouragement and Arbella, now in her mid-twenties, had spent practically all her life in the wilds of Derbyshire under the eye of her maternal grandmother, the formidable Bess of Hardwick. It would probably be true to say that outside court circles very few people were even aware of her existence and Robert Cecil meant to ensure that it stayed that way, for he was about to stake his career on stage-managing a smooth transference of power when the time came. He soon had James eating out of his hand, and once that notoriously jumpy individual was convinced that he had at last acquired a competent and trustworthy friend at court, he stopped pestering for recognition, assuring the Secretary that henceforward he would be content to wait for God's good time, rather than hazard the breaking of his neck 'by climbing of hedges and ditches for pulling of unripe fruit'.[5]

James had to wait another two years for God's good time – until the night of Saturday 26 March 1603 to be exact – when Sir Robert Carey, exhausted, muddy and 'bebloodied with great falles and bruses' having ridden nearly three hundred miles in less than three days, arrived at the gates of Holyroodhouse with the news that the old queen was dead at last.[6] Robert Cecil had done his work well and James had already been proclaimed at Whitehall and the cross in Cheapside without a dissenting voice to be heard. There had been no mention of Lady Arbella or of the family of Henry VIII's younger sister named in his controversial will, not a whisper of the Spanish claim. Bonfires were lit and church bells rung to celebrate the new reign and 'every man went about his business as readily, as peaceably, as securely, as though there had been no change, nor any news ever heard of competitors'.[7]

All the same, the new king was taking no chances. He was thirty-six now and had waited long enough for 'kingdoms, glory and immensive wealth' – long enough, too, for freedom from the everlasting self-righteous verbal bullying of the Elders of the Kirk and the ever-present dread of physical violence from his thuggish nobility. In less than two weeks he had said goodbye to his unloved native heath and set out to take possession of the promised land south of the Tweed, closely followed by a large company of hungry Scottish lords, all intent on sharing as much as possible of their master's good fortune.

The queen and the children did not go with him. James had decreed that his wife was to follow him in about three weeks' time, but that his elder son should for the present remain at Stirling Castle where he was being brought up by the Earl of Mar. The queen, however, had other ideas. She had never become reconciled to the separation from her first-born and as soon as James was out of the way, she took herself off to Stirling and attempted to remove the prince from his guardians by force. The attempt failed and as a result Anne, who was pregnant again, 'fell into such an agony of grief and indignation' that she miscarried. After this, the king decided that the family had better be reunited without delay, and by the end of May the queen, Prince Henry and Princess Elizabeth were gathered together in Edinburgh ready to take the road south. Only baby Charles, considered still too delicate to travel, was left behind.[8]

Several English 'ladies of honour' had gone at their own expense to Scotland to attend the new queen, among them Anne Harington, wife of Sir John Harington of Exton, and her daughter Lucy, the Countess of Bedford, and when the royal party reached

Berwick on 3 June they were met by an imposing number of noble personages sent by the Council to escort them to London. These included the Countess of Kildare, born Lady Frances Howard, who was appointed to take charge of the Princess Elizabeth. Separate arrangements were now made for the six-year-old princess 'in regard she was not able to undertake so great journies as her majesty did and so travelled apart from the rest'.[9]

The plan seems to have been that Elizabeth and her entourage should go quietly on at their own pace, joining up with the rest of the party whenever possible at their various stopping-places. Certainly she was present with her mother and brother when they arrived at York on 11 June. Here they rested for three days and were lavishly entertained by the city fathers, who spared no expense in their efforts to demonstrate 'their zealous love and duty'. The queen was presented with a magnificent silver cup, weighing forty-eight ounces and stuffed with gold coins. Prince Henry got a similar, smaller cup with twenty pounds in gold and Princess Elizabeth 'a purse of twenty angells of gold'.[10]

From York the journey continued through a landscape growing ever greener and more prosperous, and shimmering in a summer heatwave. All along the way the country people came crowding to stare and enjoy the rare treat of such a spectacle, for royalty was very seldom to be seen so far from the centre – even the famously peripatetic Queen Elizabeth had never ventured further north than Stamford. All along the way, too, the gentry hurried to pay their respects and satisfy their curiosity, while every gentleman fortunate enough to possess suitable accommodation was pressing with offers of hospitality.

The travellers were entertained by the Earl of Shrewsbury at Worksop and on 21 June they spent a night at Wollaton Hall near Nottingham, home of the Willoughby family. The queen and Prince Henry then made a detour to visit the Earl of Huntingdon, so that Elizabeth reached Leicester ahead of them. Here the little girl was given a formal reception by the mayor, presented with a gift of wine and sweetmeats, which cost the borough 33s 11d, and solemnly escorted to her lodgings in the house of a Mr Pilkington.[11]

The next stop was Sir Thomas Griffin's house at Dingley near Warwick, and on Saturday 25 June the queen and her train, now swollen by 'an infinite number of coaches' belonging to all the great ladies flocking to greet her as she approached nearer the capital, left for Althorp, where they were to be entertained by the wealthy sheep-farmer Sir Robert Spencer. Princess Elizabeth, meanwhile, had been carried off by Lady Harington to her family home at Combe Abbey, a couple of miles from Coventry, and made the rest of the journey independently, arriving at Windsor at the end of the month riding in a litter with her governess, Lady Kildare, and attended by a company of thirty horsemen. 'She had her trumpets and other formalities as well as the best', commented an interested observer.[12]

Two days later she was present when the king held a Chapter of the Order of the Garter, at which her nine-year-old brother was installed a knight, and young Lady Anne Clifford recorded in her diary how she and my Lady Elizabeth's grace had stood together in the shrine in the Great Hall at Windsor to see the king and all the knights sit at dinner. The diplomatic corps was present in force and so great a Court of lords and ladies that Lady Anne thought she would never see the like again.[13]

Later that day the Lady Elizabeth's grace was shown off to the French ambassador – there was already talk of a marriage with the dauphin – and M. de Beaumont reported that the princess seemed very well bred and handsome enough, 'rather tall for her age and her disposition very gentle', but the ambassador thought her 'rather pensive than gay'.[14] It was hardly surprising that the poor child should have appeared subdued – she must have been half stunned by all the violent changes which had turned her life upside-down during the past month.

She remained at Court for a few more weeks, although there is no evidence that she was present at her parents' coronation on 25 July. Most probably she was not, as by this time a worrying increase in the number of reported cases of plague had made it advisable to move the royal children further out of London, and a joint establishment was set up for them at Oatlands, the old Tudor hunting-lodge near Weybridge. This seems to have been the first time brother and sister had spent any consecutive time under the same roof and that holiday interlude in the Surrey countryside may perhaps have marked the beginning of the affectionate relationship between them.

They were not left together for long. Before the end of his first

English summer King James was once again being pursued by enemies, real and illusory, and among those accused of involvement in two plots of at least doubtful credibility were the unfortunate Sir Walter Raleigh, who was to languish protesting in the Tower for the next fourteen years, Lord Grey de Wilton and Henry Brooke, Lord Cobham, husband of the Princess Elizabeth's governess. No one suggested that Lady Kildare, who, confusingly, had continued to use her first husband's title after her marriage to Cobham, was in any way implicated in what, if anything, had been going on, but she was nevertheless relieved of her post. New arrangements were now made for the princess and on 19 October an order was issued under the Privy Seal announcing that the king had thought fit to commit the keeping and education of the Lady Elizabeth to the Lord Harington and the lady his wife. A sum of £1,500 a year was to be allowed for her board, and Harington was authorized to submit accounts for any additional charges incurred, such as travelling expenses, teachers' fees, servants' rewards and lodging, clothes and other 'necessaries for her Grace's person'.[15]

Once again Elizabeth was to be fortunate in her guardians. John Harington, who had been created Baron Harington of Exton in the coronation honours, came from an old established county family whose connections with royalty went back to the days of Edward VI. His cousin, another John Harington, had been Queen Elizabeth's favourite godson, while his wife was the daughter and heiress of Sir Robert Kelway, one-time Surveyor of the Court of Wards and Liveries under the old queen, and his son was already a friend and companion of Prince Henry. Cultured, pious, high-principled and conscientious to a fault, the Haringtons were to devote themselves single-mindedly to the 'great care and honourable charge' entrusted to them. 'With God's assistance', wrote his lordship, 'we hope to do our Lady Elizabeth such service as is due to her princely endowments and natural abilities; both which appear the sweet dawning of future comfort to her royal father.'[16]

After a brief stay at Exton, the Haringtons' Rutlandshire seat, the Lady Elizabeth was taken back to Combe Abbey. As its name suggests, Combe had been a monastic foundation which had passed into lay hands at the Dissolution and eventually to Anne Harington's father, who had converted the ancient home of Cistercian monks into an elegant and comfortable residence, furnished and decorated in the best contemporary taste and large enough to accommodate a princess and her retinue. This included three bedchamber women, a French lady's maid, a sempstress and laundress, a resident physician, two footmen, grooms of the bedchamber, presence chamber and cellar, while in the stables a score of coach, riding and baggage horses required more grooms, yeomen of the horse and sumptermen to look after them. Elizabeth's Scottish nurse was still with her at this time and since his own daughters were now married, Lord Harington recruited his niece, Anne Dudley, to be a companion for her. Then there were the tutors, the music and dancing masters. Not surprisingly, his lordship soon discovered that £1,500 a year was nothing like enough for the upkeep of such an establishment and although he was granted another £1,000 apart from what was required for wages, the honour of bringing up the princess proved an extremely expensive luxury from which his finances were never to recover.

For Elizabeth life now settled into a routine of lessons, family prayers and riding over the Warwickshire countryside. She never received any of the rigorous classical training which had been fashionable for high-born young ladies of an earlier generation and there is no indication that she was at all academically inclined, but she learned French and Italian and her early letters in those languages were probably written as exercises. Her first surviving letter, though, is a little note written between carefully ruled lines and addressed to the elder brother whom she hero-worshipped soon after her arrival at Combe Abbey. 'My dear and worthy brother, I most kindly salute you desiring to hear of your health from whom though I am now removed far away none shall ever be nearer in affection than your most loving sister Elizabeth.'[17]

In April 1604 the princess, accompanied by Lord and Lady Harington and 'many other ladies of distinction', paid a ceremonial visit to Coventry. The mayor and aldermen in their scarlet gowns rode out to greet her and escort her through streets lined with representatives of the various city companies – the mercers, tailors, cappers and drapers all standing arrayed in their best liveries – as far as St Michael's Church, where a sermon was preached before her. (No such occasion was ever complete without a sermon.)

After this the seven-year-old child, enthroned on a dais, dined in state in St Mary's Hall before retiring to the mayoress's parlour which had been specially fitted up for her reception. Here she made polite conversation with the mayoress while the mayor entertained the rest of the company to dinner. The visit ended with the presentation of a silver cup, double gilt, which cost the city £29 16s 8d, and another procession round the city – down Cross Cheaping to Bishopgate, Spon End, Spon Street and Gosfordgate as far as Jabet's Ash on Stoke Green where the mayor left her with Lord Harington and his train, 'who re-conveyed her to Combe'.[18]

After this rare bit of excitement, life at Combe resumed its regular pattern. The Harington family was much admired in official circles for its godly Protestant zeal and the routine of the household was punctuated by religious exercises. Every day began and ended with prayers, meals were preceded by a prayer, a psalm and the reading of a chapter from holy scripture; while on Sundays there were sermons fulminating against the perils of sin, the pursuit of idle pleasure and, of course, the idolatry and general wickedness of the Church of Rome. It was, therefore, unfortunate that so many of the Haringtons' neighbours should have been Catholics, or Catholic sympathizers, still clinging doggedly to the Old Faith in spite of every discouragement the authorities could put in their way. It was also an irony that the best remembered of all Popish plots should have had its origins in some of the remote rural manor houses surrounding Combe Abbey.

The embattled English Catholics had had great hopes of their new sovereign, for in the days when he had feared he might have to fight for the recognition of his title, James had taken steps to cultivate certain foreign Catholic powers and had been heard to make large promises regarding religious toleration. In July 1603 a deputation of Catholic gentlemen was received at Hampton Court and given to understand that it was his Majesty's intention to remit all recusancy fines for as long as the Catholic community remained 'upright and civil in all true carriage towards the King and State'. Then, in September, an embassy arrived from Spain to open informal negotiations over the terms of a treaty to end the war that had been dragging on now for almost twenty years. The English government wanted that treaty and was therefore prepared temporarily to relax its grip on religious dissidence at home. The results were immediate and startling. Over a hundred priests entered the country illegally during the first few months of the reign. The embassy chapels, for long centres of secret worship, were thrown open to all comers and many Catholics who had previously conformed began to venture out of the closet.

It could not go on, of course. Protestant public opinion, as represented by the House of Commons, would never have stood for it and shortly before his first parliament assembled in February 1604, the king issued a proclamation denying that he had ever given anyone cause to expect 'that he would make any innovation in matters of religion'. The proclamation went on to command all Jesuits and other priests to depart the realm, and in his speech to parliament in March James assured the members that he could not permit the increase of the Catholic religion without betraying his conscience. While the king was still apparently prepared to grant a limited amount of toleration to 'quiet and well-minded' laymen, this was a clear sign that the honeymoon was over and before the end of the summer the recusancy fines had been reimposed and a bill for the due execution of the Elizabethan penal statutes had received the royal assent. There was, in fact, no immediate crackdown on the Catholic population – the Spanish peace treaty had not yet been signed and James was still talking about his reluctance to persecute loyal subjects over matters of conscience – but it was in a general mood of disappointment and disillusion over promises broken that the Gunpowder Plot was born.

There were originally five conspirators – Robert Catesby, son of Sir William Catesby of Lapworth in Warwickshire, his friend and kinsman Thomas Winter of Huddington in neighbouring Worcestershire, John Wright, another old friend and Catholic activist, Guy or Guido Fawkes and Thomas Percy, a distant cousin of the Earl of Northumberland. These five met in London in May 1604 to discuss Catesby's remarkable plan 'to blow up the Parliament House with gunpowder' on the first day of the new session and thus kill the king, his son and heir and, with any luck, most of the Protestant establishment.

The original idea had been to dig a tunnel under the parliament building, but this proved impracticable and the plot was on the point of collapsing when, in March 1605, a convenient ground-floor store-room situated just below the chamber of the House of Lords became suddenly available for rent. It remains unclear exactly when government agents first penetrated the activities of Robert Catesby and his friends, but this would seem to mark the point at which Robert Cecil first took a hand in the affair. The conspirators, however, happily unsuspicious, hastened to transfer into their new quarters the gunpowder – some thirty barrels – together with a load of firewood, some large stones and iron bars intended to make the explosion more destructive. By about the first week of May everything was ready in place and Catesby and the others separated, arranging to meet again in London in September.

Catesby himself returned to his home base in the Midlands to organize the military operation which would have to be ready poised to follow up the carnage at Westminster. Always supposing this to have been successful and the king and Prince Henry both dead, the next in succession to the throne would be five-year-old Prince Charles or nine-year-old Princess Elizabeth. Little Charles, though still very delicate, had now been brought down from Scotland and entrusted to the care of Robert Carey's wife. Thomas Percy, who held a minor post at Court, was given the task of seizing him and carrying him off, but Charles was in London and might be inaccessible. Elizabeth, however, at Combe Abbey was no more than some twenty miles from Catesby's mother's house at Ashby St Leger and the Winter estate at Huddington. It should be a simple matter to snatch her 'by drawing friends together at a hunting near the Lord Harington's and Ashby, Mr Catesby's house'. What was needed was a troop of cavalry; local gentlemen, their servants and tenants, well armed and mounted, ready and waiting to escort the new queen to London with the least possible delay.

The plan was not quite as fantastic as it sounds. The mood in the capital in 1605 was very different from that at the time of the Essex fiasco and Catesby intended to issue a proclamation showing that but for the bold action of the Gunpowder Plotters, parliament would have ratified the projected, and deeply unpopular, union between England and Scotland; he hoped that by appealing to the current wave of violent anti-Scottish prejudice he might persuade the Londoners to support his *fait accompli*. First, though, the conspirators would have to widen their circle to include men who possessed the sort of wealth and status necessary for raising an army and, if all went well, for forming a government.

With this end in view, John Grant of Norbrook near Warwick

and Thomas Winter's elder brother Robert, squire of Huddington, had already been enrolled, and later in the summer Sir Everard Digby, Ambrose Rookwood and Francis Tresham were added to the list. These five were admitted to the inner circle of the plot, but various other 'enterprising and discontented gentlemen' approached by Catesby were told only of a plan to raise a new regiment of volunteers to serve under the Archduke of Austria in Flanders.

As autumn approached, the final touches were being put to the plan of action. It was agreed that Guy Fawkes, who had been acting as caretaker and was therefore a familiar figure in the Westminster neighbourhood, should be responsible for actually lighting the fuse that would set off the explosion, using a slow-burning match so as to give himself a margin of about fifteen minutes to get clear. The forces being prepared at the Warwickshire end would rendezvous at Dunchurch in readiness for a 'hunting match' on nearby Dunsmore Heath, last-minute details to be arranged.

After two postponements, the date for the opening of the new session of parliament had been set for Tuesday 5 November but towards the end of October a Catholic peer, Lord Mounteagle, received an anonymous letter warning him to find some excuse not to attend, for 'they shall receyve a terrible blowe this parleament and yet they shall not seie who hurts them'. Much perplexed, his lordship hurried to show this mysterious communication to Robert Cecil, now Earl of Salisbury, and was congratulated on his good sense and good citizenship. Mounteagle was well known and trusted in Catholic circles – Francis Tresham was his brother-in-law – and he was on familiar terms socially with Catesby and the others. He may or may not have been an informer and the anonymous letter may or may not have been a plant, perhaps written by Cecil himself.

Whatever the truth of the matter, the government now had a clear duty to take some action. On Monday 4 November a search began of the vaults and cellars under the parliament building and just after midnight on the morning of the fifth, Guy Fawkes was arrested at the door of the gunpowder store, lantern in hand, slow matches and touchwood on his person. Those conspirators who were still in London – Robert Catesby, John Wright and his brother Christopher, Thomas Winter, Thomas Percy and Ambrose

Rookwood – fled immediately, arriving at Ashby St Leger that same night, having covered eighty miles in a day. They were not pursued. If, as seems all too probable, Lord Salisbury already knew the names and home addresses of some at least of the wanted men, there was no need for pursuit. The local sheriffs had already been warned to expect trouble and, in any case, it would be better to hold off a little and hope to identify everyone concerned in the plot.

Meanwhile, at Combe Abbey, Lord Harington had been living through some anxious days. There were plenty of rumours going about, but little hard news. Then, on 6 November, he received a message from one of his neighbours, telling him that a number of horses had been stolen during the night by armed men believed to be papists. Harington at once wrote off to London asking for instructions; but, as further disquieting reports of papist activity began to come in, he decided to wait no longer and gathering up the Princess Elizabeth, bore her off to the greater safety of the town of Coventry. There was no pomp and ceremony about this visit, only a hurried nervous journey through muddy lanes in the gathering November dusk.

Having seen his 'great charge' comfortably settled in the house of a wealthy merchant, one Mr Hopkins of Earl Street, and guarded by the loyal citizens of Coventry, his lordship rode away in heroic mode to alarm the neighbourhood, surprise the villains and spend five days 'in peril of death'. In fact, the only peril now was for the fugitive conspirators. A correspondent writing to inform Sir Thomas Edmondes in Brussels about the antics of the 'Popish flight-Leads', reported that it was said the rebels had come 'but two hours too late to have seized upon the person of the Lady Elizabeth's grace'. But the rebels were no longer in any position to have contemplated a kidnap attempt. The 'army' which was to have gathered on Dunsmore Heath had melted away and the hard-core remnants, led by Robert Catesby, were retreating westwards with some vague idea of crossing into Wales. They got no further than Holbeach, four miles from Stourbridge on the Wolverhampton road. Here, on Friday 8 November, they were surrounded by a posse led by the Sheriff of Worcestershire and in the subsequent shoot-out Catesby, Percy and the two Wrights were killed, Thomas Winter, Ambrose Rookwood and John Grant wounded and taken prisoner.

The aftermath of the great Gunpowder Treason rumbled on for

several months and the household at Combe took some time to get over their 'sad affright'. In a letter to his cousin, written the following January, Lord Harington complained that he was still suffering 'from the fever occasioned by these disturbances', while the princess herself had not yet recovered from the surprise and was 'very ill and troubled'.[19]

No doubt it had been an upsetting experience – especially for the child of such a family – but Elizabeth seems to have been fully restored by the summer of 1606 when she came up to town for the state visit of her uncle Christian IV of Denmark. To the small girl, her mother's brother appeared as a jovial figure showering treats and presents on the children, but unfortunately his Majesty's visit was also marked by a fixed determination to drink everyone under the table – 'even the ladies abandon their sobriety and are seen to roll about in intoxication.' The other John Harington, experienced courtier and man of the world that he was, was frankly shocked. 'I never did see such lack of good order, discretion and sobriety as I have now done', he wrote, and went on, 'I do often say (but not aloud) that the Danes have again conquered the Britains, for I see no man, or woman either, that can now command himself or herself.' Sir John wished himself back at home and so, most likely, did his careful cousin, 'who doth much fatigue himself with the royal charge of the princess Elizabeth; and, midst all the foolery of these times, hath much labour to preserve his own wisdom and sobriety'.[20]

Lord Harington may well have been relieved when he was able to remove his royal charge from the neighbourhood of these unsuitable goings-on, but the quiet years at Combe were beginning to come to an end. Elizabeth was at Court again for the Christmas season of 1607 and was again inspected and reported on by the French ambassador who found her 'handsome, graceful, well-nourished and speaks French very well'. She was eleven years old now and already growing into a young lady. Although never a classic beauty, she was undoubtedly good-looking as a girl and a young woman, with regular features, large eyes, a clear complexion and a mass of bright auburn hair, but much of the fascination she was to exercise over her contemporaries came from the charm of her natural high spirits and endearing zest for life which, together with quick intelligence and the glamorous aura conferred by royalty, created a strong force-field of personal magnetism.

The princess had now begun to make regular appearances at court functions and by the spring of 1609 was living in a house belonging to the Haringtons down by the river at Kew. In April she was present with her parents at the opening of a row of shops 'richly furnished with wares' built by Lord Salisbury on land adjacent to Durham House in the Strand, and in June attended a bear-baiting at the Tower of London. Although well known to be an animal lover – the account books contain numerous references to her menagerie of pet birds, monkeys and dogs – Elizabeth would have seen nothing incongruous about this. She was, like the rest of the family, a passionate follower of all field sports and would be out on horseback with her beloved elder brother on every possible occasion.

Prince Henry was now approaching his sixteenth birthday, and on Twelfth Night 1610 was host at a grand tournament and banquet intended to mark the beginning of his public career, and show the world 'what a brave Prince they were likely to enjoy'. The tournament – the Prince's Barriers – was closely modelled on the famous Accession Day tilts of Queen Elizabeth's reign, with much dressing up by the contending knights and their retinues and much heavy classical or chivalric symbolism in the *impresas* or devices displayed on their shields. But the staging of this stylized medieval war-game was becoming more and more of a dramatic entertainment, incorporating speech, song and elaborate scenic effects. The barriers of 1610 took place indoors – a variant of the sport evolved by the gentlemen of the Inns of Court where the contestants fought on foot with sword and pike across a barrier – and were held in the Banqueting House at Whitehall. The king was guest of honour but Prince Henry had arranged a leading role for his sister, who presented prizes to the victorious knights and acted as hostess at the feast. The king went home after this, but the young people kept the party going into the small hours.

At the beginning of June came the investiture of the 'High and Mighty Prince Henry Prince of Wales' – an event celebrated by more pomp and pageantry, culminating in a spectacular court masque entitled *Tethys' Festival, or the Queen's Wake*. This remarkable production had been designed by Master Inigo Jones with spouting fountains, dolphins, whales, undersea caverns, pilasters of gold, festoons of seaweed, great shells and other suchlike marvels, and performed by the queen herself as Tethys, Queen of the Ocean, her two younger children and selected ladies and gentlemen of the household.

This was the first time Elizabeth had taken part in the amateur theatricals her mother enjoyed so much, and she appeared as one of thirteen young ladies 'in the shape of nymphs presiding over several rivers'. The princess, as befitted her superior rank, was 'the lovely nymph of the stately Thames, the darling of the ocean', while her cousin Arbella Stuart represented the nymph of Trent. The masque made little demand on the histrionic talents of its performers – mostly they were required merely to sit or stand about the stage in graceful attitudes wearing highly decorative and expensive costumes – but on this occasion considerable interest was aroused by the appearance of nine-year-old Prince Charles, wearing a short tunic of green satin sewn with gold flowerets and attended by twelve little girls, 'all of them the daughters of Earls or Barons', who danced 'to the amazement of all beholders, considering the tenderness of their years'.[21]

Although she was often to be seen with her parents in public – in September the whole family went down to Woolwich hoping to witness the launch of a great ship which unfortunately stuck fast in the dock gates – the princess continued to live at Kew in the charge of Lord Harington. In the spring of 1611 there was a scare that his son might be developing the measles and Harington wrote anxiously to Lord Salisbury that 'albeit none of her grace's servants or those that attend her come near him, yet in respect that this house is little, I have held it my duty to make this known to your lordship, and to crave your opinion whether it be fit her grace be removed or not'.[22]

Even in the seventeenth-century context it seems a trifle odd that Harington should have chosen to address himself to the king's chief minister rather than the fourteen-year-old girl's own mother, but Elizabeth's relations with her parents were of the strictly formal variety and there is certainly no evidence of any warmth of feeling between mother and daughter. Anne of Denmark had known little joy in her marriage and her childbearing record had been a wretched one, losing five babies out of eight. Perhaps not surprisingly she now devoted herself singlemindedly to the pursuit of that life of idle pleasure so deprecated by the preachers of sermons – the scholarly and fastidious Arbella Stuart had been amazed to find herself being expected to play children's games when she first came to Court – and took little apparent interest in anything else.

The king, on the other hand, liked to present himself as a caring, affectionate parent, but to his young daughter he nevertheless embodied the ultimate authority figure and the fate of her cousin Arbella was about to provide Elizabeth with an illuminating example of the ruthlessness of which he could be capable. At the advanced age of thirty-five, Lady Arbella had been unwise enough to fall in love with and secretly marry her distant kinsman William Seymour. She could hardly have made a more tactless choice, for Seymour's descent from the Tudor-Suffolk line represented yet another threat to James, who had always regarded Arbella herself with more than a shade of suspicion, and when the newly-weds attempted to escape to the Continent his suspicion that some dark doings were afoot deepened into certainty. The groom got clear away but the bride did not, and in 1611 Arbella disappeared into the Tower where she remained until her death four years later.

In the circumstances it was natural enough that Elizabeth's youthful affections should have been lavished on her pets, on kind Lord and Lady Harington, on her friend Anne Dudley but most of all on her godlike elder brother. In this she was not alone. The English people had found little to admire about King James, with his off-putting public manner, his queer shambling walk, slobbering tongue and unpleasant personal habits, and very soon the nation's hopes became fixed on the Prince of Wales who seemed to possess every attribute of the ideal Protestant monarch. He was a good-looking boy – tall and strong and well made, with tawny hair and piercing dark eyes. A fine athlete, he excelled at all the manly and martial sports and pastimes. He was also a serious-minded boy, a committed Christian of the fundamentalist variety, who was known to disapprove of the low moral tone of his father's Court and of his father's barely concealed homosexual proclivities. Friction between the king and his heir was therefore inevitable. As early as 1607 the Venetian ambassador had noticed that James was becoming jealous and had commented that the prince would have need of a wise counsellor to guide his steps.

It is not likely that the Princess Elizabeth, carefully guarded by the Haringtons, was much affected by the tensions growing within the family circle. In any case, her future lay elsewhere. In an age when alliances were still commonly sealed by marriage, the value of the daughters of a royal house was still commonly measured, even by their nearest and dearest, in terms of their usefulness as bargaining counters in the game of international diplomacy. Elizabeth Stuart was no exception to this rule and had been conditioned from her earliest years to accept that it would be her destiny to serve her country's interests abroad with her own body.

The French marriage project had lapsed since the assassination of Henri IV in 1610 but there was no lack of competition from other quarters for such a desirable prize and Elizabeth's suitors ranged from the King of Sweden's son and a couple of optimistic but obscure German princelings, to the King of Spain's nephew, Victor Amadeus, Prince of Piedmont. Even the widowed King of Spain himself declared a tentative interest. But James had already decided on a Protestant husband for his daughter and by the summer of 1611 preliminary negotiations were proceeding with the family of young Frederick V, Count Palatine of the Rhine.

Frederick's widowed mother, Louisa Juliana, daughter of the Dutch hero William the Silent and herself a lady of formidable virtue and determination, had long cherished an ambition to see her beloved son matched with the English princess. She did, however, have certain reservations, which she had confided to her brother-in-law the Duke de Bouillon, and in September 1611 the duke found an opportunity to discuss these with Sir Thomas Edmondes, the English ambassador in Paris. Louisa Juliana was concerned that her son was still only fifteen – he was, in fact, almost exactly the same age as the princess – and wondered if King James would agree to delay consummation of the marriage for a short while. Then there was the matter of Elizabeth's exalted rank. Would she be content to accommodate herself to live according to the customs of the Palatinate, or would she expect 'a more chargeable entertainment' than would stand with the constitution of their state to bear? For although that state very much desired the advancement of the match, 'so they did also much apprehend how she would conform herself in the aforesaid point; doubting that, by reason of her great birth, she would introduce the customs of her own education, which would be of too high a flight for their usance to permit'.[23]

Edmondes was reassuring, confident that all the points raised could be satisfactorily answered, but actually Frederick was far from being an ineligible suitor. In terms of ancient lineage he could more than match the house of Stuart. As far back as the tenth century his ancestors had held the office of *Pfalzgraf* or Palsgrave – the Palace-Count of the old Imperial Court. The Count Palatine was now the first secular prince in Germany and senior of the four secular princes entitled to elect the Holy Roman Emperor. He was also, or would shortly become, titular head of the evangelical Protestant Union, founded as a bulwark against the encroaching tide of Counter-Reformation in Europe. From his capital in Heidelberg the elector prince ruled over most of the rich wine-growing country bounded by the Mosel, the Saar and the Rhine. This was the Rhenish or Lower Palatinate, but he also owned the so-called Upper Palatinate, a poorish agricultural district between the Danube and the Bohemian Forest to the east, and thus controlled two key strategic vantage points on the Rhine and the Danube.

Pre-marital Anglo-Palatine negotiations now continued at a stately pace. Such matters were not to be hurried and, as Frederick was still a minor, his uncles John and Maurice of Nassau, and his chancellor, Christian of Anhalt-Bernburg, had to be consulted at every step. His mother began to worry that too much delay might lose them the prize and James hinted that the princess had received other offers and would not be available indefinitely; but these were really only well-recognized moves in the diplomatic courtship dance – King James and the princes of the German Protestant Union both wanted a defensive alliance against the threatened Catholic Bourbon-Hapsburg league – and at last, in May 1612, a deputation from the Palatinate arrived in London empowered to settle the terms of the marriage contract. James agreed to give his daughter a dowry of £40,000 and would also make her an allowance to enable her to live in the style to which she was accustomed. Frederick was to give his bride £1,500 a year pin money and provide for thirty-six male and thirteen female attendants chosen by her to be brought from England. In the event of her becoming a widow, she would have a jointure income of £10,000 a year and be free to live where she chose, but the marriage of her children, if any, were to be subject to the advice and consent of the King of Great Britain, his heirs and successors – it had to be remembered that the Prince of Wales was still unmarried and Prince Charles (now Duke of York) still delicate, and it was highly unlikely that the queen would ever have another child.

July saw the arrival of Colonel Meinhard von Schönberg – or Schomberg, as he was generally called. Schomberg was Frederick's steward, general factotum and righthand man, and brought a formal request from his master to be allowed to come to England. He also brought letters from the Count Palatine to his fiancée and future brother-in-law but, to everyone's amusement, delivered them wrongly so that, instead of a love-letter, Elizabeth found herself addressed as a future brother-in-arms. But once this little mishap had been sorted out, Schomberg's visit passed off smoothly. He was warmly welcomed by the Prince of Wales, who had been an active supporter of the marriage from the beginning, and 'kindly used' by the king. The only sour note was struck by the queen, who made no secret of the fact that she considered Frederick an unworthy match for her daughter, and teased Elizabeth by telling her she would be known as 'Goody Palsgrave'. Nevertheless, Schomberg returned home well pleased and full of enthusiastic reports of the princess's charms. But, having seen something of the grandeur and sophistication of the English Court, he warned that Frederick might be wise to acquire a little extra polish, and dancing lessons were hurriedly arranged.

The stage was now set for the arrival of the bridegroom. Everyone in England, all 'the best affected', that is, were eagerly looking forward to his coming, for the marriage with the Palsgrave of the Rhine, a young and godly Protestant prince, was a popular one and people were ready to be pleased even before they saw him.

Frederick landed at Gravesend at eleven o'clock at night on Friday 16 October, somewhat distressed by the fact that the ship carrying his wardrobe had been delayed and he would be obliged to make his first appearance at Court in his travelling clothes. But there was to be no more delay, and the young man was escorted upriver to Whitehall on the afternoon of Sunday the eighteenth. Although a chilly wind was blowing, the prince stood bravely at the open window of his barge so that the crowds which had gathered in boats and barges and on the river bank could catch a glimpse of him. A salute of eighty guns was fired off at the Tower and then the procession reached Whitehall Stairs to be greeted by Prince Charles and a posse of earls and lords ready to conduct him to the Banqueting House where the family was waiting. It must have been a fairly daunting moment for a boy of sixteen, but it was noticed that the Palsgrave's countenance was 'bold and manly', his approach and general demeanour 'seasoned with a well becoming confidence'. He bowed to the king, who descended from the chair of estate to embrace him, kissed the queen's hand, saluted the Prince of Wales in more familiar fashion and then turned at last to the Princess Elizabeth who, very properly, had not until that moment looked with 'so much as a corner of an eye towards him'. Frederick stooped and would have kissed the hem of her gown, but she made a deep curtsy and 'with her hand staying him from that humblest reverence, gave him at his rising a fair advantage (which he took) of kissing her'.

It was prettily done and soon the prince was gaining golden opinions all round. 'He becomes himself well, and is very well liked of all', wrote John Finet, the Master of Ceremonies, who had been present in the Banqueting House. 'He carried himself with that assurance, and so well and gracefully . . . that he won much love and commendation', added John Chamberlain, writing to Sir Dudley Carleton at the embassy at Venice. The king was much pleased with the 'good and discreet carriage' of his prospective son-in-law and even the queen, 'that was not willing to hearken to the match', was becoming reconciled now that she had met the good-looking, dark-haired Palsgrave. Best of all, it was plain that the princess herself had taken an immediate liking to him.[24]

Frederick had been given lodgings at Essex House in the Strand but spent most of his time in the princess's apartment at Whitehall, refusing invitations to go riding or play tennis and appearing to 'take delight in nothing but her company and conversation'. This was felt to be very suitable loverlike behaviour. Everyone was pleased by the way things were going – especially when it became known that the young Rhinelander was worth 'two hundred thousand pounds by year' – and a lavish programme of entertainments to celebrate the wedding was being planned. No one could have guessed that tragedy of the cruellest kind was waiting to strike.

It was true there had been signs that the Prince of Wales had not been enjoying quite his usual perfect health in the past few weeks, but it was not until he failed to attend a banquet at the Guildhall in honour of the Palsgrave on Thursday 29 October that any real alarm was felt. He was said to be suffering from a fever and a play scheduled for performance on the following Saturday was cancelled. Several members of the family went to see him at St James's Palace over the weekend and he was reported to be 'somewhat amended'. But any improvement was short-lived. The symptoms of fever, diarrhoea, rapid pulse, violent headaches, rigors and mounting delirium – 'alienation of braine, ravynge and idle speeches out of purpose' – grew worse and the doctors, fearful that the illness might be contagious, forbade further visits. This was especially distressing for Elizabeth, who knew that her brother had been asking for her, and she is said to have made more than one attempt to reach him. By Friday 6 November the patient had lapsed into a coma and by that evening Henry, Prince of Wales was dead.

'A jewel whom God and nature only shewed to the world, and drew in again, we being unworthy to possess him', wrote his friend John Holles. The world knew all about the inscrutable ways of the Almighty, but the sudden death of this apparently fit and strong eighteen-year-old was hard to accept and inevitably ugly rumours of poison began to circulate. But the prince was well known to have been careless of his health. He would expose himself to the dangerous night air, he would go swimming in the Thames after supper and only a few days before he was taken ill had played a strenuous game of tennis in cold autumn weather 'in his shirt, as though his body had been of brasse'. John Chamberlain, writing on 12 November, remarked that it was 'verily thought that the disease was no other than the ordinary ague that had reigned and raged all over England since the latter end of summer', and two and a half centuries later a Victorian physician diagnosed 'an historical case of typhoid fever'. More recently it has been suggested that the Prince of Wales suffered a fatal attack of porphyria, the hereditary genetic disorder which seems to have come into the royal family with James V or his daughter Mary Queen of Scots, and which was to reappear through succeeding generations – most spectacularly in the case of George III.[25]

Whatever its cause, Henry Stuart's death left the nation 'much dismayed at the loss of so beloved and likely a prince', and his family and friends shocked and grief-stricken. The Princess Elizabeth in particular was noticed to be 'much afflicted'. Very naturally, thought John Chamberlain, remembering the close relationship which had existed between brother and sister. Indeed, he had heard it said that the last words spoken 'in good sense' by the dying prince had been 'Where is my dear sister?'[26]

Her brother's death was not only a personal grief, it also looked as though it might radically affect her future. Elizabeth was now second in line of succession to the throne and those who, like the queen, had always considered the Palsgrave to be an unworthy match for her, were emboldened in their opposition. In any case, the marriage would have to be postponed until the Court was out of mourning, perhaps until the following summer, and Frederick could not possibly remain in England for so long.

But the king, who loathed all signs of gloom and mourning and who had taken a great fancy to young Frederick, was determined to sweep all obstacles aside. Christmas was kept much as usual and two days later, on St John's Day, 27 December, Elizabeth and Frederick, Count Palatine and Elector, were solemnly affianced and contracted in the Banqueting House at Whitehall in the presence of the king, but not the queen who was absent 'being, as they say, troubled with the gout'. Frederick arrived first, escorted by Prince Charles and apparelled in purple velvet, trimmed with gold lace, which was felt to be 'very fair and suitable'. Elizabeth had solved the problem of making a compromise between joy and mourning by wearing black with a little silver lace and a plume of white feathers on her head, 'which fashion was taken up the next day of all the young gallants of the court and city, which hath made white feathers dear on the sudden'. The ceremony itself was kept simple – 'the late cause of mourning took away the pomp that otherwise should have accompanied this occasion'. The king kissed the young people, gave them his blessing and then 'directed them to go down, hand in hand, some twenty paces or more, into the middle of that great room; where was a carpet spread on the floor for them to stand on'. Sir Thomas Lake, who was deputizing as Principal Secretary, then came forward to read, in French for Frederick's benefit, the words of the contract from the Book of Common Prayer. Unfortunately his translation was so clumsy and his French accent so absurd that the betrothed couple succumbed to a fit of giggles which spread to the standers-by, so that the Archbishop of Canterbury had to step in hurriedly with his solemn benediction.[27]

Frederick, now officially styled Prince Palatine and prayed for in church among the royal family, behaved with truly royal generosity over his New Year gifts. Lord and Lady Harington received gold plate to the value of £2,000. 'All the women about the Lady Elizabeth' got a medal with his picture, and her friend and companion Anne Dudley a chain of pearls and diamonds. The Palatine was equally generous towards his new relations. To Prince Charles he gave 'a rapier and a pair of spurs set with diamonds; to the King a bottle of one entire agate . . . esteemed a very rare and rich jewel; to the Queen a very fair cup of agate and a jewel' and, finally, to his fiancée, a diamond necklace, tiara and earrings, plus 'two pearls for bigness, fashion, and beauty, esteemed the rarest that are to be found in Christendom'.[28]

The betrothal ceremony was regarded as a solemn and binding contract, but Frederick and his family were anxious to set the wedding day. The Prince Palatine would have to go home soon, and he wanted to take Elizabeth with him. At last, after some haggling, it was agreed that the marriage should take place on 14 February, and that the newly-weds should leave together for Germany at Easter.

Wedding preparations now began in earnest and no expense was spared over the bride's trousseau. The embroidering of a single gown cost £200 and, by writ dated 9 January, £3,000 was advanced to the Master of the Wardrobe 'for provision of necessaries for apparel for the Lady Elizabeth's grace'. She had gowns of 'ash-coloured silk grosgraine brocaded with gold and silver', of sea-green tissue, russet cloth of gold and white cloth of silver; petticoats of green satin brocaded with gold flowers, of carnation and murray (mulberry) satins embroidered with gold and silver. She had a 'lappe mantle and cloake' of tawny velvet lined with fur, riding dresses of brocaded satin, hats of felt and beaver, bodices with 'greate sleeves of ye Spanishe facon', and negligees lined with carnation wrought satin. Everything was 'wrought' or embroidered, loaded with Venice gold and silver lace, with Spanish and Venice silk ribbons, with goldsmith's work, fringes, tassels and spangles as demanded by the current fashions which reached a peak of extravagance and ostentation in the early years of the century. The starched and goffered Elizabethan ruff had disappeared, to be replaced by the standing wired lace collar, but bodices were still rigidly stiffened by whalebone, buckram, or canvas and the French, or wheel, farthingale, surely the most ungainly and uncomfortable style ever devised, continued to be worn despite efforts to discourage it in crowded places. Ladies in farthingales were liable to become wedged in doorways and 'this impertinent garment takes up all the room at court'.

There had not been a royal wedding in England for more than half a century – not since Queen Mary Tudor had married Philip of Spain at Winchester in 1554 – and there was considerable warmth of interest, in London at least, over the marriage of this young, handsome and popular couple. There was to be a firework display and a pageant on the Thames for the general public to witness and on 4 February John Chamberlain was writing to Alice Carleton in Venice: 'Here is extraordinary preparation for fireworks and fights upon the water, with three castles built upon western barges, and one great castle upon the land over against the Court. One or two of the King's pinnaces are come already from Rochester, and diverse other vessels to the number of six and thirty are provided.'[29] A week later he wrote again: 'The marriage draws near and all things are ready. On Sunday was their last time of asking [i.e. banns] openly in the chapel. The Queen grows every day more favourable, and there is hope she will grace it with her presence. Here is a band of 500 musketeers made ready by the City to guard the Court during these triumphs, and we have extraordinary watches of substantial householders every night, and an alderman in person to oversee them.'[30]

The firework display and the mock battle on the river were staged in the week before the wedding, and although they were said to have cost upwards of £6,000, John Chamberlain was not overly impressed. The fireworks were only 'reasonably well performed' and the fight upon the water, which was supposed to represent 'a Christian Navie opposed against the Turkes', fell short, in Chamberlain's opinion, 'of that show and brags had been made of it'. There were casualties too, several unfortunates being maimed and hurt, 'as one lost both his eyes, another both his hands, another one hand'.[31]

The wedding itself, however, which took place appropriately enough on St Valentine's Day, appears to have been an unqualified success. In order that as many people as possible might have an opportunity of seeing the bride go to church, her procession followed a roundabout route through the palace, passing through the Presence and Guard Chamber and the Banqueting House, out by the Court Gate, along a gallery to the Great Chamber Stairs, through the Great Chamber and the lobby to the closet leading to the chapel. Whitehall, which covered an area roughly from Charing Cross to Westminster, was a rambling warren of galleries, presence chambers, halls, living quarters, alleys and courtyards, the whole bisected by a public right of way. John Chamberlain, that tireless observer of the social scene, was among a group of spectators watching from a window in the Jewel House and, although he complained that he had not been able to see 'the tenth part of that I wished', was still able to report that the bride and groom were both wearing cloth of silver, 'richly embroidered with silver', and that the bride 'was married in her hair, that hung down long, with an exceeding rich coronet on her head'. Her train was carried by a bevy of young ladies, also in white and silver, and she was preceded by faithful Lord Harington with two bridemen, her brother Charles and the Earl of Northampton, on either side.

In the chapel a raised platform, some twenty feet square and railed off from the rest of the congregation, had been built for the royal party and here the bride, her train managed now by Lady Harington, the groom, supported by his uncle Count Henry of Nassau, the king and queen and Prince Charles took their places while an anthem was sung and the inevitable sermon preached. The Archbishop of Canterbury performed the marriage ceremony, which this time was in English, Frederick having learned 'as much as concerned his part reasonably perfectly'. Bride and groom then went up to the altar for the benediction and Garter King of Arms called for all health and happiness and honour to 'the high and mighty Prince, Frederick, by the grace of God Count Palatine of the Rhine and Prince Elector of the Holy Empire; and Elizabeth his wife, only daughter of the high, mighty and right excellent James, by the grace of God King of Great Britain'. And as the bridal pair processed back to the Banqueting House to the sound of trumpets and cries of 'God give them joy' from the crowds of well-wishers, it seemed that this was indeed a real-life fairy-tale romance – she blonde and radiant; he dark, serious and self-possessed beyond his years, for all that John Chamberlain had pronounced him 'much too young and small-timbered' to undertake the duties of a husband. In fact, Frederick seems to have had no problems undertaking the first duty of a husband, for when the king went next morning to visit 'these young turtles that were coupled on St. Valentine's Day and did strictly examine him whether he were his true son-in-law', his Majesty came away 'sufficiently assured' that the marriage had been consummated.[32]

Although the Court was still officially in mourning, the week after the wedding was spent in non-stop partying. There were masques, revels and 'tryumphs', dancing, banquets, torchlight processions and running at the ring, through all which the 'new-married Bride' was to be seen smiling 'with much cheerfulness' and apparently enjoying herself to the full. As it was still only three months since her brother's death, such cheerfulness might seem to indicate a degree of insensitivity on the part of the bride, but at sixteen it is hard to go on grieving when you have an attentive and generous new husband at your side and an exciting new life opening up before you. In any case, the festivities were about to come to an end. James had spent an alarming amount of money on the wedding and the bills were piling up. Typically enough, his first economy was to dismiss the household he had provided for his son-in-law. The Lady Elizabeth, it was reported, 'took this very grievously and to heart; but necessity hath no law'.

It was nearly time to go. 'We are now preparing for the Lady Elizabeth's departure', wrote John Chamberlain on 14 March. 'I am of opinion her train will not be so great by many degrees as was expected; for we devise all the means we can to cut off expense, and not without cause, being come *ad fundum*, and to the very lees of our best liquor!' But it was not until Saturday 10 April that the royal party left Whitehall by barge for

Greenwich on the first stage of the journey. The river banks and the bridge were packed with cheering, waving Londoners, who had turned out to catch a last glimpse of their princess, and a salute of guns was fired from the Tower. On the Sunday, Greenwich Palace was opened to all who wished to come and pay their respects, and after church Elizabeth stood with Frederick at her side to receive the crowds of strangers who came to kiss her hand and wish her well.

On Wednesday the family was at Rochester, where the king and queen were to say goodbye. Everybody shed tears and the king, unfairly, seized the opportunity to make Frederick promise that in future his bride would be given precedence over himself, his mother and all the other German princes. Prince Charles was to see his sister safely embarked for Flushing and they got as far as Canterbury where, in a sudden uprush of filial emotion, Elizabeth wrote to James: 'I shall, perhaps, never see again the flower of princes, the king of fathers, the best and most amiable father that the sun will ever see. But the very humble respect and devotion with which I shall ceaselessly honour him, your majesty can never efface from the memory of her, who awaits in this place a favourable wind.'[33]

She had to wait nearly a week for news of a favourable wind and before it came Charles was ordered to return home. Brother and sister said an affectionate farewell – they, too, would never see one another again – and at last, on 21 April, Elizabeth and Frederick set out for Margate, where the *Prince Royal* was lying at anchor. This was the same vessel which had once stuck fast in the dock at Woolwich and was named in honour of the Prince of Wales. Did Elizabeth remember how they had once made plans together that he would come with her to Germany and find a Protestant bride there for himself?

Even now there was delay, 'the wind getting easterly and likely to be foul weather', and it was the afternoon of 25 April before the royal couple, Lord and Lady Harington, who were to accompany their princess to her destination, Anne Dudley and their personal servants were finally carried on board the *Prince*, where they were received by the old Lord Admiral. Charles Howard, Earl of Nottingham, had once commanded the fleet against the Spanish Armada and he meant the voyage to Holland taking the king's daughter to her new home to be a fitting end to his long career. They sailed with the tide, anchoring that night 'without the Foreland' and next morning Elizabeth watched the coastline of England disappear below the horizon. It was ten years since she had left Scotland. Now she was setting out on another stage of her journey. It would not be the last.

Two

The Winter Queen

We hear the Palsgrave is crowned King of Bohemia . . . God
send him good success; but surely it was a venturous part, and
likely to set all Christendom by the ears.

(John Chamberlain to Dudley Carleton)

On 25 June 1613, Mr Trumbull, the British resident in Brussels,
wrote to Sir Ralph Winwood, the British ambassador at the
Hague, that 'Sunday last, a gentleman of the Elector Palatine's
passed this way towards England, in Post, to acquaint his Majesty
with the safe arrival of our Princess at Heidelberg. Her Highness's
Physicians do report that in all appearance she should be with
Child. I pray God they prove true Prophets and that with the New
Year her Highness may be the joyful Mother of a fair Prince.'[1]

Elizabeth had reached her husband's capital after a month-long
journey which had taken her to every important town in the
United Provinces, through the Duchy of Cleves to Cologne and
finally down the Rhine to the Palatinate. Everywhere she had been
greeted with heart-warming enthusiasm – with civic receptions,
pageants, banquets and military reviews – while every spare
moment had been filled with hunting parties, fêtes, picnics and
sightseeing. She arrived at the outskirts of Heidelberg on the
afternoon of Monday 7 June, to be greeted by a deafening salute
of massed artillery and to find that all the citizens of the
picturesque little town on the banks of the River Neckar had
turned out to welcome 'the costly pearl which his electoral
highness had stolen in the kingdom of Great Britain'.

The costly pearl was conducted through streets decorated with
flowers and banners and lined with cheering crowds up the hill
to her new home – the great red sandstone castle which

dominated and guarded the town below. All Frederick's immediate family were gathered there to greet his bride, together with all the leaders of Palatinate society and all the neighbouring princes and their retinues who had been invited to join the welcoming committee. To this were now added the English nobles and their wives and attendants who had accompanied the princess, plus the commissioners who were to inspect and take possession of her dower lands. Castle and town were overflowing and it was said that some 6,000 persons were feasted at the elector's expense on the following day. A further week of celebrations had been organized, after which the house-party at the castle began to break up. The distinguished guests departed, the triumphal arches were dismantled and life slowly returned to normal. Lord and Lady Harington remained until the end of July, but at last they too had to say a reluctant farewell and Elizabeth was left, for the first time in her life, without a trusted and familiar counsellor 'able upon any occasion to advise for the best'.

Inevitably there were problems. Already there had been quarrels and jealousies between the English and Scots members of the princess's suite and between the English and German households. Over a hundred English hangers-on who had attached themselves to the travellers were still lingering in the town expecting to be fed and housed, to the understandable annoyance of the authorities, and mutterings of discontent from the good burghers of Heidelberg were becoming increasingly audible. Obviously this was an undesirable situation and since neither the princess nor her husband showed any signs of being able to deal with it, Frederick's man of business, the useful Colonel Schomberg, found himself obliged to sort out the supernumerary English and other domestic difficulties. It was not an easy task. 'I am doing my best', he wrote, 'to put the affairs and the train of Madame in good order . . . but I am fearful that I shall not succeed well. Madame allows herself to be led by anybody, and for fear of giving offence to someone, is almost afraid of speaking to anybody. This makes some of her people assume a little more authority than they should do.'[2]

But while it was an uphill struggle to persuade the charming, if distressingly easygoing, princess to take a constructive interest in household management, it proved impossible to persuade her to take any interest in, or even to admit the existence of, her pregnancy. That autumn, as careful plans were being discussed in London for sending a noble matron and a skilful midwife to Germany to attend the confinement, the Princess Palatine and her husband were out boar-hunting. It seemed as if Elizabeth was hoping that if she ignored the alarming condition which had overtaken her, it might just go away. On 1 January 1614 she felt a trifle unwell and received a visiting French envoy in her private apartments. When M. de Sainte Catherine ventured to express the hope that the New Year would soon see her a happy mother, the princess replied gaily that since everyone was so determined to think her *enceinte*, she would have to believe it herself, and hurried to change the subject. Later that same day she went into labour, without the assistance of either the noble matron or the skilful midwife, and early in the morning of 2 January gave birth to a son attended only by the local doctor, whose services proved perfectly adequate.

The arrival of Frederick junior was greeted with unqualified delight in England and Scotland as well as the Palatinate. Joyful salvoes were fired from the ramparts of Edinburgh Castle. Bonfires were lit and church bells rung in London. The 'little Palatine' was declared a naturalized Englishman and lawful successor to the throne after his mother, while King James conferred a pension of £2,000 a year on the daughter who had made him a grandfather. Prince Frederick Henry, described by his mother as 'a black babie', was christened on 6 March amid scenes of elaborate and expensive rejoicing. He had inherited his mother's robust health along with his father's dark colouring and grew rapidly into a fine sturdy boy.

The next five years were to prove the happiest of Elizabeth's adult life. True, there were still some problems. Frederick had an attack of fever that summer while attending a meeting of the Union of Protestant Princes, both of which left him in a state of deep depression, and his wife became sufficiently concerned to write, somewhat incoherently, to Sir Ralph Winwood that the elector was 'so extremely melancholy as I never saw in my life so great an alteration in any. I cannot tell what to say to it', she went on, 'but I think he hath so much business at this time as troubles his mind too much; but if I may say truth, I think there is some that doth trouble him too much, for I find they desire he should bring me to be all Dutch [that is Deutsch, or German], and to their fashions, which I neither have been bred to, nor is necessary in everything I should follow; neither will I do it, for I find there is that would set me in a lower rank than them that have gone before me . . .'.[3]

Those who wished the English princess to become all Dutch were her mother-in-law and the senior ladies of the Palatinate court, where it had already been noted with an air of faint disapproval that the princess took more pleasure in the hunting-field than in the castle of Heidelberg, charming though its situation was. But the princess, armoured by the self-confidence of youth, good looks and royal blood, remained impervious to disapproval of this kind and had no intention of giving up, or even curtailing, her favourite form of exercise in order to settle down to needlework and prudent Dutch – or German – housekeeping.

On the contrary: 'Every day people beg of Madame and, right or wrong, she cannot refuse', wrote the exasperated Colonel Schomberg. 'Everybody robs her, even to the clothes and jewels she wears; and she gives, not of herself, or from liberality, but through importunities, complaints and tears.'[4] Madame had no resolution, no consideration, was too ready to be generous to the unfortunate and undeserving. Madame, in short, was a sucker for a hard luck story. She would let the very stable boys run after her to importune her and make her believe they were ill-treated, and if any of her servants wanted to visit England, she was easily persuaded to pay their expenses.

Not surprisingly Elizabeth had been getting into debt – she was as vague about money as she was over any subject which bored her – and Schomberg was persuaded to make another attempt to put her affairs in order, drawing up a detailed set of rules for the governance of the household. The situation was made easier by the removal of several trouble-making and inefficient members of her staff and improved still further when, in the spring of 1615, the colonel finally succeeded in his long courtship of Elizabeth's lady-in-waiting. 'I have married Dudley to Colonel Schomberg', announced her mistress triumphantly, and in May she told her father that she was well contented with the service of both.

Schomberg, too, seems to have succeeded in persuading Frederick out of his black mood, though it was noticed that the elector often appeared 'cogitative, or (as they here call it) melancolique'. Young Frederick had a good deal to be cogitative about as he began to face up to the heavy responsibilities involved in his leadership of the German Protestant party, and there were other vexations nearer home arising from the promise so rashly made to his father-in-law that Elizabeth should be granted precedence not only over himself and his mother, but all the other German princes and their wives. So far the point had been reluctantly conceded out of courtesy, but in 1616 Frederick told a visiting English diplomat that he did not feel he could continue to let his wife out-rank him; it was against the custom of the country and the other electors and princes found it strange. Kings' daughters had married into his house before, he went on with unexpected firmness, and been content to give place to their husbands. In any case, on German soil, 'he did compete with the Kings of Denmark and Sweden'.[5] The problem remained a source of potential family discord, but was temporarily resolved by Elizabeth's absenting herself from formal gatherings in order to avoid social awkwardness in Germany and reproaches from King James.

The long arm of King James still reached rather more intrusively than was helpful into his daughter's affairs, and she was still applying to 'the king of fathers' for advice and approval rather more often than was wise. When Colonel Schomberg's bride died tragically in childbirth, the princess turned to England for a replacement 'lady of honour', asking her father to appoint someone of no lesser quality than her former friend and not much different in age. In fact, after some delay, the king sent old Lady Harington, now a widow and in straitened circumstances – the family fortunes never having recovered from the strain of royal wardship – but although the age difference was considerable, Elizabeth welcomed her old governess and 'bonne mère' with delight.

No doubt the Princess Palatine would have been better advised to have made a greater effort to adapt to the customs of her husband's country, but she was still very young and still suffering from bouts of homesickness. None of these early difficulties was insuperable and with a little more time and experience they would surely have solved themselves – especially as everyone agreed that on a personal level the marriage was turning out a great success. It was certainly turning out a success in one vital department. In December 1617, after a gap which was just beginning to be worrying, another 'black babie' made his appearance. Charles Louis was not at first quite so sturdy as his elder brother, but he soon began to thrive and his arrival marked a definite improvement in relations between his mother and paternal grandmother, while 'the happy news of the King's new grandchild at Heidelberg hath caused the streets in London to shine with bonfires'.

The year 1618 was to be the last carefree one that the little family at Heidelberg was to know, but it did contain one disappointment for Elizabeth, who had hoped that she and Frederick would be able to visit England in the summer. However, by the time the invitation arrived she was already too far advanced in her third pregnancy to be able to travel. She still hoped to make the trip, perhaps next year, and in the meantime there were other distractions. The devoted Frederick was building a new wing on to the castle especially for his wife and laying out an English garden for her pleasure, and in April she had received the kind of present she liked best from Sir Dudley Carleton, now *en poste* at the Hague.

Bess Apsley, one of the maids of honour and designated by her mistress as 'the Right Reverend Mrs. Elizabeth Apsley, chief governor to all the monkeys and dogs', wrote to tell Carleton that 'her highness is very well, and takes great delight in those fine monkeys you sent hither, which came very well, and now are grown so proud as they will come at nobody but her highness, who hath them in her bed every morning; and the little prince [Frederick Henry], he is so fond of them that he says he desires nothing but such a monkey of his own'. The new arrivals had been sent as companions for Elizabeth's old monkey, Jack, but he, not surprisingly, was jealous and 'will not be acquainted with his countrymen by no means; they do make very good sport, and her highness very merry; you could have sent nothing would a' been more pleasing'.[6] Her Highness continued to play happily with her monkeys and dogs – at one time she had seventeen of them – and continued to take equal pleasure in slaughtering the surrounding wildlife with her crossbow, in handling which she was said to be very skilful.

The year ended with a birth. Elizabeth's third child and first daughter was born on 27 November and named after its mother. Ominously, the early months of 1619 brought news of two deaths. The first, on 2 March, was Anne of Denmark, at the age of forty-five. Elizabeth had never been close to her mother and it does not seem likely that she was seriously distressed by this bereavement. However, she wrote very properly to James that it was an affliction so great that she had no words to express it. 'I pray God to console your majesty', she continued, 'and for me, I am very sure that I shall regret this death all my life.'

Ironically enough, it was the second death, which occurred barely a week later, that of an old man she had never seen, which was to be the indirect cause of a far more serious affliction and a real lifelong regret. The Hapsburg Emperor Matthias, hereditary Archduke of Austria, Holy Roman Emperor and King of Bohemia and Hungary by election, was childless but nevertheless determined not to allow any of his various fiefdoms to pass out of family control. Two years earlier, therefore, he had 'persuaded' Hungary and Bohemia to agree to elect his cousin and heir, the aggressively Roman Catholic Ferdinand of Styria, as their king. The Hungarians had accepted the situation without enthusiasm. The more independently minded Bohemians, who were predominantly Lutheran, had not and in May 1618 had staged a successful revolt against the Hapsburg takeover bid.

Early attempts at conciliation having failed, the Imperial armies were soon on the march and the Bohemians were only saved by the last-minute intervention of a mercenary force financed by the Elector Palatine and the Duke of Savoy, an old enemy of the Hapsburgs. Unfortunately, it was only too clear that the other princes of the Protestant Union had no intention of making a stand on behalf of the embattled Bohemians. Nor had the King of England. When applied to by his son-in-law, James made it equally clear that he regarded his alliance with the Protestant princes as purely defensive and, in any case, his financial problems just then were such that he could not possibly afford to go to war. He did, however, respond eagerly to a suggestion thrown out by Spain that he should use his good offices in the matter. 'His Majesty', wrote the reigning favourite, the Marquis of Buckingham, to Count Gondomar, 'has promised (very honourably) to do all that he can and that lies in his power, and to finish the business peaceably and quietly, if the Bohemians will listen to him, and are willing to have his advice.'[7]

It does not appear to have occurred to the British Solomon that the King of Spain, another Hapsburg bound to the Catholic Imperial cause by every tie of family and political interest, would naturally be anxious to keep England out of the approaching confrontation on the European mainland. 'The vanity of the present King of England is so great', remarked Gondomar, 'that he will always think it of great importance that peace should be made by his means.' The ambassador therefore recommended encouraging his mediation, since it could not make things any worse and might well do good, by flattering James and keeping him harmlessly occupied.[8]

An expensive – and totally useless – embassy headed by James Hay, Viscount Doncaster, at one time another of the king's young men, was fitted out, but did not leave England until April 1619, nearly a month after the old emperor's death. Considerable interest was now being taken by the English Protestants in the 'combustions' in Germany and a rumour even circulated that 'the Palsgrave shall be emperor'. Not that there was ever any question of that and in August Ferdinand was duly elected at Frankfurt. Almost simultaneously in Prague the Bohemians deposed him and amid scenes of great popular rejoicing offered their vacant throne to the Prince Palatine.

Elizabeth wasted no time in passing this exciting news on to London, writing to Buckingham, whom it was vital to conciliate, that although Frederick would not 'resolve of' the Bohemians' offer until he knew James's opinion, 'the King hath now a good occasion to manifest to the world the love he hath ever professed to the Prince here. I earnestlie entreat you', she went on, 'to use your best meanes in perswading his Majestie to shew himself now, in his helping of the Prince heere, a true loving father to us both.'[9]

Frederick now had to make a decision which would affect the future not only of himself, his family and his principality but of the whole of Germany, for no one could have any doubts that acceptance would mean war with the Hapsburgs. The prince always insisted that he had never sought the Bohemian crown for himself, but at least two members of his immediate entourage – the Duke de Bouillon, his uncle by marriage who had brought him up, and Christian of Anhalt, his most trusted adviser – had certainly considered this useful enlargement of the Upper Palatinate, whose eastern border marched with the Bohemian Forest. It was with this future possibility in mind that they had been so eager to engineer the English marriage and acquire for Frederick influential and supportive in-laws – they could hardly have been expected to foresee the early death of the Prince of Wales.

By no means everyone was in favour. King James very definitely was not, nor was Frederick's mother, who regarded the whole idea with deep misgiving. Almost all the Protestant princes and all the Palatine counsellors advised against acceptance – it was a pity that the intelligent Colonel Schomberg, whose word would have carried weight, was now dead. On the other hand, the martial uncles, headed by Maurice of Nassau, were urging boldness, as were the Prince of Anhalt and Protestant clerics from the Archbishop of Canterbury to his own chaplain. With the Bohemians pressing for an answer, the harassed Frederick hesitated, prayed for divine guidance and finally convinced himself that his was a summons from on high which must be obeyed. 'My only end is to serve God and His Church', he wrote to the Duke de Bouillon.

Afterwards, when it had all gone disastrously wrong, it was his wife who got the blame for persuading a weak-willed husband to over-reach himself to satisfy her personal ambition. This is unfair. Elizabeth may well have been attracted by the prospect of becoming a queen – that old gibe about Goody Palsgrave may still have rankled – but she loved her husband and stories of vulgar nagging have more to do with hostile propaganda than truth. As God directed all things, she wrote in reply to Frederick's anxious request for her advice, He had doubtless sent this also; if her husband felt it advisable to accept, she would be ready to follow the divine call, to suffer whatever God should ordain, and if necessary pledge her jewels and whatever else she had in the world.

Not that Elizabeth made any secret of her pleasure over Frederick's eventual decision. The Rhineland was most agreeable, of course, with its steeply wooded hillsides, picturesque castles, cosy hunting-lodges, vineyards and gardens, but it would not have been surprising if, after five years, the Princess Palatine was beginning to find it a trifle constricting and the solemn routine of the little court more than somewhat dull. Elizabeth resembled her legendary grandmother in more than charm and gaiety and the physical beauty of colour and animation which no portrait could successfully capture; she also shared the Queen of Scots' physical courage, her delight in action and adventure, and, if nothing else, Bohemia surely offered a promise of adventure.

In September 1619 the princess was seven months pregnant and her anxious husband summoned Lord Doncaster, still pursuing his fruitless peace mission round the German cities, to ask for advice on the 'disposing of her during the time of his necessary absence'. Should he leave her in Heidelberg, should he perhaps suggest that she went over to England for a visit, or should he 'lead her up with him into the Upper Palatinate, and as far farther as the importunity of the business drew him'?

Fortunately, since it would certainly not have been a propitious moment for a family reunion, Elizabeth settled the matter herself. After a conversation with her, Doncaster was able to tell Frederick that her Highness's 'owne vehement inclination . . . drew her to accompany him in the whole journey' and gave it as his opinion that to leave her behind would take from her 'the occasion of that which he estimated her greatest happiness, to express her love to him, and her desire to participate in all his fortunes'.[10]

Elizabeth was not the only one to want to share her husband's fortunes. The venture had caught the imagination of the English people, who were burning 'with great and general love towards Frederick and Queen Elizabeth'. Prayers for their success were being publicly offered, and 'there was not a soldier, an officer, or a knight, that did not beg to be allowed to go to the help of Bohemia'. Even young Prince Charles had written to Lord Doncaster that he was very glad to hear that his brother was 'of so ripe a judgement and of so forward an inclination to the good of Christendom'. 'You may assure yourself', he went on, 'I will be glad not only to assist him with my countenance but also with my person, if the King my father would give me leave'.[11] Needless to say, there was no question of any such thing. King James was seriously vexed with his son-in-law, whose rash behaviour seemed only too likely 'to set all Christendom by the ears', and was making it clear to his fellow sovereigns that he washed his hands of the whole affair.

Preparations for the journey to Prague were now well under way. It had been decided that the two younger children should be left in the care of their grandmother, but five-year-old Frederick Henry was to accompany his parents and on Sunday 6 October Frederick senior took the little boy with him to church in Heidelberg, 'there . . . with the joint prayers and tears of his people (of whom at that time he took his solemn leave) with strong cries to beseech Almighty God for his good success'. Next morning the family drove out of the castle and turned east – their possessions loaded on to 153 baggage wagons following behind. It was an emotional moment and Elizabeth shed tears, as she had done once before at the start of a journey. Now she was setting out again on another journey from which there would be no turning back, but this time she was no young bride with a powerful papa watching over her from a distance. This time she was going into the unknown, armed only with her splendidly innocent self-assurance, her cheerful conviction that somehow all would be well. 'What good man would not adventure his life, and run even in the face of death, such a lady going before, and marching in the front?' declared an excitable eye-witness.[12]

Three weeks later the new Queen of Bohemia dashed off a hurried note to the Marquis of Buckingham: 'Yesterday we arrived heire being received with a great show of love of all sorts of people . . . I will write to you more at large for I am now in hast. I pray continue still the good offices you doe me to his Majestie, I am ever Your most affectionat frend, Elizabeth. Prague, this 22 of October' (1 November N.S.).[13]

The arrival at Prague was said to have resembled a Roman triumph and as Elizabeth and Frederick approached the Hradcany Castle, the great fortified complex housing the palace of the kings of Bohemia, they were greeted by a picturesque band of peasants armed with scythes, flails, hatchets and targets. Their leader came up to make a speech in Latin, 'which being finished all the clowns cried out, with a loud voice, vivat Rex Fredericus and made such a tintamarre in clattering their weapons together, that their majesties could not abstain from laughing'.[14] This was rather unfortunate, for these were no comical rustics but descendants of the freedom fighters who had followed Zizka the Hussite in the struggle for Bohemian religious liberty two hundred years earlier.

Inside the walls of the Hradcany, which contained several palaces, monasteries, and churches, including the cathedral of St Vitus, the crowds were so dense and enthusiastic that Frederick hurriedly forbade the firing of cannon for fear of accident. Progress was slow and darkness had fallen by the time Elizabeth reached the entrance to the apartments made ready for her, to be welcomed in a flare of torchlight by a party of ladies who fell on their knees to kiss the hem of her gown and address her in a flood of complimentary but unintelligible Czech.

Frederick was crowned in St Vitus Cathedral on 4 November – the order of service being a somewhat awkward compromise between the native Lutheranism and his own more radical Calvinistic beliefs. Elizabeth watched the ceremony with her ladies and her small son from a gallery specially built for the occasion, and three days later she too was escorted to the cathedral: first to the chapel of St Wenceslaus to be attired in her coronation robes, and then up to the high altar, where Frederick presented his wife to the senior officiating clergyman – one Georgius Dicastus Mirzcovinus, administrator of the bishopric of Prague – with the request that the reverend father would 'deign to bless this our consort, joined to us by God' and to decorate her with the crown royal, to the praise and glory of our Saviour Jesus Christ'.

Elizabeth was now conducted to a throne facing the pulpit to hear the obligatory sermon. A long religious service followed, but at last the royal insignia of orb and sceptre were taken from the altar and the Stuart princess was anointed and crowned queen with the crown of St Elizabeth of Hungary. Cannon banged away from the castle walls, bells pealed from churches all over Prague and the Hradcany was packed with holiday crowds in their national dress as the new Queen Elizabeth, appearing 'very joyous', emerged from the cathedral to walk the short distance to the great Hall of Homage in the old palace for her coronation banquet. Sitting at table, being served by the great ladies of her new country, the crown on her head and surrounded by the emblems of Czech and Hungarian royalty, Elizabeth had come a long way from Combe Abbey. It was a pity that there should have been no official representative from England to witness her moment of triumph – her father was still insisting that she must be addressed only as Princess Palatine – but the ghost of Goody Palsgrave had now been well and truly laid.

A month later, between nine and ten o'clock on the evening of 7 December, the Queen of Bohemia gave birth to her fourth child and third son – yet another fine 'black babie', who was to be given the name Rupert, after his ancestor who had been elected Holy Roman Emperor and King of Bohemia in the year 1400. The queen's safe delivery was greeted with the usual thanksgivings and bell-ringing, but the queen herself was feeling low. Frederick was away visiting the neighbouring provinces of Silesia, Moravia and Lusatia, trying to rally much-needed support for the approaching confrontation with the Empire, and his wife, alone in the Hradcany, fell prey to melancholy and post-natal depression. She had very few English ladies left now to keep her company – Anne Harington had finally retired the previous summer. There was no hunting and no entertaining and she had plenty of time to brood over a disturbing little story being circulated by the Jesuits. Frederick would be a Winter King, they said, who would vanish with the snows.

However, the snows melted, spring approached and Frederick was back in Prague by mid-March in time for baby Rupert's christening and its attendant festivities. The weather improved, the king and queen were able to go hunting again and Frederick's mother came over from the Palatinate on a short visit. The Court was said to be very gay, their Majesties in good health and amusing themselves in the chase. But the appearance of cheerful normality was deceptive. Already there were signs that the people were becoming disenchanted with their new rulers. Elizabeth had unfortunately offended the good wives of Prague by failing to appreciate the significance of a gift of the special bread baked in honour of St Elizabeth, whose basket of loaves for the poor had miraculously turned into roses; while some of Frederick's subjects were scandalized by his unconventional habit of swimming with the townspeople in the River Vltava. The Lutherans resented the efforts of the Calvinists, led by Frederick's chaplain, to strip the churches of their holy images. There was a near riot when an attempt was made to remove the bronze figure of the crucified

Christ from the Charles Bridge – especially as a rumour spread that the frivolous foreign queen had spoken slightingly of this well-loved landmark.

More serious than any of these internal dissensions was Frederick's failure to attract international backing. Spain was predictably hostile, but the hoped-for support from France had not been forthcoming. In Germany, Bavaria and Saxony aligned themselves with the Hapsburgs, while the princes of the Protestant Union remained resolutely uncommitted. Most damaging was the attitude of the King of England. James still clung to his policy of trying to settle the matter by mediation, but the other European sovereigns not unreasonably concluded that if his own father-in-law refused to come to his aid, Frederick's case must surely be hopeless. And so indeed it proved, for Frederick was no war-leader. Well-meaning, conscientious but essentially weak, he was, as John Chamberlain had once remarked in a different context, much too small-timbered for his task and had fatally allowed other people to manoeuvre him into an untenable position.

By August 1620 Maximilian of Bavaria with the army of the Catholic League was moving on the Bohemian frontier. At the same time a force 25,000 strong under the command of the famous Italian general Ambrogio Spinola had left the Spanish Netherlands for an unadvertised but unsurprising destination. 'It is now too late to doubt whether Spinola's large army is designed against the Palatinate', wrote the dowager princess to the King of England; 'it is already at our door.' Louisa Juliana implored James to hasten 'a signal aid' to their dear children, for it would otherwise be impossible to preserve them 'from the bloody hand of our enemies. Your majesty will know also', she went on, 'in what pain is the queen your daughter, and that she is about to be entirely surrounded with enemies; indeed the state in which I lately left her, makes me doubly pity her [Elizabeth was pregnant again]. It is then at this juncture that your majesty may shew himself a good father, as you have always been.'[15]

Long before any response to this somewhat incoherent appeal could have been expected, Spinola had crossed into the Palatinate and the dowager fled from Heidelberg with her grandchildren, two-year-old Charles Louis and his baby sister, to seek the protection of the Duke of Würtemberg.

Meanwhile, Elizabeth's new secretary Sir Francis Nethersole had arrived in Prague and was horrified by the situation he found there. 'Considering those dangers which threaten us from all parts', he wrote on 5 September, 'the indefensibleness of this town against any enemy that shall be master of the field, and the great number of persons ill-affected within it . . . I have presumed, *ex officio*, to solicit all this king's counsellors who came from the palace, to provide in time for the safety of the queen, my master's daughter, and the prince her son, by removing them from hence to some place of surety.'[16] The king, added Nethersole, had this thought 'both in his heart and head, day and night' and was more troubled by it than all the other thorns in his crown.

It was agreed that the little prince must be sent away and six-year-old Frederick Henry departed very secretly for Holland, with his father's brother Louis Philip and as much of his mother's jewellery as could be accommodated in the carriage. But Elizabeth herself refused to budge. 'Her majesty', reported Nethersole, 'out of her rare and admirable love to the king her husband, to whom she feareth that her removing for her own safety might be the occasion of much danger, by discouraging the hearts of this people when his majesty goeth to the army . . . is irremovably resolved to abide still in this town.' In any case, the queen had remarked rather bitterly, where else was she to go? Nethersole could not suggest anywhere safer, 'nor which way to stir her, without more danger than she abideth within this place'. She did not share her secretary's confidence that Spinola would not dare to touch her. He had not hesitated to risk offending James by invading the Palatinate, why should he be afraid to seize her person 'which he may think and say her father hath in a sort abandoned'?[17]

Elizabeth had now almost given up hope of any help coming from home, but she wrote once more, to her brother this time, beseeching him 'earnestly to move his majesty that now he would assist us; for he may easily see how little his embassages are regarded. Dear brother, be most earnest with him; for, to speak freely to you, his slackness to assist us doth make the Princes of the Union slack too, who do nothing with their army; the king hath ever said that he would not suffer the Palatinate to be taken; it was never in hazard but now, and I beseech you again, dear brother, to solicit as much as you can, for her that loves you more than all the world.'[18]

James had allowed a tiny force of volunteers under Sir Horace Vere to embark for the Low Countries, but the only assistance to reach Prague was another 'embassage'. Edward Conway and Richard Weston arrived on 14 October, but although Elizabeth was happy to see them, they were able to offer no more than moral support.

The armies were very close now. 'There are these daily skirmishes', wrote Francis Nethersole from the Hradcany, 'and we can in this town hear the cannon play, day and night, which were enough to fright another queen. Her majesty is nothing troubled therewith; but would be, if she should hear how often there have been men killed very near the king . . . and how much he adventureth his person.'[19]

Frederick was still worrying about Elizabeth's safety. He had given orders for 'her necessaries to be put up in a readiness to be removed upon any sudden occasion', and wrote to her from camp on 1 November suggesting again that she should consider leaving Prague now 'in good order' rather than waiting until the enemy came nearer, when it would look more like flight. 'I beg of you, be not distressed', he went on, 'and believe that I do not wish to force you to go, but only tell you my opinion.'[20]

A week later the king was back in the Hradcany announcing cheerfully that the Bavarians were only eight miles from the city, but that his army of 25,000 was between them and it. He did not mention the fact that his army was an ill-equipped, unpaid, undisciplined rabble, whose generals were more interested in fighting each other than the enemy. On the morning of Sunday 8 November news came in that the Bohemian cavalry had spent the night in the Star Park, about three miles from Prague on the south side, 'and that the horse upon the outflanks of the army did skirmish'. However, reported the English envoy Edward Conway, 'we were invited to dine with the king, where, for aught we could discover, there was confidence enough, and opinion that both the armies were apter to decline than give battle.' After dinner Frederick had intended to go back to inspect the troops in the Star Park, 'but before the king could get out of the gate, the news came of the loss of the Bohemian cannon, and the disorder of all the squadrons, both of horse and foot'.[21]

The so-called Battle of the White Mountain – a broad-topped hill scarred with chalk pits – had lasted barely an hour and was not so much a defeat as a total disaster. Already the panic-stricken Bohemians were pouring down towards the Hradcany in headlong flight – their one idea being to put the river between them and the Imperial forces. There was no question now about leaving, and before the end of the afternoon an unwieldy procession of carriages had emerged from the palace to join the stampede on the Charles Bridge making its way to the comparative safety of the Old Town. So frantic had been the haste that the youngest member of the family was very nearly left behind. Frederick's chamberlain, so the story goes, hurrying through the deserted rooms, had come across a bundle apparently overlooked in the general commotion and, snatching it up, had just had time to throw it on to the floor of the last departing coach, whereupon it had burst into a roar and was discovered to be none other than the infant Prince Rupert.

Prague was packed with refugees and later that evening the English ambassadors, 'pressing through a confused multitude' on the streets, found Frederick 'in a principal citizen's house, accompanied with his blessed, undaunted lady'. Was the undaunted lady perhaps remembering another November day, fifteen years ago, when she had been hurried through the Warwickshire lanes to seek sanctuary in another citizen's house in another town? But this time there would be no happy ending to the story. It was obvious to their anxious advisers that Elizabeth and Frederick must be got away as soon as possible – before the people of Prague who had welcomed them so enthusiastically twelve months earlier decided to try to curry favour with the Emperor by handing them over to the Bavarian army. So, on Tuesday 10 November, the day before the first snows of another winter began to fall, the Winter King and Queen set out on their travels again. Frederick was making for Moravia, in the faint hope of being able to organize a resistance movement, while Elizabeth turned north towards Brandenburg, the territory of Frederick's brother-in-law.

It was not the best time of year for such a journey. Snow on the Silesian frontier had made the roads impassable to wheeled traffic and the Queen of Bohemia was forced to abandon her coach and her baggage waggons and cover the next forty miles riding pillion behind a young English volunteer, Captain Ralph Hopton. It can scarcely have been a comfortable experience for a woman in the seventh month of pregnancy and rumours reached England that the queen had died giving birth to a stillborn child as a result of the hardships she had suffered.

But Elizabeth was not dead. On the contrary, she arrived safely in 'the Elector of Brandenburg's Countrey' in the first week of December and wrote to Sir Dudley Carleton at the Hague with resolute cheerfulness: 'I am not yet so out of heart, though I confesse we are in an evil estate, but that (as I hope) God will give us again the victory. For warrs are not ended with one battle, and I hope we shall have better luck in the next.'[22] Her fifth child, another dark-eyed boy, was born at Cüstrin, a gloomy fortress noticeably lacking in home comforts, on 16 January 1621 and christened Maurice after his great-uncle Maurice of Nassau for, as his mother remarked, he too would have to be a soldier.

Elizabeth was doing her best to put a brave face on things, but there could be no denying that she and Frederick were now well and truly between a rock and a hard place. Bohemia was irretrievably lost. Prague had surrendered without a shot being fired and all resistance in the country had collapsed. Infinitely worse was the loss of the Palatinate – the beloved ancestral homeland – still occupied by Spinola's army and, according to the victorious Emperor, forfeited by Frederick's wilful act of rebellion. Ferdinand was on shaky legal ground here, but the princes of the Protestant Union, mesmerized by the presence of Spanish troops in the Rhineland, made no effective demur when the unhappy Palsgrave was declared under ban of the empire.

It was well known that it was not the custom of the House of Austria 'to set by any affront or forget it quickly' and the Emperor was now intent on demonstrating the truth of this adage by rubbing Frederick's nose in the dust of defeat. Placards appeared on the walls of Brussels and Vienna offering a reward for the return of a runaway king: 'Age, adolescent, colour, sanguine, height, medium; a cast in one eye, no beard or moustache worth mention; disposition, not bad so long as a stolen kingdom does not lie in his way – name of Frederick.'[23] Among the valuables lost in the chaotic aftermath of the Battle of the White Mountain was

Frederick's much-prized insignia of the Order of the Garter and the joke of the king who had run away and lost his garter was seized on with relish. Crude caricatures of Frederick in a variety of humiliating situations, but always with his stockings coming down, were sniggered at all over Europe, while rude songs mostly in Bavarian dialect –

> Oh, if you know, now tell to me,
> Where the lost Palatine can be

– were being sung in taverns and alehouses throughout the empire. Nor was Elizabeth, the king's daughter 'brought to shame for loving her kingly title too well', spared in this offensive propaganda campaign. She was depicted riding away on a swift English steed, heartlessly leaving the people of Prague to their fate; as a lioness with cubs urging her mate to find food for their numerous young; or dragging a cradle behind her, while Frederick trudged ahead grasping a pilgrim's staff.

The homeless condition of the ex-King and Queen of Bohemia was becoming a matter of some concern. 'The Foxes have holes and the Birds of the air have nests, but the daughter of our king and kingdom scarce knows where to lay her head', exclaimed an indignant member of the House of Commons. The Emperor had already made it clear that he would prefer the Elector of Brandenburg to send his sister-in-law on her way as soon as she was strong enough to travel, and it seemed there would be no welcome for her at Whitehall. King James had been seriously alarmed by a report that Frederick meant to come to London, and had sent secret instructions to Dudley Carleton at the Hague that he must be dissuaded 'by all the means you can'. As for his daughter, although his Majesty would naturally 'take great comfort to see her' out of dear and fatherly affection, 'her being here now would, for many reasons . . . be very prejudicial unto the proceedings of that business which we have now in hand for her husband's good'.[24] The last thing James wanted just then was to further inflame his troublesome Puritan subjects by the presence in their midst of their heroine the afflicted Queen of Bohemia.

Fortunately by this time the Dutch had come to the rescue. Apart from their close family ties, the United Provinces had more reason than most to fear the Spanish presence on the Rhine and the strongest motives for wishing to see Frederick recover his Palatinate. A warm invitation to the Winter King and Queen to seek sanctuary in Holland had therefore been despatched by the Prince of Orange, Frederick's uncle Maurice, together with the offer of a town residence at the Hague furnished ready to receive them. The States General even provided an escort of nineteen troops of horse to bring them safely to the end of their journey.

They reached Rotterdam early in April to be greeted 'with much demonstration of affection; the burghers and the whole garrison having been these two days in arms to do them honour'. Two days later Dudley Carleton was writing again from the Hague to report that 'the king and queen, with their whole train . . . passed in boats from thence to the halfway betwixt this and Delft, where they were met by the Prince of Orange and all his court, and so conducted to this town in coaches. The whole way, as well by water as land . . . by reason of a great concourse of people coming from all parts, being like a continued street.' Indeed, the good-natured enthusiasm of everyone 'from the highest to the lowest' showed clearly that the affection of the Dutch was not changed 'by the change of these princes' fortunes'.[25]

The kindness of their welcome came as balm to the wounded feelings of the refugees, and for Elizabeth at least the relief of being able to unpack and relax in friendly and comfortable surroundings. She had left her latest baby behind in Berlin with Frederick's sister, but little Rupert travelled with his parents and they now had the joy of a reunion with their eldest son. But although they had found a safe haven, and a generous one, for the States were granting them a pension of 10,000 guilders a month, neither Frederick nor Elizabeth contemplated making a long stay at the Hague, and Elizabeth wasted no time in appealing once again to her father. 'Your majesty will understand', she wrote, 'by the king's letters, how the Palatinate is in danger of being utterly lost, if your majesty give us not some aid. I am sorry we are obliged to trouble your majesty so much with our affairs, but their urgency is so great that we cannot do otherwise.'[26]

James was not entirely unsympathetic over the plight of his daughter and son-in-law, even though he was still of the opinion that they had brought their misfortunes upon themselves. He, too, wanted to see Frederick restored to the Palatinate and his former position at the head of the Protestant Union, but he had no stomach for military adventures. Parliament, on the other hand, reluctantly summoned in January 1621, positively burned with the desire to avenge the wrongs of its beloved Lady Elizabeth. Unfortunately, the members' zeal did not quite match their willingness – or their ability – to vote the sort of supplies necessary to finance an adequate expeditionary force and the king, greatly relieved, reverted to his preferred diplomatic methods. Yet another 'embassage' was despatched, this time to the Imperial court at Vienna, to try to negotiate the restoration of the Palatinate by peaceful means, but James's cherished long-term solution was an alliance with Spain, sealed by the marriage of his surviving son with the Spanish infanta and conditional on the return of the Palatinate to his son-in-law. He was to pursue this increasingly unpopular and unrealistic policy over the next three years, while the fortunes of the exiles at the Hague steadily declined.

It was during these years that Elizabeth first acquired the other nickname which was to cling to her for the rest of her life. 'The Queen of Bohemia', observed Maurice of Nassau, 'is accounted the most charming princess of Europe, and called by some the Queen of Hearts.' Not unlike her grandmother before her, Elizabeth in adversity was collecting a wide range of admirers. The previous summer the poet-diplomat Sir Henry Wotton had composed a classic sonnet in her honour:

> You meaner beauties of the night,
> That poorly satisfy our eyes
> More by your number than your light,
> You common people of the skies;
> What are you when the moon shall rise . . .

and the Lieutenant of the Middle Temple 'made choice of some three of the civillest and best-fashioned gentlemen of that House to sup with him, and being at supper, took a cup of wine in one hand and held his sword drawn in the other, and so began a health to the distressed Lady Elizabeth, and having drunk, kissed his sword, and laying his hand upon it, took an oath to live and die in her service: then delivered the cup and sword to the next, and so the health and ceremonie continued'.[27]

The king, it was noted, was not amused by this piece of play-acting, nor was he likely to have been any better pleased when addressed by the author of one of the numerous popular tracts promoting the cause of the distressed Lady Elizabeth: 'Sir, God hath made her your daughter, and our princess, and adorned her with so many virtues, as she rather deserves to be empress of the whole world, than lady of a small province . . . and yet will your majesty neglect her and will you not draw your sword in her just quarrel whose fame and virtue hath drawn most hearts to adore, all to admire her?'[28]

Another ally who declared himself at this time was Elizabeth's cousin Christian of Brunswick, a colourful individual commonly known as 'the mad Brunswicker', who proceeded to appoint himself the champion of the Queen of Hearts with the device 'For God and her' embroidered on his banners. He wore her glove in his helmet, promising to return it to her at Heidelberg, and was to assure her that 'as long as God gives me life, I shall serve you faithfully and expend all I have in the world for you'.

Any encouragement was welcome during the summer of 1621. Both Elizabeth and Frederick had been acutely distressed by the news reaching Holland in June of the execution in brutal circumstances of more than twenty of the leading Bohemian patriots who had invited them to Prague, and Frederick not surprisingly showed signs of lapsing into another fit of the black depression which had afflicted him in the early years of his marriage. In August, driven frantic by the inaction insisted on by his father-in-law, he had defied the disapproval of Dudley Carleton and joined the Prince of Orange's army as a volunteer in the renewed war against Spain. His absence was enlivened for Elizabeth by a brief visit from the Countess of Bedford, who had been Lucy Harington, and she was able to enjoy a few days of her old friend's company, hearing all the news from home.

Frederick was back at the Hague by October and Lord Digby, the envoy sent to Vienna, was also on his way home, exhausted by months of fruitless negotiations and convinced that the emperor had no peaceful intentions. For a little while it looked as if England might have to go to war after all and the exiles' spirits rose, only to be dashed again as Spain and Austria in the person of the Archduchess Isabella, Regent of Flanders, came up with another proposition calculated to tempt the King of England into further procrastination. Frederick, it was hinted, might yet be reinstated if he would formally renounce all claim to the crown of Bohemia for himself and his heirs, undertake henceforward to be obedient to the emperor and crave the Imperial pardon on his knees. A document to this effect was drawn up and presented to a reluctant Frederick, who was finally persuaded by Dudley Carleton and Sir Francis Nethersole to drink his cup of humiliation 'roundly and cheerfully' for the sake of a possible peaceful solution. James was also able to exert financial pressure to the extent of £30,000 to pay Horace Vere's English troops still contriving to hold out in pockets of the Palatinate, and to settle some of the debts incurred during the flight from Prague. Frederick's submission was forwarded to the emperor, but he had abased himself for nothing. Ferdinand's only response was to remark nastily that he would rather cherish a crushed snake in his bosom than see the Palsgrave restored to his former dignities.

Elizabeth was pregnant again and in April 1622 gave birth to her sixth child and second daughter. The infant was named Louise Hollandine as a compliment to the Dutch States General, who were invited to be godparents. The little princess's other sponsor was Christian, the mad Brunswicker, who presented her with a large sum of money, recently extorted as ransom from a prisoner of war. The christening ceremony, according to Dudley Carleton, 'was performed with as much solemnity as this place can afford' in the presence of the Prince of Orange and all his court, three deputies of the States of Holland and 'all the ladies of quality of this town'.[29] Christian of Brunswick was not present and nor was the baby's father.

Frederick had slipped very quietly out of the Hague about a fortnight before his daughter's birth on his way to a rendezvous with Christian, the mercenary captain Count Mansfeld and the Margrave of Baden Durlach. He was determined, 'absolutely and fully resolved', to try to regain his homeland by force of arms and, to begin with, things went reasonably well. He joined up with Mansfeld at Germersheim in the Palatinate to the delight of his former subjects and five days later they were able to repulse the forces of the Catholic League. This gave

Frederick the opportunity to return briefly to Heidelberg and have the bitter-sweet joy of revisiting his beloved castle home. It was a very brief visit. The various commanders were already quarrelling. The Margrave of Baden was heavily defeated by the Imperialist general Count von Tilly and his army melted away, while Frederick and Mansfeld marched north through the neutral territory of Hesse Darmstadt, pillaging as they went, and hoping to make contact with Christian. Unfortunately, the Brunswickers had been caught by Tilly and the Spaniards under Gonzales de Cordoba at Hochst on the River Main, a mile or so west of Frankfurt, and forced to fight a fierce engagement, losing 2,000 men and most of their baggage. However, Christian succeeded in crossing the river and joined up with Mansfeld with his cavalry and all-important treasury intact. But they were no nearer recovering the Palatinate. Mansfeld needed to pay and feed his army and insisted on crossing the Rhine and retreating into Alsace, setting fire to towns and villages as he went.

A few weeks of this was more than enough for Frederick. Desperately short of money and pursued by angry messages from London, he released Mansfeld and Christian from their contracts and by July had retired to seek sanctuary with his uncle the Duke de Bouillon at Sedan. There he passed the time bathing and playing tennis and writing love-letters to his wife. 'My thoughts are often with my soul's star, whom I love perfectly, even to death. God sends me many afflictions, and it is not the least to be so far separated from my dear heart, whose portrait I always wear most carefully. . . . Believe, my dear heart, that I often wish myself with you . . . might it please God to grant us some little corner of the world in which we could live happily together, it would be all the happiness that I could wish for myself.'[30] He was also obliged to ask his dear heart for money. 'Living is so dear here, and I have so many extraordinaries to defray for the people who followed me in the army. . . . If you could send me 4,000 or 5,000 florins more, I stand greatly in need of them. . . . If I can once get rid of my horses, of which I still have many, I hope to be a better manager. I am so afraid of inconveniencing you.'[31]

Elizabeth had spent a horribly anxious summer waiting for news. As usual she had done her best to keep up appearances but writing to her old friend Sir Thomas – 'honest Thom' – Roe she let down her guard a little. 'I see it is not good in these days to be my friend, for they have ever the worse luck.' One friend having particularly bad luck just then was Elizabeth's cousin. The mad Brunswicker had lost an arm helping the Prince of Orange to raise the siege of Bergen, but nothing daunted he sent a message to the Hague that he was busy devising 'how to make an iron arm for his bridle hand'.

At the end of September came the news which the Queen of Bohemia had been dreading for months. The garrison at Heidelberg had surrendered to Tilly. 'My poor Heidelberg taken', lamented Frederick. 'All sorts of cruelties have been committed there; the whole town pillaged and the suburbs, which were the handsomest part, burnt.'[32] Three weeks later he was back at the Hague, a place he frankly disliked, and looking so haggard and ill that, according to one report, Elizabeth suffered a fainting fit. Nor were the misfortunes of the Winter King and Queen over even yet. In November Horace Vere, who had been holding out gallantly in Mannheim with his handful of men, was finally obliged to surrender to the Spaniards and of the Palsgrave's rich and beautiful land, with its 'infinite number of good and faire villages', once so 'fruitfull of wine, corne, and other comfortable fruits for man's use', nothing now remained but Elizabeth's little dower town of Frankenthal, where a tiny English garrison was still hanging on by its fingernails.

The loss of Mannheim was almost the last straw as far as Frederick was concerned. 'Of all the ill news', wrote the sympathetic Dudley Carleton, 'which have come to him, like Job's messengers, I have observed none, since his arrival in these parts, to drive him into so much distemper and passion as this, for which the sorrow of her highness's heart (she was present at the reading of the letters), was seen in her watery eyes and silence. God send them both patience.'[33] And at the end of that miserable year of 1622 it certainly looked as if patience would be their only recourse. Dudley Carleton had told his sister, who wanted to send the Queen of Bohemia a present, that the best suggestion he could make would be 'a wheel of fortune turning, made by a cunning hand'.

In February 1623 the emperor bestowed Frederick's electorship on Maximilian of Bavaria and the cause of the Palatinate and of German Protestantism seemed to have reached its lowest ebb. Elizabeth evidently poured out some of her distress to honest

Thom Roe at the embassy at Constantinople, for he wrote in March: 'Most excellent Lady, be your owne queene. Banish all despaire and feares. Be assured the cause in which you suffer cannot perish.'[34] Elizabeth was never downcast for long – 'though I have cause enough to be sad, yet I am still of my wilde humour to be as merrie as I can in spite of fortune.' Already she was busy hatching new schemes for the restoration of their fortune. Christian of Brunswick was 'still constant' and had 'a fair array of 20,000 men'. Bethlen Gabor, the self-styled King of Hungary, her uncle the King of Denmark, the Electors of Saxony and Brandenberg, all were to unite to destroy the Hapsburgs. But without money and strong leadership these hopeful plans inevitably came to nothing, and the wits were saying that 'the Palatinate was likely to have a numerous army shortly on foot, for the King of Denmark would furnish them with a thousand pickled herrings, the Hollanders with ten thousand butter boxes, and England with one hundred thousand ambassadors'.[35]

James was still doggedly pursuing the chimera of the Spanish alliance. 'My father will never leave treating though with it he had lost us all', remarked Elizabeth bitterly. That summer saw the somewhat farcical trip of Prince Charles and Buckingham to Madrid to woo the infanta. Elizabeth's seventh child – a son named Louis in honour of the French king – was born in August as she waited anxiously for news of her brother. She wished him well but could see no good coming from a Spanish marriage, even though the restoration of the Palatinate was mentioned as a condition of the treaty. In the event, the 'courtship' was an unmitigated disaster. Buckingham quarrelled with the Spanish king's chief minister; Charles, who never got to see the infanta alone, was warned by the queen, Isabella of Bourbon, that his suit was hopeless; and the infanta herself was palpably unwilling. Whenever the Palatinate was raised everyone became strangely evasive and by October the two luckless swains were back in England, furious at Spanish duplicity; while the old king, delighted to have his two 'sweet boys' safely home, declared that 'he liked not to marry his son with a portion of his daughter's tears'.

War fever mounted again in London, encouraged this time by Buckingham. 'Since my dear brother's return into England all is changed from being Spanish', Elizabeth wrote exultantly to Thom

Roe; 'in which I assure you, that Buckingham doth most nobly and faithfully for me.'[36] The parliament of 1624 urged the king to show that the English lion had both teeth and claws, and voted three subsidies and three fifteenths, amounting to £300,000, for the support of war with Spain, declaring this to be 'the greatest aid which ever was granted . . . to be levied in so short a time'.

Money, or rather the lack of it, was always a sore subject at the Hague, where the shopkeepers were as eager as any of their most devoted adherents to see the exiles restored to their homeland. Long gone were the days when Colonel Schomberg had reckoned that the Princess Palatine could afford twenty-four new dresses a year, and have plenty over for stockings, ribbons, gold and silver lace and presents. Now, dependent on the generosity of their hosts and an allowance from England, recently reluctantly increased to £1,500 a month, the King and Queen of Bohemia were finding it more and more difficult to maintain themselves and their ever growing family in suitably dignified style. The annual addition, another boy, arrived in October 1624, but that Christmas Elizabeth experienced a new sorrow when the baby Louis, who had always been delicate, died, apparently from the 'breeding of teeth'. 'It was the prettiest child I had', wrote the queen sadly, 'and the first I ever lost.'

Three of the Palatine children, Frederick Henry, who was now ten, Rupert and Louise Hollandine, had been sent to Leiden to board with a Madame de Plessen, who had once been Frederick's governess. One of Elizabeth's daughters was later to complain that the Queen of Bohemia sent her children away because she preferred the antics of her monkeys and lap-dogs. There may have been a grain of truth in this accusation – despite, or perhaps because of, her relentless fecundity Elizabeth's attitude towards her numerous offspring was always a trifle casual – but in boarding them out she was only following the custom of her time and class, besides which accommodation was limited at home in the Wassenaer Hof on the Kneuterdijk. The rest of the family, Charles Louis, young Elizabeth and Maurice, were settled in Berlin with their grandmother and their Brandenburg aunt and uncle, but the king and queen now decided to send for their second son, always his mother's favourite, to join the nursery at Leiden.

All through the summer and autumn of 1624 Elizabeth was in her usual state of waiting – this time for news of the army being recruited in England by Count Mansfeld. That tough and resourceful individual had gone to London in search of employment and been welcomed in the streets as the knight in shining armour who would ride to the rescue of the distressed Lady Elizabeth. At the Hague the distressed Lady Elizabeth was grumbling that she and her husband were being kept in ignorance of what was happening, while Frederick was excluded from any command in the army which supposedly was to restore him.

The army eventually embarked at Dover in January 1625, but its general was hopelessly handicapped from the start by orders not to set foot in any territory belonging to Spain or her allies and to confine his efforts solely to the recovery of the Palatinate. The soldiers, 'a rabble of raw and poor rascals' scraped up from the dregs of the population, ill-equipped and untrained, were landed in Holland in the dead of winter to find nothing prepared to receive them, the States being understandably reluctant to provide for a force which had been positively forbidden to do anything to assist the Prince of Orange. Desertion, starvation and disease did their usual work – 'all day long we go about to seek victuals and bury our dead', complained one of the officers – and the survivors melted away into bands of marauders, looters and murderers.

It was another bitter disappointment for the Winter King and Queen and a humiliation for the all too obviously toothless English lion. But the war which had begun on the White Mountain – the war of Catholic against Protestant, of the Hapsburgs against the rest, which would eventually involve virtually every continental nation state from the Baltic to the Mediterranean – that war would go on and rage intermittently through Central Europe for thirty years leaving the usual trail of death, devastation, famine and pestilence in its wake.

It would not concern the King of England, who had been proud of his reputation as *rex pacificus*. James, at fifty-eight a sick old wreck of a man, died in March. 'You may easily judge what an affliction it was to me to understand the evil news of the loss of so loving a father', wrote his daughter to Secretary of State Edward

Conway: 'it would be much more but that God hath left me so dear and loving a brother as the King is to me, in whom, next God, I have now all my confidence.'[37] To Thom Roe she confided: 'I should have been much sadder, but the comfort of my dear brother's love doth revive me. He hath sent to me to assure me that he will be both father and brother to the King of Bohemia and me. Now you may be sure all will go well in England.'[38]

THREE

THE STORMS OF WAR

> Dear sister, we are, as much as we may, merry; and more than
> we would, sad, in respect we cannot alter the present distempers
> of these troublesome times.
>
> (Charles, Prince of Wales to Princess Mary)

The brother on whom the Queen of Bohemia was placing so
much reliance had grown from the delicate little boy no one had
expected would survive into a healthy, if somewhat undersized,
young man. Charles was twenty-four when he succeeded his
father. Unlike that monarch 'his deportment was very majestick;
for he would not let fall his dignity, no not to the greatest
Forraigners that came to visit him'. The moral tone at Whitehall
also changed abruptly. 'King Charles was temperate, chaste and
serious, so that the fools and bawds, mimics and catamites of the
former court grew out of fashion, and the nobility and courtiers
who did not quite abandon their debaucheries, yet so reverenced
the King as to retire into corners to practise them.'[1]

Debauchery, in short, was out and family life was in at the new
Court, for one of Charles's first acts was to complete the
negotiations already in progress with France for his marriage to
the fifteen-year-old Princess Henrietta Maria, who arrived at Dover
in June 1625. He was also deeply concerned about what to do for
his sister, who was now his heir presumptive. The restoration of
the Palatinate seemed as far away as ever and Elizabeth and her
husband and children were still living in poverty-stricken exile –
so poverty-stricken, in fact, that Charles was obliged to send
money to pay for her mourning and promised a draft of £10,000
to pay her more pressing debts.

Charles had his own financial problems but was nevertheless

determined to keep up the pressure on Spain, and the Spanish ambassador was ordered to tell his master that the Queen of Bohemia had now a king for a brother. After Mansfeld's failure grandiose plans, master-minded by the great Duke of Buckingham, were being made for a naval expedition along the lines of past exploits to seize that well-known will-o'-the-wisp the Spanish treasure fleet, and meanwhile Buckingham was sent on a mission to the Hague with instructions to assure 'our dear and only sister . . . that we intend for the good of her and hers, to make a league, offensive and defensive, with the States of the Low Countries, until both the Palatinates and Electorship be entirely recovered by arms, or otherwise restored'.[2]

Buckingham's ostensible purpose was to conclude a treaty with the Dutch, the German princes and the Protestant powers of Denmark and Sweden, but he had another alliance on his mind, that of his daughter Mary and the Palatine's eldest son, who now stood second in line for the English throne. This had previously been hinted at by the Spanish ambassador in London and angrily denied by Elizabeth but now she had to tread warily. George Villiers, Duke of Buckingham, was at the very height of his power, his influence all-pervasive. It would certainly be unwise to offend him. He was, on the other hand, the most hated man in England and any suggestion that she was in league with him would have destroyed Elizabeth's own popularity at home, still her greatest, if not her only, asset. So she was perfectly charming to her distinguished visitor and carefully non-committal. He, too, was lavish with the charm, with gifts and with promises, but they were empty promises. Charles may genuinely have wanted to help his sister, but he simply did not have the means. Parliament held the purse-strings, and the king was already on bad terms with parliament.

The year 1626 brought another catalogue of misfortunes for the King and Queen of Bohemia. News of the war in North Germany could hardly have been worse. The rising new Imperialist commander, Albrecht von Wallenstein, inflicted a heavy defeat on Mansfeld at Dessau on the River Elbe and by the end of the year the old soldier had died in mysterious circumstances – some said poisoned. Elizabeth's uncle, the King of Denmark, was also badly beaten in the field by Tilly, and in June she lost a valued friend and ally when her cousin Christian, the mad Brunswicker, died of fever.

The baby born that summer – her ninth child and third daughter – gave Elizabeth an unusually difficult confinement – Dudley Carleton's nephew and namesake, who had replaced his uncle as British resident at the Hague, wrote in July that 'the Queen of Bohemia's little infant had such a sudden and great fit of sickness on Sunday, in the evening, that everyone thought it would presently die', and Elizabeth herself told Lord George Goring 'we were fain to christen the girl in haste, she was so sick. I have called her Henriette, after the Queen, who, I hope, will esteem her god-daughter.'[3] Fortunately the baby, the only fair-haired member of the Palatine brood, survived and grew up to be the delicate beauty of the family.

Elizabeth took some time to recover from her childbed. For the first time it seemed as if her splendid constitution was feeling the strain and, according to a contemporary gossipmonger, 'the magnanimous Queen of Bohemia, who hath hitherto, with a fortitude beyond her sex, borne so many calamities undauntedly, is now suddenly marvellously dejected, and will not be comforted'.[4] In England, the Countess of Bedford, hearing that her old friend was sad and unwell, was said to have 'a purpose' to visit her, but before this kindly plan could be put into operation Lucy Bedford herself was dead and the Queen of Bohemia had lost both a link with happy girlhood days and a valuable source of information about affairs at home.

Things were changing, too, at the Hague and not for the better, 'nothing so agreeable as formerly'. Maurice of Nassau had died about the same time as King James and been sincerely mourned by Elizabeth. He had been succeeded by his brother Henry and while the new Prince of Orange was to continue to be a good friend to the exiles he, unlike Maurice, had a wife. The queen knew Amalia de Solms of old. Her father, Count Albert, had been Grand Master or chamberlain in the household of the Elector Palatine at Heidelberg and Amalia, though 'very handsome and good', had been 'one of my women'. It made for a slightly awkward social situation and Elizabeth's friends tended to be on the look-out for slights. 'I know not how it cometh to pass, but I see the wonted respect is much diminished', wrote Mr Carleton to his uncle. 'The Prince of Orange comes seldom, nor yet his wife (though she have more leisure than he), and stayeth little when they come. The French ambassador makes himself a stranger . . . and so it is almost with the rest of those that are of quality, as if all had conspired in neglect.'[5]

It was inevitable that the passage of time and repeated setbacks to her cause should have diminished the Queen of Bohemia's prestige, and important visitors came less and less to the Wassenaer Hof; but, to do them justice, the Prince and Princess of Orange did their best to show her consideration and she was invited to sponsor their son William, born in 1625. Elizabeth presented her godson with a christening gift of a solid gold basin and ewer – this despite her straitened circumstances and the family's ever-mounting debts to the long-suffering tradesmen of the Hague. On 1 January 1628 their unpaid household bills ranged from £16 for the egg-wife to £554 for the chandler, £400 for the butcher and £464 for the poulterer, though characteristically the largest amount outstanding was £1,000 for the stables, 'for oats, hay, straw, smith, etc.'. Part of the trouble was caused by the irregular payment of Elizabeth's allowance from England – and sometimes this was seized by her more determined and desperate creditors before it ever reached her – but it also had a good deal to do with the fact that she never had learned the art of management and was as casual about money now as she had been when a sixteen-year-old bride. 'I know well your custom', wrote Frederick in one of his letters, 'you cannot refuse anything to anybody.'

The King and Queen of Bohemia continued to lurch from one financial crisis to another, but in 1628, by a minor miracle of creative accounting, Frederick contrived to find the wherewithal to start building a country house at Rhenen on the banks of the Rhine in Gelderland. He and Elizabeth both yearned to escape from the stuffy confines of the Hague. In September 1627, towards the end of her tenth pregnancy, Elizabeth was complaining of the discomforts of her condition in a Dutch heatwave, and after the birth of that year's 'black babie' she felt sufficiently unwell to ask the advice of Sir Theodore Mayerne, the Stuart family physician. Not that she had ever had much faith in doctors, being sturdily of the opinion that almost any form of illness was best cured by fresh air and exercise. Out at Rhenen she would 'rumble it away with riding a'hunting'.

Elizabeth and Frederick were at Rhenen in the late summer of 1628 when news reached them that the Duke of Buckingham had been assassinated in a house in Portsmouth High Street, stabbed by an unemployed captain with a grievance. 'I am sorry for it', wrote Elizabeth to Lord Conway, 'and specially to have him die in such a manner so suddenly. It did not a little amaze me; but I am much comforted to see by your letter the care the king, my dear brother, doth continue to take in these affairs that concern me.'[6]

Elizabeth was hoping that without the hated Buckingham, her dear brother's relationship with his parliament might perhaps improve and lead to greater generosity with supplies. What actually happened was a dramatic improvement in the relationship between Charles and his wife. Their marriage had until then been a disastrous affair of public sulks and squabbles, but almost overnight Charles transferred his dependency on Buckingham to Henrietta Maria and thereafter she was to occupy undisputed first place in his heart. The predictable consequence was the queen's first pregnancy, which ended prematurely the following May with the birth of a boy who lived only a few hours.

This was a sad disappointment for the King and Queen of England but the King and Queen of Bohemia had recently suffered a more devastating personal tragedy in the death of their eldest son, drowned in a totally pointless accident in the icy waters of the Haarlem Meer. Frederick Henry was just fifteen and, by all accounts, a particularly attractive and promising youth who frequently reminded his mother of her long-dead brother. For the older Frederick, who had been with his son when their overcrowded packet boat was rammed by another craft in darkness and fog, his death came as the crowning disaster from which he never fully recovered. For Elizabeth, who had just been brought to bed of her fourth daughter, the loss of her 'poor boy' was a bitter grief, but as always it was her husband who mattered most. She was the stronger of the two and now she had to rouse herself to support and comfort him.

Meanwhile, the rest of the family was growing up. Charles Louis, now the heir, and Elizabeth the eldest girl, were eleven and ten respectively and there were six more siblings, seven including the latest baby, coming up fast behind them. So far, out of eleven pregnancies, Elizabeth had lost only one child in infancy, which was a remarkable and most unusual record. Young Elizabeth and Maurice had recently been brought over from Berlin to join the family group, but the family was still not complete.

At the end of May 1630 Queen Henrietta Maria gave birth to a fine healthy boy in St James's Palace. 'He is so ugly, that I am ashamed of him', wrote the mother of the future Charles II; 'but his size and fatness supply the want of beauty.' Later that year there was another baby in the Wassenaer Hof. 'I was born, they tell me, October 14, 1630, and being the twelfth child of the King my father, and of the Queen my mother, I can well believe that my birth caused them but little satisfaction', Sophie of Hanover was to record in her memoirs. 'They were even puzzled to find a name and godparents for me as all the kings and princes of consideration had already performed this office for the children that came before me.'[7] The problem was apparently solved by writing various names on slips of paper and casting lots for the one to be chosen. Sophie, Countess of Hohenlohe and Sophie Hedwig of Nassau Dietz were asked to be godmothers, while the Estates of Friesland were godfathers. This twelfth child, if not exactly unwelcome, cannot be said to have caused much of a stir, and her parents would certainly have been astonished to learn that her son would one day occupy the English throne and found the dynasty which occupies it to this day.

Sophie's mother had more immediate matters on her mind that year. Elizabeth does not seem to have been much concerned by the fact that she was no longer her brother's heir. She was, however, very much concerned by the reports which had been circulating for several months that Charles was planning to make peace with Spain. 'I hear the treaty with Spain goeth on', she wrote to the Earl of Carlisle, once Lord Doncaster, but known to the Queen of Bohemia as 'camel's face'. She did not believe the Spaniards would do anything, 'except it be upon dishonourable conditions', but retained a touching confidence in her dear brother's love and his promise 'not to forsake our cause'.

Sadly, her illusions were to be shattered in the summer of 1630 when Sir Henry Vane arrived in the Hague on a mission of extreme delicacy. He had, in short, to inform the exiles that the Anglo-Spanish treaty, which was about to be signed, contained no mention of their restoration, indeed no mention of the Palatinate other than a vague general promise that the King of Spain would do his best to further Frederick's interests with the Emperor.

It was too much for Frederick, who burst into angry tears and had to be restrained from physically attacking the unfortunate envoy. 'That evening', reported Sir Henry, 'I waited upon the queen, whom I found a little distracted betwixt the love of a husband and a brother; but after I had spoken a while with her, she was very well satisfied, and submits herself, in this and all things else that may concern her, absolutely to your majesty's wisdom.' She had little choice but to do so and to listen to Vane's tactful explanation that really Charles, too, had no choice. He could not rescue the Palatinate single-handed, not without ruining his own kingdom, though he would, of course, continue to do everything possible through diplomatic channels. There was also the point that since the king had now parted company with his disobliging parliament and embarked on his eleven-year experiment of personal rule, any further military adventures abroad were effectively put out of the running.

On the following day Vane saw Frederick again: 'and the first word he said unto me was, that he was reduced to that want and necessity, by the non-payment of the queen's pension, as that, if I had not brought money with me, to supply their present wants, he was resolved to put away all his servants, himself to live obscurely with a couple of men, and to send the queen by the next passage to England, to throw herself at your majesty's feet; for that he was not able to put bread into her mouth.'[8] Frederick had only £200 left in the world, he declared, and did not know where to turn for more, while their creditors had taken to pursuing them in the street.

Vane could only express surprise and regret, and put the blame on the inefficiency of the Lord Treasurer and his officials in London – who in turn protested that the exchequer was empty and credit non-existent. Meanwhile, Elizabeth, 'with tears in her eyes', begged Vane, 'if it were possible, to avoid further disputes', that he would engage his credit and take up £4,500 for the three months that were in arrears. This he did, telling Charles that he 'judged nothing so unfit at this time as to hazard the publishing of these particularities, or the endeavouring of sending your sister for England, which nothing but this course would have prevented'.[9]

Temporarily relieved of her most pressing financial problems, Elizabeth's spirits rose again. The house at Rhenen was now ready for occupation and Henry Vane was invited to stay. 'The situation is agreeable', he wrote, 'and both their Majesties take great delight therein.' Soon they were to have another, more substantial reason to be more cheerful, for by 1631 it had become apparent that the Protestant cause had at long last acquired a champion capable not only of uniting the various factions but of actually winning battles.

Gustavus Adolphus, King of Sweden, had once been suggested as a suitor for the Princess Elizabeth. Now his army was cutting a swathe through North Germany and he was showing an active interest in helping Frederick to regain the Palatinate. In an unusually strongly worded letter, Elizabeth implored her brother to lend his support, 'for if this opportunity be neglected, we may be in despair of ever recovering anything'. If Gustavus became disheartened and made his own peace, 'we shall never have anything, but live to be a burden to you, and a grief and affliction to ourselves and posterity . . . if you do nothing now but treat, I beseech you give me leave to say, that the world will wonder at it'.[10]

But Charles had already allowed the Marquis of Hamilton to raise a small force of Scots and English to serve with the Swedes and had promised to pay for it, on condition that his name did not appear. He was in no position to do any more, so when Frederick went to join Gustavus at Mainz he was obliged to pawn his remaining plate and accept a hand-out of 20,000 francs from the Prince of Orange in order to equip himself for the journey.

The Winter King has always had a bad press from historians for being weak, indecisive and unsuccessful but now, although worn down by misfortune and in failing health – he had been seriously unwell on and off during most of the past two years – Frederick had not hesitated to offer himself as a volunteer, waiting only for the birth of his thirteenth and last child in January 1632 before setting out once more on his travels. Once more Elizabeth was left waiting for news and at first the news was good. Gustavus's triumphal progress continued through the spring and summer and most of the Palatinate was now in his hands. Early in October

Frederick was able to visit the Rhineland again, though everywhere he found devastation, starvation and disease. Oppenheim, where he and Elizabeth had stayed on their wedding journey, was almost unrecognizable. Half the town had been burned and the house they had occupied lay in ruins. But he was still optimistic. The damage would be easy to restore, he wrote. Meanwhile he was moving back to Mainz, where he had been offered accommodation in the castle. He was still there on 16 November when the King of Sweden engaged Wallenstein's army at Lutzen, fifteen miles west of Leipzig. The result was a decisive victory for the Swedes but Gustavus's luck had run out and he was killed on the field of battle. A fortnight later Frederick, too, was dead of a fever – said to be the plague, which was certainly prevalent in the Rhine towns. He was thirty-six but already an old man, worn out with illness, disappointment and the dreadful knowledge of his own inadequacy.

Christian Rumph, the old family doctor who had delivered Elizabeth's first baby, was deputed to break the news to the widow. 'Though Dr Rumph told it me very discreetly', she said later, 'it was the first time that ever I was frighted.' For three days she remained in shock, 'as cold as ice' and unable to cry or speak, eat, drink, or sleep. Her friends feared seriously for her sanity, if not her life. 'I cannot but let you know', wrote Sir John Meauty to a correspondent in England, 'what an afflicted and grieved lady the Queen of Bohemia is for the death of the king. . . . Certainly no woman could take the death of a husband more to heart than this queen doth.' 'Whether the queen will long be able to bear the grief thereof, they who are nearest about her do much doubt', added William Boswell, the new English ambassador at the Hague.[11]

But after a week's seclusion, Elizabeth rose from her bed and prepared to return to the world. She told her brother that she would always be the most wretched creature that ever lived, 'having lost the best friend that I ever had, in whom was all my delight'. She had fixed her affections so entirely upon him that she should have longed to follow him, 'were it not that his children would thus have been left utterly destitute'. Charles had written urging her to make her home in England – 'my dearest sister, I entreat you to make as much haste as you conveniently can to come to me' – but it was not possible. Elizabeth knew that she would now have to fight for the rights of her eldest surviving son as once she had fought for Frederick's and to do that she must stay as near to the scene of the future action as possible. 'I must prefer the welfare of my poor children to my own satisfaction. The last request that their father made me, before his departure, was to do all that I could for them; which I wish to do, as far as lies in my power, loving them better because they are his, than because they are my own.'[12] The children's welfare thus became a sacred trust and gave Elizabeth a much-needed purpose in life. She was missing Frederick more and more every day and told Thomas Roe that she would grieve for him as long as she lived. 'Though I make a good show in company, yet I can never have any more contentment in this world.'[13]

There would be no more little Palatines, but the family of Charles and Henrietta Maria was now increasing steadily. Their second child and first daughter was born at St James's Palace in the early hours of 4 November 1631 and was baptized immediately in the name of Mary because, according to one account, she seemed unlikely to survive. Others hinted that the hasty private ceremony had been intended to save expense. Whatever the reason, the baby soon began to thrive and 'as well our young princess as her majesty are in good and perfect health, so as nothing is wanting to make this joy entire'. The King's second son, James, Duke of York, arrived two years later, and a second daughter was born at St James's on Monday 28 December 1635 and christened Elizabeth by Archbishop Laud in another private ceremony on the following Saturday. So far the queen had been fortunate in her childbearing, but Anne, born in March 1637, was always delicate and died before her fourth birthday 'of a suffocating catarrh, with inflammatory disposition of the lungs'. Another daughter lived for only a few hours but in July 1640 a healthy boy, Henry, Duke of Gloucester, was born at Oatlands without any complications.

The children lived mostly at St James's, or out at Richmond or Hampton Court, but they saw a good deal of their parents and were generally considered to be an unusually close and happy family. Mary's first public appearance was at a family occasion, the christening of her brother Henry. The two elder children were godfathers, while eight-year-old Mary was the only godmother.

By this time, however, troubles were already beginning to crowd in on the royal family. Three years before, the Scots had openly defied the king's ill-advised attempt to foist Archbishop Laud's English prayer book on them, and his equally ill-advised attempt to assert his authority by force of arms had dissipated the reserves accumulated during a decade of prudent housekeeping, so that he had been driven to summon a parliament which proved to be every bit as disobliging as its predecessors. Charles was now in urgent need of friends abroad and was consequently forced to consider for his eldest daughter a match which in normal times he would have rejected as unworthy. He and the queen had hoped to marry the Princess Mary to the King of Spain's heir and perhaps give Elizabeth to Prince William of Orange. But the Spanish negotiations had stalled and in the winter of 1640/1 Prince William's father, ambitious for his son and aware that Charles was desperate for the alliance, upped the bidding, asking instead for the King of England's older daughter. Elizabeth, after all, was barely five years old and said to be a sickly child.

The queen was against the idea and the king usually did what the queen wanted, but the Prince of Orange was prepared to advance him a considerable sum of money, as well as offering a suggestion of mediation with parliament and even perhaps military aid if necessary. There were other advantages. The match would be a popular one. The fifteen-year-old bridegroom was reported to be a good-looking boy, healthy and well advanced for his years, and Mary would have the support and guidance of her aunt Elizabeth when she went to her new home. Charles and Henrietta had little choice but to accept the Orange proposal and by mid-January the bargain had been struck. It was agreed that William should come to England in person for the wedding, but that the princess would stay with her parents until her twelfth birthday. There was the usual formal exchange of letters and portraits, and the commissioners who came over in March to sign the marriage treaty were granted an audience with the queen and Princess Mary. Henrietta Maria expressed a hope that God would bless the union, and when asked if she was willing to have William as her husband, Mary replied very properly: 'Yes, since the queen my mother desires it; and I wish the prince would come to England that we might meet.'[14]

Arrangements for his journey were already in hand and he and his retinue landed at Gravesend at the end of April 1641, to be greeted by the Lord Chamberlain and escorted to Whitehall. Everyone was perfectly civil, but it was noticed that the prince was not permitted to kiss the queen and that his fiancée offered him only her hand and not her cheek. Anyone who could remember the arrival of the young Palsgrave nearly thirty years before must have reflected that then as now there had been reservations as to the bridegroom's worthiness, but this bridegroom too could more than match the Stuarts in matters of ancient lineage.

Originally the Roman colony of Aurangium, Orange, the little city state in Provence, had been recovered from the Moors by Charlemagne in the eighth century and, according to tradition, bestowed on his kinsman Guillaume au Court-nez, whose exploits are celebrated in the romantic *chansons de gestes* of the early Middle Ages. In the twelfth century, Bertrand des Baux, Count of Orange, was given the title of prince by the Emperor Frederick Barbarossa and his descendants played an active part in the complex and blood-stained history of their region, but it was not until the early sixteenth century, when Claude, sister of Philibert, Prince of Orange, married Henry, Count of Nassau, that the interests of the house of Orange shifted north. It entered the international arena when William, called the Silent, who inherited the title in 1544, became the renowned Protestant hero who led the Dutch people in their epic struggle against their Spanish overlords and effectively founded the ruling dynasty in Holland.

The hero's grandson was now making an excellent impression in London. As with his cousin Frederick before him, his pretty manners, his Protestantism and the knowledge that he was a very wealthy young man, all added to his general acceptability. There, however, the parallels ended. True, in the autumn of 1612, family bereavement had cast a shadow over the wedding preparations, but in the spring of 1641 Court and City were engrossed in a political crisis which threatened to develop into a major confrontation between king and parliament. The Earl of Strafford, the king's ablest and most trusted adviser and regarded by the Commons as their most dangerous enemy, lay in the Tower awaiting the passage of a bill of attainder which would mean his execution for high treason – unless Charles could find a way of saving his life.

Understandably in the circumstances nobody was in party mood, and the wedding which took place at Whitehall on Sunday 2 May was a very low-key affair. The nine-year-old bride, in silver tissue and pearls, was escorted to the chapel by her brothers, the princes Charles and James, while the bridegroom, very smart in a suit and cloak of Utrecht velvet embellished with silver and lace, had been fetched from his lodging at Arundel House in the Strand by a posse of lords. The marriage service was conducted by the Bishop of Ely, following the simple form set out in the Book of Common Prayer, 'for so the king had before directed'. Charles gave his daughter away and William put a plain gold ring on her finger.

The Catholic Henrietta Maria watched the Protestant ceremony from the window of her private closet and another member of the family was also absent from the congregation. Charles Louis, the dispossessed and unrecognized Prince Palatine, had been haunting his uncle's court on and off for the last five or six years, the perennial poor relation, and had returned uninvited a few days before the wedding, announcing that he hoped to further his interests by his presence during the meeting of parliament and the negotiations of the Dutch ambassadors. According to the Venetian ambassador, the king and queen were not pleased, and their annoyance was increased when Charles Louis began to spread it around that he had always believed his cousin Mary was promised to *him* – an optimistic notion in which his mother seems to have encouraged him – and ostentatiously stayed away from the chapel.

The ceremony was followed by a family dinner party and afterwards the queen and the young people walked in Hyde Park until suppertime. Later that evening the newly married couple had to go through the ritual of being ceremonially put to bed. Mary was undressed in the queen's chamber in the presence of her mother and as many of the high-ranking peeresses as could squeeze into the room, and arranged in the state bed with its blue velvet curtains and gold and silver fringe. Prince William, in dressing-gown and slippers, was then led through the crush by the king and the princes and, after kissing the princess, lay down beside her for about a quarter of an hour 'in the presence of all the great lords and ladies of England, the four ambassadors of the

United [Dutch] States, and the distinguished personages who had attended him to London'. In order for the marriage to be pronounced officially 'consummated' the children's bare legs had to touch, and when it was discovered that Mary's nightgown reached modestly to her ankles, the queen's dwarf, Geoffrey Hudson, produced a pair of shears to slit the garment, amid much merriment from the standers-by.

Young William seems to have been pleased with his bride. 'At the beginning we have been a little serious', he wrote to his father, 'but now we are very free together. I think she is far more beautiful than her picture, and love her very much and think she loves me also.'[15] They had about three weeks to get to know each other, but there were none of the festivities which would normally have accompanied a royal wedding. Instead the streets around Westminster and Whitehall seethed with hostile crowds baying for the blood of the unfortunate Earl of Strafford, and threatening to invade the precincts of the palace itself. Finally, on 10 May, the king was forced to surrender to overwhelming pressure. He signed the attainder and Strafford was beheaded two days later. Not that the sacrifice did anything to appease the House of Commons which, led by the implacable John Pym, was now busy attacking the independent power of the Crown by every means open to it.

The Catholic queen was, of course, a prime target and when, in July, Charles attempted to send his wife abroad for the sake of her health and to take Mary to the Hague, the Commons objected – suspecting, quite correctly, that she meant to stir up trouble in foreign parts. A committee was set up to cross-examine her doctor, who failed to satisfy the members that there was anything much the matter with the queen, apart from an unquiet mind. As for the princess, they positively could not agree that she should join her husband until she was old enough to be a wife. The plan had, therefore, to be abandoned and Henrietta retreated gloomily to Oatlands, while the king embarked on a journey north where he hoped to conciliate the Scots.

By the time he returned, towards the end of November, public opinion had shifted in his favour and there seems to have been a general feeling that things had gone far enough. The tradition of reverence for the monarchy lay very deep in the English psyche – besides which the more thoughtful element of the propertied, taxpaying class was beginning to have an uncomfortable suspicion that parliament could prove just as heavy-handed and expensive a master. At all events, it was clear that a significant number of his subjects were prepared to give the king another chance.

The queen and the children had gone out to meet him at Theobalds, the Cecils' old palace in Hertfordshire, and when they entered the City at Moorgate they found the streets gay with hangings, the conduits running with wine and the people, who barely six months earlier had been ready to form a lynch mob, cheering a loyal welcome. The family was entertained at a civic banquet at the Guildhall – Princess Mary, now just ten years old, sitting between her mother and the young Duke of York – and afterwards rode back to Whitehall in something very like triumph. At St Paul's the choir came out to greet them with an anthem and all the way home down Fleet Street and the Strand more cheering crowds lit their way with torches through the November dusk.[16]

Sadly this demonstration of 'great acclamations and joy of the giddy people' was a passing phenomenon. John Pym and his party had gone too far now to retreat, even if they had wanted to, and the king's habitual bad luck and bad judgement continued to combine fatally against him. Rebellion in Ireland that autumn, together with reports of a massacre of the Protestant settlers, provoked a fresh outburst of anti-Catholic hysteria. It was persistently rumoured that the queen had been in contact with the Irish chieftains and that she, too, was to be impeached. London was once more in an uproar and once more angry mobs roamed the streets shouting 'No bishops' and 'No popish lords'. There were some ill-tempered confrontations between the king's officers and City apprentices, on the loose over the Christmas holidays, and for the first time the opprobrious epithets of Roundhead and Cavalier were being flung around.[17]

The old year ended in disorder, bitterness and fear. The new year began with the disastrous fiasco of the Five Members. On 4 January, the king, in a desperate bid to regain the initiative descended on the House of Commons at the head of several hundred armed guards. He entered the Chamber hoping to arrest the five members he regarded as ringleaders, only to find that the birds, forewarned, had flown.

This was the end of London. Charles had committed the ultimate folly of engaging in a violent and unlawful act, and failing. On 10 January the king and queen with the three older children left precipitately for Hampton Court in what looked very like flight. The next day the five members emerged from their hiding-places in the City and returned to Westminster in triumph. As they passed the deserted royal apartments there were derisive cries of 'Where is the king and his Cavaliers?'[18]

The king and his family had passed an uncomfortable night at Hampton Court, which had been quite unprepared for their arrival so that they had been obliged to share one room and one bed. They moved on to Windsor, but it was now obvious that the queen would have to leave England. As long as he was afraid for his wife's safety, Charles would be hopelessly hampered in his dealings with his enemies; besides which Henrietta intended to take her own and her husband's personal jewellery, together with as many of the Crown jewels as possible, in order to raise money for the armed struggle which could not be long delayed. As before, the excuse of taking Mary to the Hague was used and on 7 February a formal announcement was issued to this effect: 'His majesty being very much pressed by the States' ambassador to send the princess his daughter immediately into Holland, and being likewise earnestly desired by his royal consort the queen to give her majesty leave to accompany her daughter thither, hath thought fit to consent to both desires, and to make this his majesty's consent and her majesty's resolution known to this parliament.'[19]

This time parliament made no objection. The Venetian ambassador thought they believed the king would be more amenable if the queen's influence were removed, and preparations for the journey were made as quickly as possible. 'Things are done in such post-haste', wrote one royal official disapprovingly, 'that I never heard of the like for the voyage of persons of so great dignity.'[20] Certainly not a moment was being wasted. The travellers set out on 10 February and spent a few days at Greenwich on the way to Dover, where they had to wait for a favourable wind.

Mary's opinion of this hurried, almost furtive departure was not asked and her feelings are not recorded. She had enjoyed none of the special attentions normally paid to a royal bride and does not appear even to have had much of a trousseau, so perhaps she was not entirely sorry to be leaving the unhappy and stressful atmosphere of home. But when the actual moment of leave-taking arrived on Monday 23 February, everyone was in tears. The king embraced his daughter fondly, saying he was afraid he would never see her again. In fact, it seemed highly doubtful just then whether the family would ever be united again. The parting with the queen was particularly affecting. 'His Majesty', wrote the Venetian ambassador, 'accompanied his wife as far as the shore, and did not know how to tear himself away from her, conversing with her in sweet discourse and affectionate embraces, nor would they restrain their tears, moving all those who were present.'[21] At last the small fleet had to put out to sea and Charles rode along the water's edge, waving his hat in farewell until the sails faded into the distance.

The crossing was a stormy one and at the entrance to the harbour of Helvoetsluys one of the ships foundered, taking with it all the queen's chapel plate and the wardrobes of several of her ladies. Prince William, with his cousins Rupert and Maurice, was waiting to escort his bride to Rotterdam by water, but Henrietta Maria had had more than enough of the sea, so it was agreed they should make instead for the palace at Honselaersdijck before going on to the Hague.

The Queen of Bohemia had driven out to meet her sister-in-law and niece, taking her youngest daughter with her. 'I was chosen out from among my sisters as being the fittest companion for the young princess, who was but little younger than myself', recalled Sophie complacently. She was, however, deeply disappointed at sight of her aunt. 'The fine portraits of Van Dyck had given me such an idea of the beauty of all English ladies', she wrote, 'that I was surprised to find the Queen a little woman with long, lean arms, crooked shoulders and teeth protruding from her mouth like guns from a fort.' Luckily, Henrietta was tactful enough to say she thought Sophie resembled the princess her daughter which, since Mary was considered the best-looking member of the family, pleased the youngest Palatine so much that she was prepared to consider her Majesty 'quite handsome' and, after careful inspection, found 'she had beautiful eyes, a well-shaped nose and an admirable complexion'.[22]

The newcomers were given a polite, though not ecstatic,

welcome. The oligarchy of Dutch burghers who made up the States General of the United Provinces and wielded the real power of an increasingly wealthy and important nation, were less impressed by the grandeur of the English alliance than the Prince of Orange, who received his daughter-in-law 'as did become the daughter of so great a king' and always approached her 'with a reverence more like a subject towards his sovereign than the freedom of a father towards his son's wife'.[23] His own wife, conscious of her less than royal origins, was not surprisingly inclined to take offence, and relations between Mary and her mother-in-law were thus strained from the beginning.

The Dutch were resigned to accepting young William's bride, even though she seemed likely to prove an expensive luxury, but her mother was a different matter. Stolid Calvinist citizens stared suspiciously from under their hat brims at the vivacious little queen, sat down uninvited in her presence, and sometimes just walked away without bowing or speaking. Henrietta was in no position to object to these uncouth manners. Having delivered her daughter safely to the Orange family, she now concentrated all her energies on what had always been the prime purpose of her journey – collecting money and support for the king's cause – and for that she was prepared to shrug off any amount of boorishness from 'brewers, bakers and felt-makers'.[24]

Owing to the scrambling haste of the departure from England, no definite arrangements had been agreed for the payment of Mary's dowry, or for her maintenance and living accommodation, and after a state visit to Amsterdam and a trip down to Utrecht for a grand military review, the princess was left at the Hague in the charge of her governess, Catherine Stanhope, widow of Henry Stanhope, son of the Earl of Chesterfield. Lady Stanhope had recently remarried, to Baron Heenvliet, the former Dutch ambassador to London, now appointed Grand Superintendent of Mary's household, and a detailed list of rules to be observed by husband and wife was presently compiled by the Prince of Orange with the object of ensuring that his son's wife would at all times be treated with 'the respect due to a princess of her quality and extraction'. She was also to be instructed 'how she ought to behave to those who visit her', how to distinguish between 'persons of condition', and to become accustomed 'to caress those of this country, and make them good cheer as much as she possibly can'. Whenever the princess appeared in public, her lady governess, or some other suitably qualified person, was always to be with her to keep guard over her and make sure no one behaved improperly in her presence. Care was also to be taken that Mary herself was never, 'from negligence, inattention or want of thought', allowed to be guilty of 'any unseemly and uncivil actions'.[25] Considering her youth and inexperience, these regulations seem reasonable enough, but Mary was not happy and complained that she was being spied on.

Her only contact with home in those first months was a letter from the Prince of Wales, hardly calculated to cheer her up. 'My father is very much disconsolate and troubled', wrote young Charles, 'partly for my royal mother's and your absence, and partly for the disturbances of this kingdom. Dear sister, we are, as much as we may, merry; and more than we would, sad, in respect we cannot alter the present distempers of these troublesome times. My father's resolution is now for York, where he intends to reside, to see the event or sequel to these bad unpropitious beginnings. . . . Thus much desiring your comfortable answer to these my sad lines, I rest your loving Brother, Charles Princeps.'[26]

These were troublesome times for the whole Stuart family. The Queen of Bohemia, watching her sister-in-law's fund-raising activities, was increasingly afraid that civil disturbances would soon erupt into civil war. 'I find', she wrote to her old friend Thom Roe that April, 'by all the Queen's and her people's discourse, that they do not desire an agreement betwixt his majesty and the parliament, but that all be done by force.'[27]

Elizabeth had good reason to dread the outbreak of civil war and feared both Henrietta's violence and the strength of her influence over Charles. 'The Queen is against any agreement with parliament but by war, and the King doth nothing but by her approbation.' The Winter Queen also felt herself excluded from the family problems. When Will Murray, her brother's lifelong friend and gentleman of the bedchamber, came over to confer with Henrietta in May, his business was kept a close secret, even from Elizabeth. 'He is very reserved to me', she told Thomas Roe, 'which he need not be, for I am not curious to ask what I see is not willing to be told.'[28] Nor can she have much enjoyed the spectacle of her sister-in-law haggling with the Dutch pawnbrokers over the family jewels. 'You may judge, now, when they know we want money, how they keep their foot on our throat', Henrietta told her husband bitterly.

The Queen of England spent a year in Holland, pleading, cajoling, nagging anyone and everyone, from the King of Denmark to the Jews of Amsterdam, who looked as if they might be good for a loan or a promise of aid. Her success was only moderate. Although the Prince of Orange did reluctantly provide some financial assistance from his private funds, she was greatly disappointed by the Dutch response to her appeals and relations were further strained when the parliamentary party in London sent an envoy to the Netherlands. Although not officially recognized, he was, despite Henrietta's furious protests, received by a committee of the States General. 'If I do not turn crazy, I shall be a great miracle', she wrote in one of her endless letters home, and by the time she finally left for England in February 1643 the Hollanders at least were thankful to see her go. Elizabeth, in a letter telling Thom Roe of the queen's impending departure, remarked that she 'continues still her kindness and civilities to me', but after a year of listening to her sister-in-law's grievances and hearing her and her friends 'rail abominably at the parliament', it is probable that the Queen of Bohemia, too, felt only relief.

Elizabeth was in a particularly awkward predicament with regard to the parliament, for that body now disposed of all the revenues derived from the customs duties known as tonnage and poundage which were normally granted to the Crown and from which her monthly allowance was paid. Her sympathies naturally lay with her brother and his cause, but the widowed queen could not afford to alienate what was virtually her only source of income – not when she considered her brood of nine surviving children. The young people themselves kept remarkably cheerful, though they had to depend on home-made amusements in the increasingly shabby surroundings of the Wassenaer Hof – a solemn deputation of English Puritans visiting the Hague had been scandalized to find the family engaged in some rowdy amateur theatricals – but their prospects were scarcely encouraging. The two eldest girls, Elizabeth and Louise, were now of marriageable age, but again no one could pretend that these exiled and penniless princesses, however well connected they might be, had much hope of attracting suitable husbands; while the boys, to their mother's dismay, seemed doomed to the lives of soldiers of fortune.

Not Charles Louis, though – that cautious individual had dissociated himself from the royalist colours and come quietly home. Almost simultaneously the Palatine princes Rupert and Maurice were crossing the sea in the opposite direction, and when the royal standard was finally raised at Nottingham on a damp August evening in 1642, the king's nephews were beside him. Rupert at twenty-three was already experienced in warfare, and his early successes in the field, coupled with his reckless enthusiasm and romantic good looks, soon earned him the sort of reputation which did nothing to help his mother and sisters at the Hague.

Elizabeth's correspondence with her sons was being intercepted and hearing that the Commons had taken offence, she was forced to write a placatory letter to Mr Speaker Lenthall, asking him to explain to 'the honourable House of Commons' that, although she could not remember exactly what she had written, 'if anything did perchance slip from my pen, in the private relation between a mother and a son, which might give them the least distaste, I entreat them to make no worse construction of it then was by me intended; having never admitted of any thought or resolution which hath not been sincere and constant to the public peace and prosperity of the kingdom'. She went on to urge 'the honourable House' to be satisfied with this assurance, and not give her enemies occasion to rejoice by stopping 'those necessary supplies, which, by the love of the king my father and king my brother, I have hitherto enjoyed, and without which I have no other subsistence in this world'.[29]

The year 1643 was an anxious one for the Queen of Bohemia. She was worried about her sons, telling Thomas Roe that she had not much approved of Charles Louis's desertion of his uncle because she thought 'his honour somewhat engaged in it'. On the hand, reports that she had encouraged Rupert and Maurice to join the king were 'verie false' – she had, in fact, tried to find Maurice employment elsewhere. But she had to admit that she no longer had any authority over her wayward offspring. Charles Louis was 'now of an age to govern himself and choose better councells than mine are', while the fiery Rupert, now commanding the royalist cavalry, was clearly beyond any mother's control.[30]

Elizabeth continued to be harassed by money worries. Despite repeated appeals to both Houses of Parliament, only a fraction of what was due from her allowance reached her during the summer, and in September she was writing to Honest Thom to tell him that she was 'in no small straits. I am still just in hope I shall have money, but yet I have none, and the proportion is very small beside, for it is but three thousand pounds.'[31] Two of her daughters were seriously ill that winter and she herself was laid up with a bad attack of pleurisy.

While the Queen of Bohemia faced the all too familiar perplexities of an empty purse, problems of a similar kind were just beginning to afflict another unfortunate Stuart princess. When the king and queen made their hasty exit from Whitehall in January 1642 they doubtless did not intend to abandon their two youngest children to the enemy, but that, in fact, is what they had done. The Princess Elizabeth, then just six years old, and Henry, Duke of Gloucester, aged eighteen months, were living at St James's Palace, and after their mother's departure to Holland and their father's to Yorkshire they passed into the hands of parliament.

No attempt was made to victimize them and they remained undisturbed, until, that is, the question of their maintenance arose. Lord Saye and Sele advanced them a loan of £780 but in the autumn of 1642 the princess's governess, the Countess of Roxburgh, was driven to petition the Commons for a regular allowance to be made to the children, who were, she declared, 'in want of everything'. Speaker Lenthall made enquiries and then informed the House that 'the destitution of the royal children was such that he should be ashamed to speak of it, or have the particulars publicly known'.[32] After this, the Commons consulted with the Lords and it was agreed that the sum of £800 a month should be allotted for the maintenance of the king's children.

Unfortunately, however, there were strings attached to this act of generosity, for some time in the spring of 1643 the Commons issued an order for a careful investigation to be made into the characters and doctrines of the clergy who preached in the chapel at St James's, and also into the religious and political affiliations of all members of the household. It was further ordained that no persons who were not willing to subscribe to the Covenant – that is, the undertaking to uphold the Presbyterian form of worship – would be allowed to remain. Since this meant, in effect, that almost all the royal servants would be removed and, presumably, replaced by nominees of the House of Commons, the Princess Elizabeth, who was still only seven, turned to the House of Lords for help. 'I account myself very miserable', she wrote (or dictated), 'that I must have my servants taken from me, and strangers put to me. You promised me that you would have a care of me, and I hope you will show it, in preventing so great a grief as this would be to me. I pray, my lords, consider of it, and give me cause to thank you, and to rest Your loving friend, Elizabeth.'[33]

This touching appeal, which may or may not have been all her own work, was handed to the Earl of Pembroke by the princess herself, with a request that he should present it to the Lords. Their lordships were surprised and affronted to discover that the Lower House had taken it upon themselves to displace the royal servants in this high-handed fashion, nor were they appeased by the excuse that there had been reports of a royalist plot to snatch the children. They considered that the privilege of their House had been breached and proceeded to appoint a committee headed by the Earls of Northumberland, Pembroke, Manchester and Salisbury to visit St James's and examine and report on the state of the household. The Commons replied huffily that since their lordships had been pleased to take the affairs of the king's children into their own hands, they might consider the need for economy as well as changes.

Eleven servants were dismissed, but the establishment presently agreed was a reasonably generous one. The Countess of Dorset, who had been in charge of the Prince of Wales's nursery, was appointed governess and Lady Southcote lady of the bedchamber to the princess. There were, in addition, two cofferesses, four chamberwomen, a laundress, two physicians, six chaplains and one domestic chaplain, two gentlemen ushers and four pages. The Lords' committee ruled that family prayers were to be read morning and afternoon and two sermons preached on Sunday. The gates of the palace were to be locked each evening at sunset and on no account to be opened after ten o'clock without special permission. There was, of course, to be no unauthorized contact with the Court, now at Oxford, and their lordships reserved the right to make any alterations to the size or regulation of the household that they might deem necessary.

Elizabeth and her little brother appear to have remained at St James's until the summer of 1644, when they were moved out temporarily to Sir John Danvers's house at Chelsea, before being taken back to Whitehall. There had, meanwhile, been another addition to the family. Henrietta Maria had spent an adventurous few months after leaving Holland. 'Mam's ill fortune at sea' was proverbial among her children, and a frightful storm had forced her back on to the Dutch coast. She had insisted on setting out again as soon as possible and this time succeeded in making a landfall in Bridlington Bay. Here a blockading parliamentary fleet bombarded the town, so that the queen was obliged to take shelter in a ditch. Undeterred, she had moved on to York and, styling herself 'Her She Majesty Generalissima', had presently led a force of several thousand new recruits down through the Midlands, joining up with the king and her two elder sons at Oxford in July.

The reunion with Charles had its predictable result and by the winter Henrietta knew she was pregnant again. Oxford was not thought safe or suitable for her lying-in – the parliamentary armies were too close and the city could not stand a siege – so, in April 1644, there was another unhappy parting. To make matters worse, the queen felt extremely ill, wracked with rheumatic pains and dreading her confinement. After some indecision she made for Exeter, which was held for the king by the trusted Sir John Berkeley and well garrisoned. She arrived safely at the beginning of May, but reports of her symptoms were now so alarming that Charles dashed off his famous frantic note to the royal physician Theodore Mayerne in London – 'Mayerne, for the love of me go to my wife.'

Henrietta herself was convinced she was dying, but on 16 June she gave birth to a daughter at Bedford House, the Russell family mansion. The baby was healthy, 'a lovely princess' according to the French agent de Sabran, who saw her when she was a week old, but the unfortunate queen was still suffering acutely, with 'a seizure of paralysis in the legs and all over the body' and such a constriction round the heart that she thought she would suffocate. 'At times I am like a person poisoned', she told the king. 'I can scarcely stir and am doubled up.'

Nevertheless, news of the approach of the Earl of Essex and his army stirred her into action. She was terrified above all things of being captured by the enemy, knowing that Charles would consider no sacrifice too great to rescue her, and leaving her infant daughter in the care of her friend Lady Dalkeith, she travelled painfully down to Pendennis Castle by the port of Falmouth *en route* for France. The night before she sailed, Henrietta wrote again to the king. 'I am giving the strongest proof of love that I can give; I am hazarding my life that I may not incommode your affairs. Adieu my dear heart. If I die, believe that you will lose a person who had never been other than entirely yours.'[34] But again she did not die. In spite of determined efforts by ships of the parliamentary navy to intercept her, and her usual bad luck with the weather, she reached the coast of Brittany and, in the sympathetic surroundings of her native country, began slowly to recover her health.

The king was now advancing westward, forcing Essex to withdraw into Cornwall. On 26 July the royalists reached Exeter and Charles was able to make the acquaintance of his youngest and, so it was said, prettiest daughter. He also arranged for her to be baptized in the cathedral. She would be named Henrietta after her mother and Anne, as a compliment to the kindly Queen Regent of France who had sent the royal midwife to attend the afflicted Queen of England, as well as a much-needed gift of money and baby clothes, and was now offering her sanctuary. The king stayed only briefly in Exeter and the baby Henrietta Anne remained at Bedford House in the care of her governess.

Lady Dalkeith – her husband was the eldest son of the Earl of Morton – had been born Anne Villiers and was related to the murdered royal favourite Buckingham. She possessed a fair share of the Villiers good looks but, more importantly, proved to be strong-minded, brave, resourceful and devoted to her charge. When Exeter came under siege by the parliamentary army under Thomas Fairfax in the autumn of 1645, she made an attempt to take the princess to Cornwall, but everyone's attention just then was concentrated on getting the Prince of Wales safely away and Henrietta Anne stayed where she was. The poor woman was to be most unfairly blamed by the queen for exposing the child to danger but found a champion in Edward Hyde, who declared her to have been 'as punctual, as solicitous and as impatient to obey the queen's directions, as she could be to save her soul'.

The siege came to an end the following April, when Sir John Berkeley was obliged to surrender the city, but Lady Dalkeith was allowed to leave freely and given a safe conduct to take the princess with her household, plate and money to any place she chose. Her ladyship, having 'his majesty's allowance to remain with the princess for some time about London, in any of his majesty's houses', chose Richmond as the fittest but was directed instead to Oatlands. As usual, the problem was money. Contrary to the assurances she had been given before leaving Exeter, no provision had been made for the princess's maintenance and Lady Dalkeith found herself being forced to meet the household expenses out of her own pocket. Appeals to Sir Thomas Fairfax, to parliament and finally the committee of justices for the county of Surrey at Kingston produced no result. Then an order came that the household was to be broken up and the young princess brought to London to join her brother and sister at St James's, where care would be taken to see that she wanted for nothing.

But Anne Dalkeith was not going to be parted from her nursling without a struggle. She wrote again to both Houses of Parliament begging them to consider that the king himself had entrusted the princess to her care, that she had 'preserved her highness – not without many cares and fears – from a weak to a very hopeful condition of health' and was best acquainted with her constitution. All she asked was to be allowed to remain with her charge, 'without being any kind of burden to the parliament', her 'interest and inclination being both in this service'. But if that was not possible, she went on, 'I have only these requests, that I may be reimbursed the money I have laid out during my attendance . . . and that I may have a pass to send one to his majesty to know his pleasure, without which, in honour and honesty, I cannot deliver up his child.'[35]

Evidently afraid that she would, in the end, be forced to deliver up the princess, Lady Dalkeith now came to the bold decision that she would somehow contrive to smuggle the child over to the queen in France. Taking only two trusted servants into her confidence, she disguised herself in a shabby gown and cloak, with a bundle of rags stuffed into one shoulder to give her a hunchbacked appearance. Posing as a Frenchwoman, and accompanied by a French *valet de chambre* as her 'husband', the valiant governess set out on 25 July to walk to Dover, carrying the little princess, who was passed off as a boy named Pierre. A few hours after their departure, a letter was carried back to Oatlands addressed to the gentlewomen of the Princess Henrietta's household, requesting them, as a great mark of their faithfulness and kindness to their mistress, to conceal her being gone for as long as they could. The gentlewomen waited faithfully for three days before raising the alarm, but it seems that the authorities in London were frankly relieved to be spared the expense and responsibility of another royal child, and there was no pursuit. The travellers were therefore able to go on their way undisturbed, their only anxiety being caused by the two-year-old Henrietta, who insisted on telling all and sundry that her name was not Pierre but princess, and that the rough clothes she was wearing were not her own. On reaching the port, they crossed to Calais by the ordinary French packet and were presently rapturously received by Henrietta Maria at St Germain. 'O, the transports of joy! O, the excessive consolation to the heart of the Queen! She embraced, she hugged, she kissed again and again that royal infant.'[36] For better or worse, Anne Dalkeith's fierce loyalty and devotion to duty had effectively determined the future course of the princess's life and from now on the destiny of Henrietta Maria's '*enfant de bénédiction*' would lie in her mother's country.

The eldest and youngest of the king's children were now at liberty – the Prince of Wales having arrived in France shortly before his little sister. Their siblings still in England were less fortunate, although it was true that some changes for the better had been made in the household at St James's. After the death of the Countess of Dorset in the spring of 1645, the Princess Elizabeth and her brother had been transferred to the guardianship of the Earl and Countess of Northumberland. Algernon Percy, tenth Earl of Northumberland, had been one of the leaders of the opposition in the House of Lords from the earliest days of the Civil War, but he was still a great nobleman who had once been familiar with the Court and who knew how things ought to be done. He had insisted on being given permission to treat his charges as the children of a king and was also able to take them out to Syon, his house on the river at Isleworth, which, although it had some unfortunate associations with those tragic royal ladies Queen Katherine Howard and Lady Jane Grey, was still a pleasant place in the country.

Parliament continued to keep a sharp eye on the budget, and in September Northumberland's original allowance of £9,500 a year was reduced to £5,000, which was to cover all expenses except the physicians' salaries and the servants' wages. The earl had been empowered to choose Whitehall, Somerset House, or St James's as a town residence and to take such furniture, bedding and plate from the royal stores as he considered necessary. The children were therefore living in comfort and being treated with the respect due to their rank, but their future prospects were bleak and Elizabeth at least was now old enough to be aware of this. A serious-minded, studious girl, she would be ten that December, the same age as her sister Mary was betrothed, and although the parliament had always insisted that they were wards rather than prisoners, the distinction must often have seemed a fine one.

Any news reaching the princess from the outside world just then would have brought her little consolation. After the disastrous defeats at Marston Moor and Naseby, and the loss of such key towns as York, Exeter, Bristol and Chester, the king's cause had never looked more hopeless, and when the last royal army was destroyed at Stow-on-the-Wold in March 1646, Charles wrote to the queen that he no longer had 'force enough to resist nor sufficient to escape to any secure place'. What he did was to slip unobtrusively out of Oxford with only two companions in the early hours of 27 April and give himself up to the Scots army camped near Newark. The last of the royal garrisons surrendered during the summer. Oxford, site of the wartime Court, opened its gates to Thomas Fairfax at the end of June and the king's second son, twelve-year-old James, Duke of York, came to join his brother and sister in London.

The Scots, meanwhile, had retreated to Newcastle, taking the king with them, but whatever hopes he had, or had been encouraged to have, of coming to some accommodation with the Covenanters were soon dispelled. At the beginning of 1647 they handed him over to the parliamentary commissioners who had gone north to negotiate terms and who then escorted him as far as Holdenby House in

Northamptonshire. By this time, however, another war was breaking out between the parliament and their victorious New Model army, and in June a businesslike troop of horse arrived at Holdenby to take the king into their possession. The children were at Hampton Court, where they were to spend the summer, but as soon as the news of the army coup reached Westminster, hasty orders were issued to fetch them back to St James's in case they, too, might be seized.

The king, attended by the army commanders Oliver Cromwell, Thomas Fairfax and Henry Ireton, was brought as far as Windsor. He wanted to see his children, and when General Fairfax gave his word that they would be returned after two days, the House of Commons reluctantly agreed. A rendezvous was arranged at the Greyhound Inn at Maidenhead, and Elizabeth and her brothers, accompanied by the Earl of Northumberland and a strong guard of the City of London militia, drove into the town in a procession of three coaches, to be greeted by welcoming crowds and streets decorated with flowers and green branches. Elizabeth had not seen her father for more than five years and seven-year-old Harry, Duke of Gloucester, had no memory of him. 'Do you know me, child?' asked the king, and being told 'No', replied mournfully, 'I am your father, and it is not the least of my misfortunes that I have brought you and your brothers and sisters into the world to share my miseries.'[37] At this, not surprisingly, everyone burst into tears and Oliver Cromwell, himself a family man, who witnessed the reunion, was much affected by 'the tenderest sight that ever his eyes beheld, which was the interview between the King and his children'.[38] The party dined at the Greyhound and afterwards went on to Lord Craven's house at Caversham, where they stayed for the two days stipulated by parliament.

The usual summer outbreak of plague caused Northumberland to apply for permission to move the children out to Syon but parliament, increasingly suspicious of the army's intentions, insisted that they should instead be brought into the City and lodged in the Mansion House under the eye of the lord mayor himself. But Cromwell and the army were now taking control, and after a very few days Northumberland was able to take his charges back to the country.

The king was now installed at Hampton Court, being treated with careful deference by his captors, who were still hoping to persuade him to agree to the Heads of the Proposals they had put before him. Charles had given his parole that he would not try to escape, so he was allowed a good deal of liberty and saw the children regularly, either at Hampton Court or Syon, which he visited twice during August. The *Weekly Intelligencer*, writing on 13 September, records that 'his majesty's children came yesterday in the afternoon to Hampton Court, to ask blessing of him'; adding that they were a long time in the garden, running and playing before the king who 'expressed much joy to see them with him'. Another correspondent, also writing from Hampton Court that week and probably describing the same occasion, remarked on the affection shown by the family. 'The Duke of York sat on his majesty's right hand; his majesty is very fond of him, and loving to all the children; he bears the young lady often in his arms.'[39]

With the approach of autumn the children were moved back to St James's for the winter and Charles wrote to Thomas Fairfax asking that 'my lord of Northumberland may be authorized, once in ten days, or some such time, to give us the same satisfaction of letting our children visit and remain with us here for a night or two; the distance from London, winter weather, and shortness of days, not permitting such returns as they have hitherto observed'.[40]

There was some delay while this request was considered and finally agreed, for on 27 October Charles wrote to Elizabeth to explain that 'it is not through forgetfulness, or any want of kindness, that I have not all this time sent for you, but for such reasons as is fitter for you to imagine, which you may easily do, than me to write; but now I hope to see you upon Friday or Saturday next'.[41]

The visit took place, but Elizabeth is said to have complained that the sentries patrolling in the palace at night were keeping her awake. The king summoned their commander, Colonel Whalley, and asked him to move his men further away. Whalley explained that the guards already had strict orders to be as quiet as possible and had told him that they 'stepped so softly' they did not think the princess could have been disturbed. However, he offered to move them further off, if the king 'would be graciously pleased' to renew his engagement not to attempt to escape. Charles replied that this involved a point of honour, adding, 'You have my engagement. I will not renew it.'[42]

On 11 November, a few days after the children had returned to London, the king escaped from Hampton Court, but he got no further than the Isle of Wight and by Christmas was a close prisoner in Carisbrooke Castle. The following April the young Duke of York escaped from St James's. Assisted by Colonel Joseph Bamfield, said to be 'a man of wit and parts', he slipped away during the evening of Friday 20 April under cover of a game of hide-and-seek with his brother Harry, and wearing girl's clothes, succeeded in reaching Gravesend where a Dutch boat was waiting to take him to Holland.

There is no evidence that Elizabeth had had, or was suspected of having taken, any active part in organizing her brother's flight, though it is difficult to believe that she had no previous knowledge of it, and the Earl of Northumberland was presently exonerated from blame. As he reminded the Lords, while being prepared to take every reasonable care of the king's children, he had always refused to be responsible for preventing their escape or rescue.[43] He and his wife were confirmed in their guardianship and Elizabeth and Harry were taken to the country as usual for the summer.

There was to be no further communication with their father, although an occasional letter was smuggled out of the Isle of Wight – Sir Thomas Herbert, the king's confidential servant, acting as postman for one sad little note addressed to Elizabeth in October. 'Dear daughter', Charles had written, 'It is not want of affection that makes me write so seldom to you, but want of matter such as I could wish, and indeed I am loth to write to those I love when I am out of humour (as I have been these days by-past) lest my letter should trouble those I desire to please; but having this opportunity I would not lose it, though at this time I have nothing to say but God bless you. So I rest, Your loving father, Charles R. Give your brother my blessing, with a kiss, and commend me kindly to my Lady Northumberland by the same token.'[44]

The king's tragedy was now moving inexorably towards its end. In November 1648 he was transferred from Carisbrooke to Hurst Castle on the mainland and from there to Windsor. On New Year's Day, the House of Commons, recently 'purged' of those members who opposed the army, passed an ordinance for the trial of 'Charles Stuart, the now King of England' on a charge of treason. Still there was hesitation, as men shrank from the unknowable consequences of adopting the final solution to their problem. In the end it was Oliver Cromwell who put an end to discussion. Cromwell had tried patiently for more than a year to reach a negotiated settlement with an adversary who patently regarded negotiation as no more than a legitimate ploy for gaining time and advantage. The experience had convinced him that he and his colleagues were destined to be the instruments of God's providence and that there was only one way to deal with the slippery Charles. 'I tell you we will cut off his head with the crown upon it,' he shouted famously to one objector.

The king came back to his capital, which he had last seen almost exactly seven years before, on 19 January and was lodged at St James's. His 'trial' opened in Westminster Hall on the following day and lasted for a week. On Saturday 27 January, sentence was pronounced and on Monday 29 January his children were brought up from Syon House to say goodbye. Charles kissed them both and gave them his blessing and then turned to thirteen-year-old Elizabeth, who was already in tears. 'He told me he was glad I was come, and although he had not time to say much, yet somewhat he had to say to me.'

Elizabeth's recollection of her father's words, set down immediately after the event, still echoes poignantly across the years. 'He wished me not to grieve and torment myself for him', she wrote; 'for that would be a glorious death that he should die; it being for the laws and liberties of this land, and for maintaining the true Protestant religion. . . . He told me, he had forgiven all his enemies, and hoped God would forgive them also; and commanded us, and all the rest of my brothers and sisters to forgive them. He bid me tell my mother, that his thoughts had never strayed from her, and that his love should be the same to the last. Withal he commanded me and my brother to be obedient to her. And bid me send his blessing to the rest of my brothers and sisters, with commendation to all his friends.'[45]

'Sweetheart, you'll forget this,' said Charles to his weeping daughter. '"No" (said she), "I shall never forget it while I live." And pouring forth abundant tears, promised him to write down the particulars.' The king then took the little Duke of Gloucester on his knee and said, '"Sweetheart, now they will cut off thy father's head." (Upon which words the child looked very steadfastly on him.) "Mark, child, what I say. They will cut off my head, and perhaps make thee a King. But mark what I say, you must not be a King, so long as your brothers Charles and James do live; for they will cut off your brothers' heads (when they can catch them) and cut off thy head too at the last; and therefore I charge you, do not be made a king by them." At which the child, sighing, said "I will be torn in pieces first."' Which, according to the account printed in the *Eikon Basilike*, 'falling so unexpectedly from one so young' – Gloucester was still only eight – 'made the King rejoice exceedingly'.[46]

Charles gave the children some of his few remaining pieces of jewellery and, perhaps in an attempt to comfort them, told them once more not to grieve for him, 'for he should die a martyr'. He was sure that God would settle the throne on his son and they would all be happier than they could have expected to be if he had lived. He kissed both children again before turning away to go into his bedroom. But a fresh outburst of grief from Elizabeth brought him back for one last embrace. 'Most sorrowful was this parting', wrote Thomas Herbert, who witnessed the scene, 'the young princess shedding tears and crying lamentably, so as moved others to pity that formerly were hardhearted; and at opening the bedchamber door the King returned hastily from the window and kissed them and blessed them; and so parted.'[47]

FOUR

THE EXILE

> I am just now beginning this letter in my sister's chamber, where
> there is such a noise that I never hope to end it, and much less
> write sense . . . I shall only tell your majesty that we are now
> thinking how to pass our time, and in the first place of dancing.
>
> (Charles II to the Queen of Bohemia)

King Charles's execution, though scarcely unexpected, still sent a
seismic wave of shock horror resonating through the courts of
Europe. For while Charles was far from being the first reigning
monarch to die violently at the hands of subjects, to his fellow
sovereigns there was something peculiarly atrocious in the idea of
a reigning monarch being tried by subjects and judicially
executed. It struck at the very foundations of the institution of
monarchy, desecrating the concept of the divine right of kings
bestowed by God alone.

The news took some ten days to reach King Charles's widow.
France was at that moment distracted by the so-called wars of the
Fronde – a series of civil disturbances born out of a general
resentment against the power of central government and in
particular the all-pervading influence of the queen regent's chief
minister, the Italian Cardinal Mazarin. In the winter of 1649 Paris
was surrounded by the insurgents, and the queen and her young
son, the ten-year-old Louis XIV, had retreated to St Germain. But the
Queen of England insisted on remaining at the Louvre, believing
that news from London would reach her more quickly there.

Her situation was extremely uncomfortable. Her pension from
the French government had not been paid for several months and
now, with the royal family absent and the city in a state of siege,
the Parisian shopkeepers were refusing to extend her credit any

further. The weather had turned very cold and when Cardinal de Retz, leader of the Frondeurs, as the rebels were styled, came to visit her early in January, he found the queen shivering in a fireless room with her four-year-old daughter, who had been kept in bed for warmth. Greatly shocked, the cardinal hastened to the rescue. 'You will do me the justice to believe that the daughter of England did not stay in bed the next day for want of firewood', he wrote in his memoirs, and he persuaded the Paris parlement to authorize an immediate grant of 40,000 livres.[1]

Henrietta Maria's most urgent problems might have been solved, but she remained in a state of acute anxiety. She had written, via the French ambassador, to both Houses of Parliament begging for a safe conduct to see her husband, but her letters were not even opened and at last the news of his death had to be broken to her by her worried attendants, who were afraid it might send her out of her mind. According to her confessor, Cyprien de Gamache, 'she stood motionless as a statue, without words and without tears. . . . To all our exhortations and arguments our queen was deaf and insensible. At last, awed by her appalling grief, we ceased talking and stood around her in perturbed silence.' It was not until evening, when the Duchess de Vendôme, Henrietta's sister-in-law and close friend, came in weeping to kiss her hand, that the widow's frozen silence melted into tears. Princess Henrietta Anne was the uncomprehending spectator of all this adult grief, 'some sighing, some weeping, all with mournful looks', and kind Father Cyprien believed her childish prattle was the afflicted queen's greatest consolation.[2]

By an ironic stroke of fate, news of the King of England's execution reached the Hague just as the Orange and Palatine families were preparing to celebrate the ratification of the Treaty of Westphalia which had finally brought to an end the war begun in Bohemia thirty years ago. For Elizabeth this meant that at long last her son would be restored to his father's hereditary estates – or to some of them. By the terms of the treaty only the Lower Palatinate was being returned to its previous owners, nor was the Palsgrave any longer to be the first elector of the empire. That honour, together with the Upper Palatinate, remained firmly in the grasp of Maximilian of Bavaria and an eighth, very junior, electorate had been created as a consolation prize for Charles

Louis. However, he would now be able to go home to Heidelberg, even though the castle was no longer habitable and the Rhineland devastated by war. His sisters might now be able to find husbands and Elizabeth herself could hope to receive her dower income.

The news from England put an end to all rejoicing. The Queen of Bohemia had not seen her brother since that day at Canterbury half a lifetime ago when she had said goodbye to a shy, stammering boy of thirteen. He had often disappointed her in the past by his failure to help her and Frederick and she had remained deliberately neutral throughout the Civil War, but Charles was still her little brother and there was nothing neutral about her reaction when she heard of his death. From that moment on she became furiously and openly partisan, refusing to recognize the existence of the Commonwealth government in London and announcing that if anyone who had any connection with it ventured to come to her house, they would be thrown down her stairs and kicked out of doors.

This was going to make for an awkward reunion with her eldest son. Charles Louis had been living in England for the past four years, apparently on excellent terms with the new regime, and when he returned to the Hague that April he faced a very unpleasant quarter of an hour with his mother, who insisted that he must immediately break off relations with his parliamentary friends and pay his respects to the new King of England.[3]

Since there were strong suspicions in diplomatic circles that the Palsgrave had at one time been hoping parliament might decide to offer him his uncle's crown, this, too, had all the makings of an awkward social occasion. But the new King of England was notoriously easygoing. He received his cousin with his usual urbane good manners and an embarrassed Charles Louis hurried away to Heidelberg to make the best of his severely curtailed patrimony.

All Elizabeth's sons had now flown the nest. Rupert and Maurice, who had been expelled from England after the surrender of Oxford, had taken to the sea and for the next few years led an adventurous life as freelance privateers. Rupert was to live to see the Stuarts restored at Whitehall, but Maurice disappeared in 1652, when his ship foundered in a Caribbean hurricane off the Virgin Islands. Rumours persisted for more than a decade that he had somehow survived and been taken prisoner by Algerian pirates, but although it was a long time before his mother and brother gave up hope, there seems no real reason to doubt that the prince born in the cold discomfort of Cüstrin Castle had perished in the wild seas of the New World.

Edward and Philip, the two youngest Palatine princes, both proved a serious disappointment to the Queen of Bohemia. In 1645 Edward had married a French heiress eight years older than himself and committed the very nearly unforgivable sin of converting to Rome. But Elizabeth found it hard to stay angry with Ned, the best-looking and most amiable of her sons, who at least would never now need to ask her for money, and in due course she allowed herself to be reconciled.

Six months after Edward's defection, Philip caused a much more reverberating scandal, when he took exception to the attentions being paid to his mother by a smooth young Frenchman, with ingratiating manners and a reputation as a womanizer. Elizabeth found Jacques de l'Epinay an amusing companion, was probably flattered by his interest and appears to have seen no harm in a little mild flirtation. Her sons thought otherwise, and when de l'Epinay refused to be warned off and even boasted of his 'bonnes fortunes' with both the queen and Princess Louise, Philip challenged him to a duel. This was frustrated by the authorities, but further encounters followed, ending in a street brawl in which Philip killed the insolent Frenchman with his hunting-knife.

The affair naturally caused something of a sensation and a good deal of ill-natured gossip in the small, enclosed society of the Hague. Philip fled to Germany and refused to obey repeated summonses to return and give an account of himself, but the French embassy was apparently disinclined to press charges and after a while the matter was allowed to drop. Elizabeth herself was said to be furious with Philip for exposing her to the scandalmongers and Charles Louis wrote to her in July 1646 urging her to forgive his brother. 'The consideration of his youth, of the affront he received, of the blemish had lain upon him all his life-time if he had not resented it; but much more that of his blood, and of his nearness to you' were, the Palsgrave felt, a sufficient excuse. Philip had, after all, only been defending his mother's honour and that of his house.[4] He was able to return to Holland for a visit in 1648, but he had by then drifted into a not very distinguished career as a mercenary captain – a career which ended in his death two years later at the age of twenty-three in a minor Franco-Spanish skirmish somewhere in the Ardennes.

The Palatine girls were all still at home. Elizabeth, according to her sister Sophie, had black hair, a dazzling complexion and sparkling brown eyes, with a sharp aquiline nose 'which was rather apt to turn red'. Poor Elizabeth, she was very learned – 'she knew every language and every science under the sun' – and corresponded regularly with the philosopher Descartes, 'but all her philosophy could not save her from vexation when her nose was red'. Louise, who was lively and unaffected, 'devoted herself to painting' and had considerable artistic talent. She studied under Gerard van Honthorst and it is said that some of her pictures were signed by the master and sold to supplement the family finances. But while painting others, observed Sophie, Louise neglected her own appearance sadly, so that 'one would have said that her clothes had been thrown on her'. Henriette, the third sister, was the beauty of the family, with fair flaxen hair and a complexion, 'without exaggeration, of lilies and roses'. Her talents lay in the direction of the kitchen and stillroom and young Sophie had happy memories of enjoying the fruits of her confectionary labours, though she also recalled that the family was 'at times obliged to make even richer repasts than that of Cleopatra, and often had nothing at our court but pearls and diamonds to eat'.[5]

The Queen of Bohemia's violent outburst of hostility against the Commonwealth had led unsurprisingly to the final cutting-off of all payment of her parliamentary pension. For a time the blow was cushioned by Lord Craven, a wealthy English peer who had long been her devoted slave – there was a rumour that they were secretly married – but unfortunately Craven's obvious sympathies soon resulted in the sequestration of his estates and Elizabeth began to know real poverty. Already, in the summer of 1649, she was forced to face the fact that she could no longer afford her lifelong favourite recreation of riding a'hunting and had the heartrending task of disposing of her beloved horses. Almost all her jewellery was in pawn and in August 1650 she told Charles

Louis that she was 'in very ill case and though I have put away as many of my servants as I can, yet I am in great want'.[6]

The year 1650 had begun badly for the Stuart cause with the failure of Montrose's attempt to raise the Scottish Highlands for the king. This was an especial grief for Elizabeth, who had felt an instant rapport with the soldier-poet James Graham, Marquis of Montrose during his short visit to the Hague the previous spring. They had both feared that young Charles might be driven to throwing in his lot with the Scots Presbyterians, the Brethren as Elizabeth called them, who were Montrose's bitter enemies. These fears proved only too well founded. Cromwell's brutal suppression of any possible royalist resistance in Ireland did indeed propel the inexperienced king into an agreement with the Covenanters involving the repudiation of Montrose, notwithstanding the fact that he had already given the marquis his commission for a landing in Scotland. The Queen of Bohemia prayed God to send her friend safety and success but the expedition was a disaster. Montrose sailed for the Orkneys from Scandinavia in March. In April he was defeated at Corbiesdale and betrayed to his arch-enemy, the eminently dislikeable Marquis of Argyll. A month later the gallant marquis had been hung, drawn and quartered in the Grassmarket in Edinburgh. Charles himself arrived in Scotland that summer, but his cynical flirtation with the Brethren was to have unhappy consequences for others besides Montrose.

In the weeks immediately following their father's death, young Elizabeth and Henry were taken back to Syon, but a change in their guardianship was now being considered. The Earl of Northumberland had been one of the small handful of peers who had opposed the king's execution and was no longer felt to be quite sound by Parliament, while he himself was anxious to be released. Like so many minders of royalty before him, he was finding it an increasingly thankless and expensive business, and in April 1649 wrote to the Council of State complaining: 'I have, for some months past, been put to maintain the Duke of Gloucester and his sister out of my own purse; and, for want of those allowances which I should have received by appointment of the Parliament, have run myself so far out of money, that I am altogether destitute of means to provide longer for them, or indeed for my own poor family.'[7]

On parliament's receipt of this *cri de coeur*, the matter of the children's custody was laid before the House of Commons. Elizabeth had already asked to be allowed to go over to Holland to her sister the Princess of Orange, but her petition, presented in the tense weeks leading up to her father's trial, had been ignored. Now, facing the prospect of a new and perhaps less sympathetic guardian, she renewed her request. It was debated by the Commons but this humane and, as someone did not fail to point out, economical solution to the problem of her future was rejected; a small majority voting that the Princess Elizabeth 'should not have liberty to go beyond the seas'. After some delay, Northumberland succeeded in persuading his sister Dorothy, wife of Robert Sidney, Earl of Leicester, to agree to take over his charge, and Elizabeth and her little brother came to Penshurst, 'abode of the noble Sidneys', on Thursday 14 June.

Penshurst Place in the Weald of Kent was an idyllic spot, standing 'in the midst of a wide valley on a pleasant elevation, its woods and parks stretching away beyond', but the arrival of the noble Sidneys' royal guests had been preceded by a reverberating domestic row, caused by the earl's determination to reduce his wife's housekeeping money of £700 a year. Parliament was allowing her £3,000 for the two children and their servants and, considering this 'great accession' of her means, together with all the extra personal expense and inconvenience he would be put to, his lordship thought it 'very reasonable to abate a great part of that £700 a-year; and so from midsummer, 1649, I resolved to take off £400 a-year. This caused a huge storm in the house', he recorded in his diary, 'but I persisted in it.'[8]

As England was now a republic, all royalty and royal titles and dignities were considered to be abolished. The Countess of Leicester, therefore, received strict instructions to see that her charges were accorded no more respect than the children of any noble family. No one was to bend the knee or remain uncovered in their presence, and their meals were no longer to be served with special ceremony.

The various royalist propaganda sheets were naturally full of lurid reports regarding the projected degradation of 'Bessy and Harry Stuart'; how they were to be put away in some charity school or hospital; how Elizabeth was to be married to one of

Cromwell's sons 'to see if they can beget a new royal progeny to heir the crown when they have killed all the rest'; while Harry would be apprenticed to some menial trade – Cromwell, it was said, had suggested setting him up as a cobbler or brewer. 'Thus', raged *Mercurius Pragmaticus*, 'these royal infants are likely to be tossed about as their father of happy memory was in his lifetime, until these devils have an opportunity to murder them as they did his majesty.'[9]

In fact, although young Gloucester came to be addressed as Mr Harry by his attendants, his sister was always given her title. As for Lady Leicester, that kind and strong-minded soul continued to treat both children in the privacy of the household with as much deference as she thought proper, and the ailing Elizabeth at least with particular tenderness. The princess had never been strong and the emotional trauma surrounding her father's death seems to have drained the last of her reserves, for it was noticed how from that time 'she fell into great sorrow, whereby all the other ailments from which she suffered were increased'.

The quiet months at Penshurst came to an end in August 1650. News that Charles II had landed in Scotland under the patronage of the Kirk caused a flurry of alarm in Whitehall, where executive power now rested in the hands of the new Council of State. This body had no intention of allowing either king or Presbytery to be foisted on it by the Scots, but as Cromwell prepared to take the army north to deal with the Covenanters, rumours of royalist plots in the West Country began to circulate, causing nervous members of the Council to consider the wisdom of taking further precautions. A letter signed by the President, John Bradshaw, was therefore despatched to Colonel Sydenham, Governor of the Isle of Wight, informing him that 'the parliament hath appointed that the two children of the late king, who are now at the Earl of Leicester's at Penshurst, shall be sent out of the limits of the Commonwealth'.[10] At the same time, orders went to Anthony Mildmay, Governor of Carisbrooke Castle, that he and his wife were to collect the children from the Countess of Leicester and escort them over to the island.

The party landed at Cowes on 13 August, but Elizabeth's stay in the castle where her father had spent the last full year of his life was destined to be brief. It is said that she and her brother were playing bowls on the green which had been constructed for King Charles when they were caught in a summer rainstorm. The princess got very wet and next day was complaining of the chill which led to her death. In fact, it seems pretty certain that she was already in the terminal stages of tuberculosis when she came to Carisbrooke. She took to her bed within a few days of her arrival, and although the Mildmays summoned Dr Bagnall from Newport and sent urgent requests for assistance to old Theodore Mayerne in London, Elizabeth was beyond medical help. She died on the afternoon of Sunday 8 September at the age of fourteen years and eight months.

They buried her in the parish church at Newport, the place marked only by the letters E.S. cut into the stone of a nearby wall, and she lay there forgotten until 1793, when vault and coffin were discovered as another grave was being prepared. In the 1850s the coffin was once more brought to light during the rebuilding of St Thomas's Church. This time it was opened and the corpse examined by 'the learned Ernest Wilkins MD', who pronounced that the princess had suffered from 'softening of the bones, called rickets' and that their appearance indicated some deformity. Her hair had been preserved round the skull and was 'of considerable length and silky fineness, of a fine light brown, approaching to auburn hue'. The remains were respectfully reinterred and Queen Victoria had a marble monument erected to the memory of the Princess Elizabeth, daughter of Charles I, as 'a token of respect for her virtues and of sympathy for her misfortunes'.[11]

There is no evidence that Elizabeth was ever treated with deliberate unkindness or neglect. Indeed, Mr Speaker Lenthall was later to deny that there had ever been any want of duty on his part towards either of the king's children. On the contrary, he declared, 'there was no opportunity but I made it my care to get necessaries and conveniences for them'.[12] That may be so, but still it is not pleasant to think of a sick child being posted from one reluctant set of guardians to another, and dying at last among strangers, far from those who should have cherished her. From the few glimpses of her that have survived, a picture emerges of a sensitive, affectionate girl, whose intellectual gifts might have come to equal those of her Palatine cousin and namesake.

Ironically enough, when it was too late, parliament finally agreed that the Lady Elizabeth should, after all, be granted liberty to join her sister Mary in Holland, with a pension of £1,000 a year, provided she continued to 'act inoffensively' towards the Commonwealth. News of her death caused a wave of sympathy for the exiled Stuarts in the Courts of Europe and the queen her mother, it was said, 'could not learn her melancholy death without shedding many tears'. But apparently the principal cause of regret among her elder brothers and sisters was that they had 'looked upon her as an instrument that might contribute to the re-establishment of their royal house, by means of some high marriage'.[13]

Mary's marriage – that which had once been planned for Elizabeth – had not been a success. Her husband was consistently unfaithful and she remained on bad terms with her mother-in-law. Her father-in-law, Frederick Henry, the last of William the Silent's sons, died in 1647 and William II and Mary became Prince and Princess of Orange. But Mary was no happier. Of all King Charles's children she was most like her father in appearance and had also inherited much of his obstinacy and self-centredness. She seems to have laboured under a permanent sense of grievance and pined constantly for England and her own family.

Things might have been different if there had been children, but after a serious miscarriage when she was fifteen, Mary did not conceive again. Then, in the spring of 1650, after a visit to Spa, where the waters had far-famed restorative properties, the Princess of Orange was reported to be *enceinte*. Her husband was not with her during the final stages of her pregnancy. Instead, William, who possessed none of the statesmanlike qualities of his distinguished predecessors, was engaged in an unwise and ultimately damaging attempt to impose his authority by force of arms on the independent citizens of Amsterdam. He returned to the Hague in the autumn, unsuccessful and out of sorts, and developed a fever which was presently diagnosed as smallpox. Only a mild attack, said the doctors, but the doctors were wrong and it killed him. Ten days later, on her nineteenth birthday, his widow was delivered of a son.

Throughout these ordeals of bereavement and childbirth, the Princess of Orange was faithfully supported by her aunt Elizabeth

– 'my poor neece is the most afflicted creature that ever I saw, and is changed as she is nothing but skin and bone.' The Queen of Bohemia was very fond of her 'poor neece'. True, she sometimes found Mary's tendency to hypochondria rather tiresome, complaining that she was 'deadlie lasie' and would soon be well if only she would take exercise, but in general she seems to have got on better with her niece than with her daughters. As it happened, only one of her daughters now remained at home. Henriette, or 'Nennie' as her mother called her, had been married that summer to Prince Siegmund Rakoczy and had departed to his Transylvanian castle. It proved a very happy marriage but pathetically brief, for within six months poor, pretty, fragile Nennie was dead.

Charles Louis, now established at Heidelberg though living in a house in the town, the castle being still uninhabitable, and now himself married to a princess of Hesse Cassel, had invited his eldest and youngest sisters to visit him. Sophie accepted the invitation eagerly, rather to her mother's annoyance. During his last visit to the Hague, King Charles had paid marked attention to his cousin and the unquenchably optimistic Winter Queen had begun to dream of wedding bells. Sophie herself, a practical young person with a healthy estimation of her own worth, did not seriously consider the penniless and exiled King of England as husband material. 'He and I had always been on the best of terms as cousins and friends', she wrote, 'and he had shown a liking for me with which I was much gratified.' But she was not impressed when Charles started a desultory flirtation – telling her, among other things, that she was handsomer than his mistress, the notorious Lucy Walter – and began to avoid him, 'having sense enough to know that the marriages of great kings are not made up by such means'.[14] Sophie had no intention of being left on the shelf like her two unfortunate elder sisters and believed, correctly as it turned out, that she would have a better chance of finding a partner at her brother's court than by staying in the Hague. She therefore left for Heidelberg in August 1650 and was presently joined there by the eldest Palatine princess, so that by the time the Princess of Orange was brought to bed only Louise remained at the Wassenaer Hof.

In the end, the Queen of Bohemia saw her youngest daughter depart without too much regret. 'As for Sophie's journey, I will never keep any that has a mind to leave me, for I shall never care for anybody's company that doth not care for mine.'[15] Elizabeth was now taking a close interest in the affairs of her 'best neece' and in January 1651 told Charles Louis that 'tomorrow the Princess of Orange and I Christen my little Nephew with the States; his name will be William Henry'.[16]

In fact, the baby's name represented a defeat for his mother in the three-cornered battle between herself, her mother-in-law and the States General currently being fought over his cradle. Mary had wanted to call her son Charles, but the dowager objected that it was an unlucky name and had insisted on another William. This, however, was a minor skirmish in the feuding over 'la tutelle', or the guardianship of the child, which was being claimed by his grandmother, the dowager princess, and his uncle by marriage, the Elector of Brandenburg, on the grounds that his mother was herself under age and too immature for so important a responsibility. Mary had countered by producing her late husband's will, which contained a codicil dated December 1649 conferring on his wife the office of tutrix to his children, should he leave any, and increasing her dower revenue to £20,000 a year if she had a child. Attempts by the dowager to have this declared invalid were unsuccessful and Mary was able to supply another useful piece of evidence from William's private cabinet. This was a copy of a secret letter of instruction from the prince to Count Dohna, governor of the town of Orange, requiring him to hold the place for the Princess Royal his wife in the event of his death, and to act according to the orders she should give him. Unfortunately, Dohna was related to the dowager princess and preferred to take his orders from her, but Mary could still claim with some justification that her husband had shown he considered her fully capable of bringing up their son and administering his estates.

The matter was referred by the States to the Court of Justice which presently decreed that Mary should be sole guardian of her son's person and have the power to appoint the officers of his household, while the dowager princess and the Elector of Brandenburg were to be joint inspectors of his property. The Queen of Bohemia was delighted that her niece had got just sentence 'of being declared absolute tutoress to her son', but Amalia de Solms, supported by the elector, appealed the decision and the court finally ruled that Mary must share the guardianship with her mother-in-law and the Brandenburgs. Mary was not happy with this compromise arrangement, but had little choice but to acquiesce. She had never been popular in Holland, having never troubled to conceal her poor opinion of all things Dutch, and her position was consequently vulnerable.

The House of Orange itself was on somewhat shaky ground just then. As the United Provinces, led by Holland, grew stronger and more prosperous, so their sense of obligation towards the family which had defended their liberties against the Spain of Philip II inevitably began to wane and the tide of republicanism to rise. To be fair, this revulsion of feeling had quite a lot to do with the behaviour of the last two princes of Orange. Frederick Henry's judgement had been seriously impaired by mental illness in the last years of his life, and William II's clumsy attempts to extend his authority over the provincial assemblies had roused considerable resentment among the merchant class, which now saw its opportunity to curb Orange pretensions. The offices of Stadtholder and Captain General had been made hereditary in gratitude for the services rendered by William I, but now the States positively refused to confer them on a young child – especially one brought up by a mother 'whose family interest shall swallow up all other, and ever be preferred before those of our state, our trade, and our own welfare'.

Mary's well-known devotion to her family's interests was understandable enough in the circumstances, but scarcely tactful for a princess of the house of Orange at a time when the Dutch were hoping to negotiate an alliance with Commonwealth England, and it was to involve her in some humiliating clashes of will with the States. On the anniversary of her father's execution, which royalists everywhere kept as a solemn day of mourning, the princess and her aunt Elizabeth were forcibly prevented from having a sermon preached in the English Church and obliged to retreat to continue their devotions in Mary's private apartments – something which an anonymous correspondent regarded as 'an unparalleled affront'.

Not long after this, a diplomatic mission arrived from the republican government in London which, for the first time, was given official and public recognition by the States General.

Needless to say, the occasion was ostentatiously boycotted by the Princess of Orange, who retired to her dower residence at Breda taking her baby son with her. There were, however, a couple of unfortunate incidents involving the young Duke of York and Prince Edward Palatine, who encountered members of the ambassadorial party on the streets of the Hague. Insults were freely offered and Ned was made to apologize, although his mother considered he had merely called Cromwell's creatures by their true names, while it was made clear to both princes that in future their room would be preferred to their company. Times, in short, were changing, and the days when the house of Orange had been able to offer unrestricted hospitality to dispossessed royal Stuarts and their hangers-on were rapidly coming to an end.

The summer and autumn of 1651 was an especially anxious period for all dispossessed royalists as they waited for news of their king. At the beginning of August, after enduring a miserable twelve months of being bullied, prayed over and preached at by the Covenanters, Charles had at last begun to advance into England at the head of an unenthusiastic Scottish army. They were pursued by Cromwell's Ironsides, who had already trounced the Scots once at Dunbar the previous year and were fully prepared to give a repeat performance at the first available opportunity. This occurred on 3 September at Worcester – Cromwell's 'crowning mercy' and the latest, worst and seemingly conclusive defeat for the royalist cause.

News of Worcester reached France and the Low Countries in a matter of days – then nothing for nearly seven weeks. Nothing until a tired, desperately shabby young man with a brown complexion, close-cropped black hair and only one companion turned up in Rouen, begging money and clothes from a couple of English merchants in the town. The king's apparently miraculous return from the dead produced a brief spasm of euphoria among the exiles, but in truth their prospects had never looked bleaker and Charles himself soon lapsed into a fit of deep depression. The French gave him sanctuary for his mother's sake, but there was no disguising the fact that he was a failure, a penniless outcast living on the fringes of the Court, dependent on the charity of his mother's relatives, an object of pity mixed with a certain amount of barely concealed Gallic scorn.

But if nothing else, Charles was a survivor. He learned to cope, to hide his despair behind a façade of carefree charm, to sing for his supper and take his pleasures wherever he could find them. A definite bright spot in those first grim months was the uncritical affection of his youngest sister. Henrietta Anne, christened Minette, or 'little puss', by Charles, was seven years old now, a delicate pretty child who hero-worshipped her glamorous grown-up brother and happily became his pet and playmate.

Minette and her mother were now established in a suite of rooms in the Palais Royal, Cardinal Richelieu's old house, but with the help of her sister-in-law the queen regent and some other anonymous donors, Henrietta Maria had managed to acquire a small, rather rundown château out at Chaillot, then in the suburbs of Paris on the north bank of the Seine. There she installed a dozen nuns of the Order of the Visitation, founded by St Francis de Sales especially to meet the needs of ladies of gentle birth, and often stayed there herself for several weeks at a time, taking Minette with her.

The widowed Queen of England was finding increasing consolation in her religion, but her determination to bring up her youngest child, her *enfant de bénédiction*, in the Catholic faith caused deep disquiet in the family. Charles's attempts to remonstrate with his mother on the subject had only resulted in a scene from which he hastily retreated, passing on the unpleasant task of speaking freely with the queen to his Chancellor and principal adviser, Sir Edward Hyde. Poor, faithful, pompous, conscientious Hyde did his best, 'as well as I could have done had it been to save my life', he wrote plaintively to the king's secretary Edward Nicholas. 'I told her the evil it might do the king by making his own religion suspected, the damage and prejudice it would bring her in the affections of England, and the irrecoverable ruin it would be to the princess.'[17]

But Henrietta, who loathed Hyde anyway, was unpersuadable. The late king of sacred memory had himself given her permission to raise her last child in her own faith she declared unanswerably. 'In a word, she was resolved, and it should not be in any body's power to hinder her.' Faced with so much 'passion and resolution' Hyde, too, retreated, only extracting a promise that the queen would not seek to put her daughter in a nunnery.

That was easily given – Henrietta Maria had more interesting plans for Minette's future.

It was obvious that nothing could be done – for the present at least – to rescue the princess from the toils of Rome. Charles was in no position to provide a home for his sister, even if the queen had been willing to let her go, and Sir Edward could only advise patience, pointing out that in any case it would be several years before the child was capable of understanding much about religion. Here, however, he underestimated the efforts of Father Cyprien, to whom Minette's religious education was entrusted and who found her an exceptionally apt and eager pupil – although she failed in her juvenile attempt to persuade her much-loved governess Lady Dalkeith, now Countess of Morton, to follow her in the paths of salvation.

According to Father Cyprien's own account, the queen, happy to see her daughter 'so warm in the cause of religion, had said to her, "My dear, as you have so much zeal, why do you not try to convert your gouvernante?" "Madame", replied the princess, in her childish innocence, "I do as much as I can. I embrace my gouvernante, I hug her, I kiss her, I say to her: Lady Morton, be converted; be a Catholic: you must be a Catholic to be saved. Father Cyprien tells me so very often; you have heard him as well as I: be a Catholic, ma bonne dame, and I will love you dearly."'[18] But Lady Morton, always a staunch Protestant, was proof against this type of blackmail. In the summer of 1651 she asked for leave of absence to attend to family affairs at home. There, sadly, she succumbed to an attack of fever and died without seeing her princess again – a clear instance, in the opinion of Father Cyprien, of the judgement of God and an awful warning of the dangers of not responding to His call when it was given.

Henrietta Maria might have been able to get her own way with Minette, but when she tried similar tactics with her youngest son there was a serious family row. Ever since the death of the Princess Elizabeth, the young Duke of Gloucester had been left at Carisbrooke Castle, seemingly almost forgotten. Then, early in 1653, the government in London decided that 'Henry Stuart, the son of the late King, should be sent out of the realm, for lessening the charges for his keeping by the Commonwealth'. A more compelling reason may have been recent signs of an upsurge of royalist interest in the twelve-year-old Gloucester, who was said to be a serious-minded, intelligent boy who might perhaps, some people thought, prove a more suitable candidate for the throne than his rackety eldest brother.

Accordingly, in March, 'little Mr. Harry' arrived in Holland with Richard Lovell, his faithful tutor, and £500 in cash. The Princess of Orange was delighted to see him and wanted to keep him with her, offering to provide for him and give him a good education. But from Paris came pathetic pleas from the queen for a reunion with the son she had not seen since he was a baby. It was difficult to refuse and Charles reluctantly agreed that his brother could come for a visit. Gloucester was an attractive youth, handsome, energetic and with plenty of Stuart charm. He was an immediate success at the French Court, and after his lonely, restricted life in England he blossomed in the general atmosphere of praise and approval.

There was quite a family gathering in Paris that summer, for the Duke of York, now an officer in the French army, was home on leave. But to Henrietta Maria's acute distress, France had begun to move towards an understanding with Cromwell's *de facto* republican regime, and by the spring of 1654 Cardinal Mazarin was indicating that it was time for Charles to move on. Charles himself was glad enough to get away from the endless feuding and intrigues of the exiles surrounding the queen and for once, thanks to Mazarin, he was in funds. He was not happy, though, about leaving young Harry in his mother's care and asked her with unusual earnestness to promise that she would not try to convert the boy. 'It is not in my thought that any such attempt should be made', she replied.

Charles left Paris in July on his way to Spa, where he had a joyful meeting with Mary, whom he had not seen for four years. Brother and sister had always been especially close and now they were planning a holiday. An outbreak of smallpox at Spa caused them to move on to Aachen, where they were very civilly entertained by the local dignitaries and shown the treasures of the cathedral, which included Charlemagne's skull, his sword and iron crown. The Landgrave of Hesse joined them for a visit and the time passed delightfully with hunting and hawking, sight-seeing expeditions and dancing in the evenings until the beginning of October, when Mary had unwillingly to start for home.

According to the agent of Cromwell's spymaster John Thurloe, who had been shadowing them all summer, 'R.C. [Charles], his sister royal, and their trains, bag and baggage, and I, close to them, parted from Aiken [Aachen] and lodged that night in Julick [Juliers]'. Next day the travellers came to Cologne and were put up in the house of a Protestant widow; 'very fair and curious, full of decent rooms and with pleasant gardens'. Cologne was a predominantly Catholic city but here, too, they were given a courteous welcome: 'The senate sent two hundred musketeers to give R.C. three volleys of shot at his door after his arrival, and did him much honour', reported the spy, adding that 'he and his sister, Saturday last, were invited by the Jesuits to their college, where they had a comedy prepared for them and a banquet after.'[19]

Brother and sister moved on to Dusseldorf, where they were royally entertained by the Duke and Duchess of Neuberg, and then Mary had to say goodbye. She was in floods of tears at parting and Charles, too, was plainly distressed. He went back to Cologne, where he was planning to spend the winter, to find letters from Paris informing him that the Duke of Gloucester was about to be received into the Catholic Church.

The news sent alarm bells ringing all round the family. Even Mary, a notoriously reluctant correspondent, was moved to write to Edward Hyde wishing some way could be found to hinder the misfortune likely to fall upon them 'by my brother Harry's being made a Papist. . . . Certainly there could not have happened a more fatal thing to his majesty at this time; but I hope God will give us some means of preventing it.'[20] The Queen of Bohemia was equally concerned. 'I am sorry', she wrote, 'the king has so much cause of grief . . . I believe my dear nephew has a good resolution, but there is no trusting to one of his age. I confess I did not think the queen would have proceeded thus.'[21]

Unfortunately, however, when it came to advancing the cause of her Church, the queen showed neither compunction nor common sense, and had been subjecting her teenage son to a relentless campaign of propaganda designed to persuade him to 'turn'. Surrounded by her priests and separated from his tutor and Dr Cosin, the Anglican chaplain in Paris, young Henry became deeply unhappy and bewildered. Theological argument was beyond him, but the memory of that dreadful January day at St James's Palace when he had leant against his father's knee and heard him speak of maintaining the true Protestant religion would always remain with him, so that even when he was sent away to the abbey at Pontoise, his resolution held firm.

From Cologne, Charles, roused for once to real anger, wrote to his mother that he could only suppose she wanted never to see him restored, and to his brother that he need never think to see England or him again if he changed his religion.[22] The king had also sent the Duke of Ormonde to Paris to find out what was going on and to bring Gloucester away. There were angry scenes with the queen who, realizing that she had lost the battle, ordered the boy to get out of her sight. 'I will not own you as a son!' she screamed. When Gloucester, much distressed, waylaid her the following day to ask for a parting blessing, she ignored him, and when he tried to see Minette to say goodbye, the poor child burst into hysterical tears and refused to speak to him.[23]

As a result of this sorry episode, Henrietta was temporarily estranged from her family. Harry joined Charles in Germany and later, together with his brother James, followed a career as a professional soldier. Charles himself remained based at Cologne for another year and Mary, who had been forbidden to receive him in Holland now that the States had signed a treaty with the Commonwealth of England, joined him for another holiday in the summer of 1655. This time, taking Harry and a small retinue with them, they went on what was supposed to be a private visit to the famous Frankfurt Fair, travelling from Bonn on one of the Rhine river barges. The correspondent of the republican news-sheet *Mercurius Politicus* was much impressed by the convenience of this method of transport, 'for besides the greater', he wrote, 'they had two lesser boats fastened to it. In one they conveyed all their beds, trunks, and wardrobe, and they made a kitchen of the other, which was a very fine accommodation for this water voyage, that continued for four or five days, having all their victuals dressed at hand, and at table there was no state nor distinction among them, eating all together (as I hear) to make the more merry. In the acting of this frolic, they would needs pretend to pass incognito, yet carried the matter so notoriously that it was known all abroad.'[24]

Although the king's prospects showed no sign of improvement – on the contrary, an attempted royalist rising in England that spring had failed disastrously – Charles continued to be merry in public, especially when he had congenial company. He began a letter to his aunt Elizabeth 'in my sister's chamber, where there is such a noise that I never hope to end it, and much less write sense'. He would only tell her Majesty that they were thinking how to pass their time, 'and in the first place of dancing', in which there were two difficulties, the one for want of fiddlers and the other for want of someone to teach them the new dances. They were waiting for the fiddledidees, and in the meantime had to content themselves 'with those that make no difference between a hymn and a coranto'.[25]

Mary stayed till the middle of November before returning, reluctantly as usual, to the Hague. For the sake of her son's future she dared not openly defy the authority of the Hoghens Moghens – the 'high mightinesses' of the States General – but her resentment over their attitude towards her beloved brothers continued to smoulder and although Cromwell's agents regarded her court as a vipers' nest of disaffection, the princess continued to provide whatever help and support she could to the numerous distressed Cavaliers struggling to survive in the Low Countries. She had already given sanctuary to Jane Lane, the royalist heroine who had played such a vital part in the king's escape after the Battle of Worcester, and was also employing Edward Hyde's daughter Anne as one of her maids-in-waiting – a gesture which was to have far-reaching consequences for the family.

Life at the Hague had its compensations – at Christmas and the carnival season of Kermesse it could be quite gay and the Queen of Bohemia's letters mention balls and masquerades, at one of which the Princess of Orange appeared very becomingly dressed 'like an Amazone'. But in December 1655 Mary was writing to Charles: 'I have not been well since I came home, and I know nothing so well able to cure me as to see you in Flanders, which I am very sorry to find is not so near as you expected when we parted. . . . I beg your pardon if I do not say much at this time; for truly, writing troubles my head, and I must give a little relation to the doctor of my health; for now from the green sickness I begin to fancy I shall fall into a consumption, though none is of my opinion; which I believe they disguise, because they would put that fancy out of my head.'[26] The Queen of Bohemia was sorry to see her 'best neece' looking so poorly and also privately feared consumption, but clung to her belief that exercise was the best medicine – one of the more bizarre remedies which she recommended to Mary was sawing wooden billets!

There were no holiday jaunts abroad for the Winter Queen. 'I must stay here, having no money.' Any hopes that her financial problems would be solved by Charles Louis's restoration had quickly faded, and the next ten years were spent in a wearisome and increasingly acrimonious battle fought out on paper between mother and son over the non-payment of her widow's jointure. 'I am not so unreasonable to think that you have the same revenues out of the Lower Palatinate as the king had', she told him in 1650, 'but yet I believe you will think too, that I cannot live upon the air.'[27]

Elizabeth may have been genuinely trying to be reasonable, but she never fully comprehended the extent of the devastation left by the wars; that Frankenthal, her dower property, lay in ruins and that Charles Louis, with the best will in the world, would have been in no position to pay her anything like the income that had originally been settled on her. Charles Louis did not, in fact, have the best will in the world. 'I did not think that I should be put to dispute with you for my maintenance', his mother wrote bitterly. The 'pitiful small' sums which trickled through from Heidelberg were never anything like enough, 'and if all the world were judge, I am sure they would not say but that I have no small cause to complain, since I ask not so much as is my due, and yet cannot get that'.[28]

In April 1651 the queen was able to congratulate her son on the birth of an heir. 'I wish you all happiness with your boy.' She was only sorry she could not afford to send her grandson a christening present, 'for truly all my jewels almost are at pawn, only such left that I cannot give away, keeping them for your father's and my eldest brother's sake . . . and I have no means to buy anything, being already so much in debt.'[29]

It was agreed that Rhenen, now deserted and rapidly falling into ruin, should be sold, but when 'the stuff belonging to my chambers' arrived at the Hague, it was found that the caretaker left in charge had stolen all the valuable gold and silver lace, 'about forty ells of it', which had once decked the queen's bed, and allowed most of the furniture and hangings to rot. The house itself was in such bad condition that Elizabeth doubted if anybody would buy it.

Charles Louis had also suggested as an economy measure that his mother should come and live with him and his wife at Heidelberg. Elizabeth was not enthusiastic. 'As for my resolution of going into Germany, I am willing enough to go, but there are many considerations to think upon before I resolve, for I must see how I may leave this place handsomely, how to content my creditors, and in what manner my jointure shall be settled in money or lands and what houses I shall have to dwell in.'[30]

When she realized that there was no question of dwelling in either Frankenthal or her other dower house at Fridesheim, which she remembered from her early married life as having a very fine garden, and that she would have to be content with a corner of the castle at Heidelberg – when, that is, it had been put into some sort of repair – she sent the faithful Lord Craven to the Palatinate to plead her cause with Charles Louis. The results were not encouraging and the queen wrote to his lordship in November 1653:

I have received and read both your letters, and find little comfort in them concerning my own particular; it may be my next will tell you I have no more to eat: this is no parable but the certain truth, for there is no money nor credit for any; and this week, if there be none found, I shall neither have meat, nor bread, nor candles. I know my son would have me to be rid of all my jewels, because he thinks he doth not deserve so well of me that he should share in them after my death. . . . I believe he means to starve me out of his palace, as they do blocked towns. I know he may do it, and has already begun pretty well; but he will have as little comfort as honour by it; for if I will be forced by ill usage to go, I shall be very ill company there.[31]

But whatever happened, 'let him be as tyrannical as he will be to me', she was not going to face the rigours of a winter journey. She could not possibly be ready to move before May at the soonest and in the meantime renewed her pleas for more money, 'for you cannot imagine what shifts I am put to here'.

Elizabeth was by now more or less resigned to the prospect of moving. 'I assure you it shall not be my fault if I do not go from hence to you to Heidelberg', she told Charles Louis in January and began to make anxious enquiries about her lodgings. 'I pray you let me have those that have most chambers upon one floor.' She would need to have her women as near to her as possible, and two 'cabinets', one to sit in and the other to put all her things in.[32]

But the Queen of Bohemia never did get to see Heidelberg or the Palatinate again. When her creditors heard about her planned departure, they raised such a storm of protest that it was clear there would be no question of her being able to leave the Hague, handsomely or otherwise, in the foreseeable future. As a last resort, and only 'the most urgent necessity hath been able to force it from us', she appealed to the States for help in settling her debts – at least until her creditors could obtain their just demands from England, or 'we may so manage our business in the Palatinate as to have wherewithal to content them'.[33]

The Dutch, who knew a bad investment when they saw one, would not pay her debts, though they agreed to make her an allowance of a thousand guilders a month 'for my kitchen', and the queen was thrown back on writing yet more begging letters to her unresponsive son. 'You did always promise me that as your country bettered, you would increase my means, till you were able to give me my jointure. I do not ask you much', she went on pathetically. 'If you would add but what you did hint, you would do me a great kindness by it, and make me see you have still an affection for me.'[34]

Although she continued to complain fluently about the many difficulties of her melancholy existence – 'my poor servants are almost starved for lack of board wages . . . I have not a smock but is all broken, nor other linen which is not in the same case' – the Winter Queen retained a keen interest in the world around her and never missed an opportunity for getting out and about. 'I was at Delft to see the wreck that was made by the blowing up of the powder magazine. . . . It is a sad sight, whole streets quite razed . . . there is scarce any house in the town but the tiles are off.'[35] On another occasion she contrived to make an expedition to Antwerp, where she caught a glimpse of the eccentric Queen Christina of Sweden, daughter of her one-time champion Gustavus Adolphus. 'She is extravagant in her fashion and apparel, but she has a good well-favoured face, and a mild countenance', was Elizabeth's verdict.

In January 1655 the Queen of Bohemia was writing to Edward Nicholas, 'I believe you will hear at Cologne how I have been debauched this last week sitting up late to see dancing. . . . Yesterday was the christening of Prince William[of Friesland]'s child. I was at the supper; my niece, the princess dowager, the little prince and Prince Maurice were gossips.' The little prince was the four-year-old William of Orange and his great-aunt recorded that he appeared at the supper 'and sat very still all the time; those States that were there were very much taken with him'.[36]

Elizabeth followed the careers of all her martyred brother's children with anxious attention. She could not always approve of Charles's life-style but never failed to accord him the respect due to him as sovereign and head of the family. Young Gloucester was her 'sweet nephew', but her favourite seems to have been her godson the Duke of York whom she had nicknamed Tint for reasons which remain obscure. When Mary was in residence at the Hague aunt and niece were regular companions, but early in 1656 the princess, having apparently recovered from her malaise of the autumn, was preparing to set out on a trip to Paris.

This project had been the cause of some friction with her brother and his friends, who pointed out that since the French government had now signed a treaty with Cromwell and Charles was negotiating with France's enemy Spain, this would hardly be a tactful moment for Charles's sister to appear at the French Court. Charles himself tried to persuade her at least to postpone her journey – apart from anything else, it was going to cost a great deal of money for which he could have found a better use. But Mary was not to be deflected. This was a purely private family visit. She had not seen her mother since she was a child and Henrietta had written so kindly pressing her to come 'that truly if I should deny her majesty, it were very barbarous in me'.

Socially the visit of the Princess of Orange was a glittering success. 'There is great preparation and disposition to pay her all the honours that she had cause to expect at her arrival, and to divert her during her stay', wrote Lord Jermyn to the king. 'The

117

great balls and the masque are reserved for her, and much of the good company of the place resolved to pay her all sorts of respects and civilities, especially those more particularly related than others to you and her.'[37] Mary was, after all, a granddaughter of France and first cousin to Louis XIV, and she certainly had nothing to complain about in the civilities with which she was received. 'She pleases all here, from the greatest to the least', wrote her mother on 4 February; 'she has been today so overwhelmed with visits that I am half-dead with fatigue.'

Although their relationship had never been especially close, there had been an affectionate reunion between mother and daughter, and Mary also had the opportunity of meeting her little sister for the first time. Minette was now approaching her twelfth birthday and beginning to attract favourable notice among the *cognoscenti* for her grace and charm and musical talent. She had made her first public appearance at the age of nine, when she had been honoured with a small part in a ballet given at a grand fête celebrating the marriage of one of Cardinal Mazarin's nieces. This remarkable production, which featured King Louis in his favourite role of Apollo, had been an immense critical success, with Minette's performance as Erato, muse of love and poetry, being singled out for special praise. Some sentimental souls began to whisper that his majesty might do worse than to marry the amiable and accomplished princess of England, but the teenage king had very different ideas and caused much embarrassment at a private party by refusing to dance with his cousin, saying sulkily that he did not like little girls.

There was another Stuart gathering in Paris during that carnival season for, despite the recent Anglo-French *entente*, the Duke of York was still serving in Turenne's army and was able to escort his mother and sisters when they went to visit another of their relations, Anne-Marie de Montpensier, daughter of Henrietta Maria's brother Gaston d'Orleans, known as 'La Grande Mademoiselle'. Mademoiselle – a great heiress with whom the Queen of England had tried long and unsuccessfully to match her eldest son – was inclined to look down on the dispossessed Stuarts, but even she was quite impressed by Mary. 'The Princess of Orange', she remembered, 'wore the most beautiful diamond earrings I ever beheld; very fine pearls, clasps, and large diamond bracelets, with splendid rings of the same.' The princess's mother evidently considered this display to be rather vulgar. 'My daughter of Orange', she told Mademoiselle, 'is not like me; she is very lofty in her ideas, with her jewels and her money. She likes splendour.'[38]

Mary was to have all the splendour her heart could desire in the dazzling succession of balls and ballets, masques and banquets that filled the next few weeks. According to the strict rules of conduct for widows laid down by the queen mother, Anne of Austria, she was not able to take part in the dancing, but it was noticed that Queen Anne showed the Princess of Orange every courtesy, even to the extent of inviting her to sit on a *fauteuil* (a chair with arms) – a privilege usually reserved for crowned heads.

This was Mary's first experience of court life on so brilliant and sophisticated a scale. Her obvious appreciation of their hospitality – 'I never, in all my life, received half so much civility' – made her popular with her hosts and, like her brother Harry before her, she bloomed in the unaccustomed atmosphere of gaiety and admiration. 'The Princess of Orange out-shone all our ladies', gushed a contemporary gossip columnist, 'although the Court was never more crowded with handsome women.'

Mary was still only twenty-four and a very eligible widow, so there was naturally talk of her remarriage. The Duke of Savoy and Ernest Augustus of Brunswick Luneberg, who were both in Paris at the time, were mentioned as possible suitors but Mary was not interested. How she would have reacted had she received a proposal from someone she considered to be of suitable rank remains a matter for conjecture – it had been rumoured that her real purpose in coming to Paris was to set her cap at King Louis – but she does not seem to have been thinking of marriage. She told La Grande Mademoiselle that as soon as her brother Charles was settled in one place, she meant to go and live with him. But although the Princess of Orange may not have been thinking of romance, nevertheless romance was in the air, for it was during this time that her brother James and her maid-in-waiting Anne Hyde first became lovers – a fact they were both very careful to conceal from their respective families.

Mary's stay in France prolonged itself through the summer, and it was well on into the autumn before she finally tore herself away. Charles was now established at Bruges in the Spanish

Netherlands, having signed a treaty with Spain whereby Philip IV agreed to work for his restoration in return for a promise of future help against France. Young Gloucester was with him and he had summoned James to join them, so that when Mary arrived on her way home to the Hague, there was another family reunion. Mary had brought some money with her and all the gossip from Paris, and they amused themselves by going to see a travelling company of French players much patronized by the king.

With her brothers now based in Flanders it was easier for the Princess of Orange to keep in touch and she was able to offer them an occasional refuge at her house at Breda, which lay outside the Dutch border in territory known as the Generality. John Thurloe's agents were convinced that she meant to break up the Anglo-Dutch alliance and was working to collect a fleet for a royalist expeditionary force. In fact, of course, both these undertakings would have been far beyond Mary's power to achieve and, although she continued to devote her energies to the family cause and to be more than generous with her own and her son's revenues, her relations with Charles were no longer quite as affectionate as they had once been.

The king was beset with problems, personal and political, which were trying even his usual relaxed temper to its limits. Apart from having to stall his new allies, who were urging him to convert to Catholicism, while at the same time persuading them to go on paying him a pension, he was engaged in a bitterly fought battle with his former mistress Lucy Walter over the custody of their son James. He had also fallen out with the Duke of York, who resented having to give up a promising career in the French army, and was beginning to find Mary's constant complaints against the Dutch and her attempts to involve him in her quarrels with her in-laws more than a little tiresome.

As a result brother and sister were drawn into squabbles over trivialities. Charles thought Mary's friends, Lord and Lady Balcarres, were intriguing with Cardinal Mazarin, and accused her of using Lord Balcarres 'much better since I have been unsatisfied with him than ever you did before'. Mary denied the charge indignantly. It was 'as false as those that report it of me' and she felt Charles was being unreasonable. A few months later there was trouble over Harry Jermyn, nephew of Henrietta Maria's close friend, counsellor and, some said, lover. Young Jermyn visited the Princess of Orange at the Hague and rumours of an undesirable degree of intimacy between them began to circulate. Charles, who detested all the Jermyns, immediately ordered his sister to send the young man packing and Mary, who appears to have been quite innocent of any impropriety, was hurt and furious. 'I hope you will give me leave to desire you to consider what consequences your severity will bring upon me', she wrote, adding that Jermyn's sudden departure would only encourage the scandalmongers.[39] But none of these misunderstandings lasted for long. The king was hampered by his recurrent need to borrow money from Mary, while she remained too dependent on his company and goodwill to hold a grudge. Indeed she was to spend more and more time following him about, seizing every excuse for a trip to Antwerp, Brussels, or Bruges.

Back at the Hague, marooned in her ramshackle Court where rats could be seen scurrying freely behind the threadbare soft furnishings, where the undisciplined servants often 'fought like gladiators' and robbed their mistress of everything from the silverware to the best beer, the Queen of Bohemia sadly missed her niece's companionship – and soon she was to be even more alone. A few days before Christmas 1657 the Princess Louise Hollandine failed to put in an appearance at the noon dinner hour. No one had seen her since the night before and it looked as if she had left the house in darkness, alone and on foot. A frantic search of her bedchamber produced a letter addressed to her mother which was hardly calculated to set that lady's mind at ease. It seemed that with the approach of the Christmas festivals, Louise had felt obliged to remove herself 'from fear of being desired to receive the sacrament against my conscience, since at length it has pleased God to discover to me the surest way of salvation, and to give me to know that the Catholic religion is that only way'. She begged her mother's pardon for taking a course inspired 'by a power which the powers of earth vainly resist', and went on to assure her Majesty that she had no other aim 'than that of securing a tranquil retreat where I may have full leisure for the service of God'.[40]

Elizabeth had always got on well with the artistic, unconventional Louise, the most congenial of her grown-up daughters, and this totally unexpected act of betrayal came as a stunning shock. It subsequently transpired that Louise had gone first to the English Carmelites at Antwerp and from there to Queen Henrietta Maria at Chaillot – hardly a tactful choice in the circumstances. She received a civil, if somewhat surprised, welcome from the French royal family, and Henrietta wrote promising to care for the defector as if she were her own daughter and asking for her afflicted sister-in-law's understanding and forgiveness. This was too much. After all, how would Henrietta have felt, 'if she had had the same misfortune'?[41] Deeply hurt and aggrieved over Louise's 'unhandsome' behaviour, the Queen of Bohemia suffered the added mortification of having to deny the slanderous rumours, which spread quickly round the Hague, that the Palatine princess had been obliged to seek shelter in a convent in order to conceal an illicit pregnancy. Mother and daughter never met again, and although Elizabeth did eventually agree to forgive and forget, it was only, she made quite clear, at the insistence of the King of England and his mother.

Louise herself appears never to have regretted her flight. She presently took the veil and ended her career as abbess of the convent at Maubuisson near Pontoise, where she lived out an unusually long life in the tranquillity she had sought in so dramatic a fashion. 'It is indescribable how pleasant and playful the princess of Maubuisson was', wrote one of her nieces. 'She said she had always liked a country life, and fancied she lived like a country girl.'

Another family scandal, which had been threatening for several years, came to a head in the winter of 1657 when Charles Louis and his wife finally separated and he consoled himself with a morganatic marriage. His mother, who held old-fashioned ideas about the sanctity of marriage – 'if everybody could quit their husbands and wives for their ill humours, there would be no small disorder in the world' – was shocked and saddened by her son's domestic problems and inclined to side with her daughter-in-law. She was also worried about Sophie, who was still living under her brother's roof, but could hardly 'with any honour' remain, now that his wife had left him and he was openly keeping a mistress.[42]

Fortunately Sophie solved the problem by becoming engaged to be married to Ernest Augustus of Brunswick Luneberg, a younger brother of the Duke of Hanover. It was not a brilliant match but, as Charles Louis remarked, 'in the present condition of our family we must be satisfied to take hold of what we can'. As for Sophie, she was now approaching her twenty-eighth birthday, and told her brother frankly that a good establishment was all she cared about. However, when Ernest Augustus arrived at Heidelberg for the wedding in October 1658, Sophie 'being resolved to love him, was delighted to find how amiable he was'. Charles Louis had made a great effort to give his sister a good send-off, and she went to the altar dressed 'according to the German fashion' in white silver brocade, with a long train borne by four maids of honour, and a diamond crown on her head.[43] The youngest Palatine now departed to live with her new family in Hanover and her mother, hearing that she had been 'very handsomely received there', wrote to King Charles asking him to consider bestowing the Garter on Ernest Augustus. 'He will take it for a great honour . . . and it will oblige all that house.'

Naturally no one at the time had any idea of the immense dynastic significance of Sophie's marriage, and in any case the whole of the expatriate English community was still in a ferment of excitement over news which had reached them early in September, for Oliver Cromwell, Lord Protector, great beast and murderer, was dead at last. In Amsterdam they were mad with joy. 'The young fry dance in the streets at noon-day. "The Devil is dead", is the language at every turn; and the entertainment of the graver sort is only to contemplate the happy days approaching.'[44]

In a very secret meeting at the Hague, George Downing, Cromwell's ambassador to the States General, knelt before the king to seek pardon for past offences and the Queen of Bohemia told Charles Louis that 'all the French court went to congratulate this monster's death with the Queen my sister', and Cardinal Mazarin himself had called him 'this viper'.[45]

In Paris and Cologne, Brussels, Antwerp and Ghent, wherever the exiled royalists had been eking out a miserable, poverty-stricken existence in cold, uncomfortable lodgings, glasses were being raised and optimistic plans made for the happy days now surely approaching.

FIVE

A GREAT MIRACLE

> There is no other news here but all are overjoyed at the news of
> England. It is not to be believed how all from the highest to the
> lowest are overjoyed.
> (Elizabeth, Queen of Bohemia to Charles Louis, Elector Palatine)

The rejoicing which greeted the news of Cromwell's death quickly
subsided. England remained quiet. Oliver's son Richard succeeded
him as Protector, and the European powers were apparently
content to go on dealing with the republican regime at
Westminster. It looked as if nothing had changed. Charles
remained a shadow king, 'having no part to act upon the theatre
of the world', and Edward Hyde thought his condition had never
appeared so hopeless, so desperate.

The disappointment was very hard to bear and, to make matters
even worse, the embattled Stuarts were once more falling out
among themselves. Charles had recently been paying court to the
Dowager Princess of Orange in the hope of being accepted as a
suitor for her daughter Henriette. He was unsuccessful, but when
Mary heard about it she was furious that he should ever have
contemplated an alliance with the Orange-Nassauers, whom she
regarded as her enemies. The Harry Jermyn affair, too, still rankled.
The princess would not brook any more interference in her private
life. She was not her brother's subject but a free woman and could
marry whom she pleased.[1] York and Gloucester seem to have taken
her side and during the wretched winter of 1658, when the family
fortunes were at their lowest ebb, James and Harry were living in
comfort as Mary's guests at Breda, while Charles, alone and
virtually penniless in Brussels, was reduced to selling the last of his
plate and eating his one meal a day off a pewter dish.

The Queen of Bohemia's financial situation showed no sign of improvement either, even her wedding ring was in pawn by this time, and a steady stream of letters about 'the necessity of my affairs' continued to flow from the Hague to Heidelberg. In April 1659 she wanted very much to meet Sophie and her new husband at Utrecht, but could not afford the expense of even so short a journey.

However, she did somehow manage to get herself to Brussels in June, 'all incognito'. She stayed in the house of the Palatine agent, 'who is the best man that can be and so is his wife', and wrote to Charles Louis, with a touch of complacency, 'I cannot enough tell you how welcome I am to all my nephews'. Sophie arrived from Amsterdam and the queen thoroughly enjoyed her little holiday. Everyone was being amazingly kind – 'I do nothing but ramble up and down with my nephews and other good company' – and Charles, whom she had not seen for nine years, was especially attentive, coming every day to fetch her to dinner.[2]

She was back in the Wassenaer Hof by the end of the month, but Sophie had promised to visit again, 'towards winter', and meanwhile there were other distractions, such as a jaunt over to Leiden and supper out at Honselaersdijck with her niece. 'I believe it will be morning before I come back, for her maids and gentlemen act a comedy in French, and there shall be a masque danced after it.'[3]

Mary was busy just then with supervising arrangements for her son's education. The Prince of Orange was eight years old, a solemn, dark-eyed little boy beginning to show signs of unusual promise. 'You cannot imagine the wit that he has . . . a very extraordinary child and very good-natured,' wrote the Queen of Bohemia. Unhappily, Piccinino, as his mother called him, was also a very delicate child and there had been more than one occasion in his infancy when he had not been expected to survive. But although he was never robust, and suffered from asthma and other chest problems all his life, young William had overcome convulsions, measles and other hazards of early childhood, so that by the time he was eight or nine his health was no longer giving serious cause for concern.

Mary has often been accused of being an uncaring mother, putting the interests of her own family before those of her child. It is true that she once told Charles that she could not love her son above all things in the world as long as Charles himself was alive, but there is nothing to suggest that she did not also love her son, or that she ever neglected his welfare. On the contrary, she kept him at home with her for longer than was usual at that time, and William was almost nine before he left his nursery at the Hague to go to the university town of Leiden, where a separate establishment had been set up for him. Even then Mary brought him back for a few days' private leave-taking at Breda, which suggests she was finding it as hard to part with him as any mother seeing her baby off to boarding-school for the first time.

William was still at the Hague when Sophie arrived for her promised visit, bringing with her Charles Louis's seven-year-old daughter Elizabeth Charlotte, or Liselotte as she was known in the family circle, and the two became playmates. Many years later Liselotte was to remember vividly going with her grandmother to the Binnenhof to pay a call on the Princess of Orange. Gazing round at the throng of strange ladies and gentlemen, she had asked Prince William, 'Who is that woman with the very red nose?' only to be told with a giggle, 'That is my mother, the Princess Royal.' Liselotte was struck dumb with embarrassment at this dreadful gaffe, but a kind young English lady, a Mademoiselle Hyde, came to her rescue, suggesting that she and William should go and play in the next room until the Queen of Bohemia was ready to leave. 'We played at all sorts of games', recalled the older Liselotte. 'We were both rolling about on a Turkey carpet when I was summoned. I jumped up and ran into the drawing room, but the Queen was already in the ante-chamber. I quickly pulled the Princess Royal back by her skirt, and, making her a pretty curtsey, walked in front of her, following the Queen to the carriage. Everyone laughed, I didn't know why.' As soon as they got home, Elizabeth, still in fits of laughter, regaled Sophie with the story of Liselotte's outing and Sophie, who did not greatly care for Mary, enjoyed the joke even more.[4]

Much to her family's amusement, the Queen of Bohemia had become quite besotted with her bright, pretty little granddaughter, who apparently reminded her of her poor dead Nennie. 'You know I care not much for children', wrote the mother of thirteen with unconscious humour to Liselotte's father, 'but I never saw none I like so well as her, she is so good natured and witty. . . . I can assure you I love her extremely. . . . She is a very good child and not troublesome . . . very apt and willing to learn anything. . . . You may believe me when I commend a child, she being one of the few I like.' Liselotte could dance the saraband with castanets – 'You cannot imagine how well she dances.' She could read and understand French and was learning some English.[5] Liselotte, in short, could do no wrong and Sophie told her brother that the queen talked no more of sporting dogs and monkeys, but only of Liselotte 'for whom she has taken a violent fancy'.

Elizabeth was able to enjoy the company of her new favourite until the spring of 1660, when Sophie, who was now well advanced in pregnancy, returned to Hanover to prepare for the birth of her first child. By this time, however, the Queen of Bohemia was beginning to receive exciting news from England, where the government of Cromwell's son had collapsed. Tumbledown Dick had returned thankfully to private life and now there were reports that the army commander, General Monk, was planning to declare for a restoration of the monarchy. In March Elizabeth heard that the streets of London were full of people lighting bonfires and drinking the king's health 'by the name of Charles the second and to his happy return'.

King Charles, meanwhile, had been on a private visit to Spain, or at least as far as the frontier town of Fuenterrabia, where Franco-Spanish peace talks were in progress and where he had been hoping, vainly as it turned out, to pick up support from one side or the other. On his way home he had stopped to see Henrietta Maria, who was now living at her new country house at Colombes, a few miles out of Paris. Mother and son had not met for five years, not since the unfortunate conversion attempt on the Duke of Gloucester, but now they embraced affectionately, past differences apparently forgotten.

Charles was also able to renew his acquaintance with his little sister. Minette was fifteen now, and a Yorkshire gentleman who had recently ventured to visit the Court of the widowed Queen of England and her daughter, recorded that the young princess had treated him 'with all the civil freedom that might be. She danced with me,' he continued, 'played on the harpsichord to me in her own apartment; she suffered me to wait on her when she walked in the garden, and sometimes to toss her in a swing between two great trees; and, in fine, to be present at all her innocent diversions.'[6]

According to an enthusiastic Frenchwoman, writing in 1658, the Princess Henriette was growing up to be a paragon of beauty and virtue. Her hair was 'of a bright chestnut hue, and her complexion rivals that of the gayest flowers. . . . Her eyes are blue and brilliant, her lips ruddy, her throat beautiful, her arms and hands well made.' Her wit was lively and agreeable. She was gentle, obliging and kind-hearted. She danced with incomparable grace, sang like an angel, 'and the spinet is never so well played as by her fair hands'.[7] Old Father Cyprien joined in the chorus, praising his former pupil's rare beauty, sweet temper, noble spirit and religious devotion.

Allowing for a generous measure of flattery – up until the autumn of 1659 there was still just the faintest chance that she might have married King Louis – Minette was clearly developing into an unusually attractive and talented young woman, with a full share of Stuart family charm. She was not strictly beautiful. One shoulder was slightly higher than the other, although this defect was so cleverly camouflaged that few people were aware of it, and she was always painfully thin. But she possessed an irresistibly appealing, fragile, waif-like quality and her brother Charles, that well-known connoisseur of the female sex, was instantly captivated. He stayed at Colombes for about a fortnight, and during that time the bonds of an enduringly affectionate relationship between brother and sister were forged.

To Minette, familiar with all the immensely elaborate, rigidly formal intricacies of French court etiquette, and with a system in which men competed fiercely for the privilege of performing the most menial tasks at the royal *levée* and *coucher*, her brother's informality was a delicious novelty, as was his willingness to laugh at himself and his misfortunes, and his refusal to take offence at slights – neither of which was a noticeable characteristic of the French royal family. To a princess brought up on stories of her father's martyrdom and her mother's afflictions, Charles was naturally invested with all the glamour of a wronged romantic hero. She could hardly have been expected to realize that behind all that easygoing geniality lurked a coldly calculating brain and a quite ruthless sense of self-preservation. As for Charles, he was truly charmed by the grown-up Minette, by her pretty manners, her eagerness to please and her touching delight in his company; he became genuinely fond of her, while at the same time recognizing a valuable potential asset in his exquisitely Frenchified little sister.

The king was back in Brussels before Christmas, but was soon writing that 'the kindness I have for you will not permit me to lose this occasion to conjure you to continue your kindness to a brother that loves you more than he can express . . . dear sister be kind to me and be confident that I am entirely yours'.[8] Minette felt he did her too much honour in writing so often. 'I am afraid it must give you trouble, and I should be sorry that your Majesty should take so much trouble for a little sister who does not deserve it, but who knows how to be grateful for that honour and is delighted with it. I hope that the peace [the Franco-Spanish treaty signed in November] will give you all the happiness you can wish for. . . . It is a great joy for me, since it gives me the hope of seeing your Majesty, which is a thing passionately desired by your humble servant.'[9]

Charles wrote again, a cheerful gossipy letter sent by the hand of Janton, 'the best girl in the world', who sang delightfully and was teaching him all the new songs. 'We talk of you every day and wish we were with you a thousand times a day.' He wanted to know how Minette had been spending her time, 'for if you stayed long at Chaillot in this miserable weather you must have been not a little bored'. Finally, he urged her not to treat him with so much ceremony in future, or address him with so many Majesties, 'for between you and me there should be nothing but affection'.[10] This letter, which is endorsed 'for deare deare sister', was written in February 1660, a few days before General Monk entered London with two regiments of horse and three of foot. 'What he will do none knows,' wrote the Queen of Bohemia, 'it may be not himself.'

The winter in Flanders was bitterly cold and the exiles, huddled over their meagre fires, waited with grim patience while the general, a dour and uncommunicative man, slowly made up his mind. The so-called Rump, the fifty-odd survivors of the 1648 purge of the original Long Parliament, was sitting again at Westminster and fighting a determined rearguard action, but the tide of public opinion was running high and strong for the return of the king and by March it was irresistible. The Queen of Bohemia, who was taking a keen personal interest in developments taking place across the North Sea, told her son that Monk had begun 'to show himself an honest man'. He had gone to the parliament house with the 'secluded' members – that is, those expelled in Pride's purge – 'and there they have annulled all that has been done since 1648, the year before the king's murder, and called a free parliament, of which they say there shall be lords and commons, for the rump is dissolved, and I hope shortly all will be in England whom I wish there'.[11]

Although there were still a few dissentient voices in the background, events now took on a momentum of their own. The free parliament elected in the spring of 1660 resolved that the government of England properly consisted of king, lords and commons and, having received a conciliatory message from Charles, proceeded to beg him to come home.

Charles was at Breda with his brothers and sister when the summons came, and Mary wasted no time in informing the high and puissant lords of the States General that her brother had been invited by the parliament of Great Britain to return to his dominions. Congratulatory messages flowed in from all sides and within a very few days a deputation arrived from the States of Holland, beseeching his Majesty to grace that province with his royal presence at the Hague, and promising that his reception 'would testify the great joy of their hearts for the Divine blessings which Providence was showering upon his head'.[12]

It was a sweet moment of triumph for Mary who had for so long suffered the mortification of seeing her beloved brother scorned and rejected, and who had been prevented from offering him hospitality even in the privacy of her own home. To the Queen of Bohemia it was 'a great miracle to see so sudden a change'. 'It is not to be imagined how all here are joyed at this,' she wrote, 'the very common people are as hot for the king as any of us.'[13] The family's journey from Breda turned into a triumphal progress and they entered the Hague at the head of a procession of seventy-two coaches with little Prince William, who had been brought from Leiden to play his part in the ceremonial, sitting on his uncle James's knee.

In the hectic week of banquets, balls, receptions, fêtes and military reviews which followed, the English royal family dined in public every day, with the place of honour on the king's right hand occupied by the Queen of Bohemia – 'he useth me more like a Mother than an Aunt' – while out in the streets bonfires blazed, church bells pealed, cannon roared and crowds of hopeful sight-seers gathered day and night. Nothing, it seemed, was too good for the King of England – 'if he were their own king the States could do no more for him' – and valuable presents, from a yacht to a state bed, rained down on him. Probably, though, the most welcome gift was the trunkful of gold coin thoughtfully provided by the English commissioners at Breda. Samuel Pepys heard they had been horribly shocked to find 'in what a sad, poor condition for clothes and money the King was' and how he had been so overjoyed to see the gold that he had called the Princess Royal and the Duke of York 'to look upon it as it lay in the Portmanteau before it was taken out'.[14]

An English fleet was now lying off Scheveningen, waiting for a wind to carry the king away, but meanwhile the Hague was full of English visitors and the Queen of Bohemia was so much in demand that she scarcely had a moment to herself. Among those queuing up to kiss her hand was Mr Pepys, present in his capacity of secretary to the admiral, Lord Montague. The great diarist pronounced her Majesty to be 'a very debonair [affable] lady', but commented on the plain style of her dress.

At last, wind and weather were favourable and everyone set out on the short journey to Scheveningen. The sands were black with people, and the air thick with smoke and the reek of powder as muskets popped and cannon fired salvoes from the shore and the guns of the fleet thundered in salute. As the king went aboard the flagship the *Naseby* – hurriedly rechristened the *Royal Charles* – a great shout went up from the crew: 'We have him! We have him! God bless King Charles!'

The family dined together privately 'in a great deal of state' in the coach – an apartment adjoining the admiral's cabin under the poop deck – and made, so Sam Pepys thought, 'a blessed sight to see'. Everybody was in expansive mood and the Queen of Bohemia was told not to worry any more about her debts. Of course parliament would pay them, the king would see to it himself. 'All those of them that were here have promised to do their best, and all in general beg of me to go into England, not one that was here but still sung that song.'[15]

But now it was time to say goodbye. Charles embraced his nephew and blessed him, bade farewell to his aunt and kissed and hugged his sister. All differences between them were long forgotten and Mary clung to her brother in floods of tears, while he tried to console her with promises that she should soon come to England. In the end she had to be practically torn out of his arms and was rowed ashore, still weeping and supported by a sympathetic Queen of Bohemia.

The next thing was an anxious wait to hear how the king had been welcomed home. He landed at Dover on 25 May according to the English calendar, to be received 'with all imaginable love and respect at his entrance. . . . Infinite the Crowd of people and the gallantry of the Horsemen, Citizens and Noblemen of all sorts', wrote Pepys. 'A Canopy was provided for him to stand under, which he did; and talked awhile with General Monk and others; and so into a stately coach there set for him; and so away straight through the town toward Canterbury. . . . The Shouting and joy expressed by all is past imagination.'[16] At Canterbury Charles snatched a moment to scribble a note to Minette, but 'my head is so dreadfully stunned with the acclamations of the people, and the vast amount of business, that I know not whether I am writing sense or nonsense; therefore pardon me if I say no more than that I am entirely yours'.[17]

Three days later, on his thirtieth birthday, the king entered his capital, where another chronicler of the passing scene, John Evelyn, stood in the Strand to see 'the ways strewed with flowers, the bells ringing, the streets hung with tapestry, fountains running with wine; the Mayor, aldermen and all the companies in their liveries, chains of gold, banners; lords and nobles, cloth of silver, gold and velvet everybody clad in; the windows and balconies all set with ladies; trumpets, music and myriads of people flocking the streets and ways as far as Rochester'.[18] With all this excitement going on in England, it is hardly surprising that the birth of Sophie's son George Louis in distant Hanover should have passed almost unnoticed.

One of the last things Charles had done before leaving the

Hague had been to commend his sister and nephew, 'two persons whom I esteem beyond measure', to the special favour and protection of the States General, and Mary took advantage of her son's enhanced status as nephew to the restored king and fifth in succession to the English crown to renew her campaign to persuade the States to recognize his right to the reversion of his father's honours. She had several conversations on the subject with John de Witt, Grand Pensionary and effective ruler of the province of Holland, and found him polite but non-committal. As he told the French ambassador, it was hardly advisable to promise such great offices to a nine-year-old boy, who might or might not grow up to be worthy of them; let his mother ensure that her son was educated so as to fit him for his future responsibilities before trying to claim them – and with that Mary had to be content.

The States of Holland did, however, revoke the so-called Act of Seclusion. This had been insisted upon by Cromwell, who had had no desire to see the late king's grandson wielding power in the Low Countries, and had made it a condition of the 1654 treaty that the prince and his descendants should be permanently debarred from office. The Act had always been highly unpopular with the Dutch, who saw it as an unwarranted interference in their affairs, just as popular feeling at grass-roots level had always run strongly in favour of the house of Orange. In that triumphant summer of 1660 even the republican citizens of Amsterdam invited William and his mother to pay their town a state visit and received them in royal style.

A good deal less satisfactory was the recent annexation by France of the ancestral land of Orange. Mary, driven to distraction by constant disputes with its uncooperative governor, had been unwise enough to ask Louis XIV for help in establishing her 'legitimate authority, and the tranquillity, that the violence of his lordship, Count Dohna have impaired'. Louis, only too pleased to be offered an excuse for removing an irritating (and Protestant) enclave from within his dominions, had proceeded to take the principality under his protection – in the interests, naturally, of young William, his esteemed neighbour and kinsman. This had not been at all what Mary had intended, but she was powerless to prevent the French action which, not surprisingly, was to be the cause of much future bitterness and contention.

But that was for the future. In the late summer of 1660 the princess was busy preparing for her forthcoming journey to England and making provision for her son's welfare while she was away. With this in mind, she had managed to persuade the States to agree to appoint a panel of commissioners to supervise his education, thus extracting a tacit admission that William's training in the 'princely virtues and exercises' had now become a matter of national concern. This counted as a victory, but Mary was still not quite easy in her mind. Although she and William had often been parted before, this time it seemed harder to say goodbye, and once more she sent for him from Leiden to spend a few days with her before she sailed. At the last moment she wrote again to the States General asking them to take special care of the child, 'the being who is dearest to us in the world', and as she embarked at Helvoetsluys on 29 September she begged the Queen of Bohemia, who had come to see her off, to keep a motherly eye on him.

Poor Mary's eagerly anticipated return home began disastrously, for hardly had she stepped on board the yacht *Tredagh* which was to carry her across the North Sea than she was met by the news that Henry, Duke of Gloucester had died of smallpox only a few days before. The death of 21-year-old Gloucester came as a dreadful shock to everyone and was, in the opinion of his aunt Elizabeth, 'a great loss to our house'. It is true that after his famous victory over his mother's priests he had become rather obnoxious for a while, but in the circumstances that was perhaps understandable and forgivable. Four years later he had fought bravely – 'as bravely as any of his ancestors had ever done' – alongside the Duke of York at the Battle of the Dunes, and the good-looking, high-spirited boy might very well have developed into a valuable asset to the royal family.

For his brothers and sisters, his mother and aunt, his death brought a sadness which dimmed much of the joy of the Restoration. Henrietta Maria would now never have an opportunity of being reconciled with her youngest son, from whom she had parted in anger six years earlier. The Queen of Bohemia, who had loved him, she said, as her own child, mourned the loss of her dear nephew, 'the best natured youth that could be'; while Mary was prostrated and remained in a grief-stricken stupor throughout the whole of a stormy and uncomfortable journey.

The malign fate which sometimes seemed to pursue the house of Stuart was especially active that autumn, and young Gloucester had no sooner been buried in Westminster Abbey than bereavement was followed by scandal. By early October rumours were spreading that the child being all too visibly carried by Anne Hyde had been fathered by the Duke of York and – worse – that the couple were secretly married. The Queen of Bohemia did not believe it. She knew, of course, that the unfortunate girl had gone to Dr Rumph as early as the previous May with a story of food poisoning and asking for strong physic 'to carry all away'; also that the good doctor, who had not attended the queen through thirteen pregnancies without learning to recognize the signs, had very properly refused to prescribe anything which might be harmful. To Elizabeth this seemed conclusive, for 'if it had been a marriage she would not have sought to destroy the child'.[19]

However, it presently appeared that there had indeed been a marriage, performed very privately but legally, in the presence of two witnesses, and a furious family row ensued. The bride's father, now the king's chief minister, was beside himself with rage and mortification, declaring that he would rather see his daughter the duke's whore than his wife and hoping the king would send her to the Tower. Edward Hyde's enemies, of whom there were many in the royal circle, lost no time in putting it about that Anne was a loose woman, notoriously free with her favours, and York began to panic and talk of repudiating her. In the middle of all this uproar Anne gave birth to a son and the queen mother arrived from France with the expressed intention of 'unmarrying' James. The matter was settled by the king, who alone behaved with generosity and common sense, taking the attitude that since the business was done they must make the best of it. He refused to listen to malicious gossip, visited the new Duchess of York at her lying-in, and conferred a peerage on her father. Even Henrietta, advised by Cardinal Mazarin who wanted to keep on good terms with Hyde, was eventually persuaded, albeit reluctantly, to accept the situation.

Henrietta had come to England, accompanied by her youngest daughter, partly to try to set her own financial affairs in order, but principally to obtain a suitable dowry for Minette, who was now engaged to be married. The previous August the Queen Mother of England had received a visit from the Queen Mother of France bringing a proposal on behalf of her younger son, Philippe, Duc d'Orleans. Henrietta Maria was overjoyed. Failing King Louis, who was marrying the Spanish infanta, this was just the sort of match she had dreamed of for Minette and she wrote off at once to London asking Charles to give his consent. 'I assure you that your sister is not at all displeased about it; and as to Monsieur, he is violently in love and quite impatient for your reply.'[20]

Charles was only too pleased to approve, and by the time mother and daughter reached London in November the affair was as good as settled. 'As for the marriage of Monsieur with the Princess of England,' reported the French envoy charged with the task of arranging the formalities, 'I regard it rather as a family and domestic matter, than as an affair of state. The King talks so publicly about it every day, and sees all its advantages so clearly, that there is scarcely any doubt about the matter.'[21]

The political advantages were certainly clear enough. Friendship with France, the largest and most powerful European state, could work only in England's favour and more especially in favour of England's monarch. Charles placed little reliance on the continued docility and enthusiasm of his subjects, and knew there could well come a time when his survival might depend on having wealthy and influential friends abroad. The fact that he was condemning his sixteen-year-old sister to marriage with a notorious homosexual seems not to have troubled him at all.

Minette herself raised no objections to the plans being made for her future. She would, of course, have known Philippe from a distance virtually all her life, but it is highly doubtful whether she had grasped the significance of her fiancé's effeminate appearance, his delight in cross-dressing, painting his face and adorning himself with jewels, earrings and patches. It is true that in an age when even the most irreproachably macho men about the court habitually wore satin and lace this idiosyncrasy would have been less conspicuous, while Philippe's obsessive interest in matters of dress and ceremonial generally was regarded as a bit of a joke. When La Grande Mademoiselle's father, Gaston d'Orleans, died in February 1660, King Louis informed her that she would

Princess Elizabeth aged about ten: miniature by Nicholas Hilliard c. 1605
(Courtesy of the Board of Trustees of the V & A)

Princess Elizabeth's parents, James VI and I, and Anne of Denmark: John
de Critz (Courtesy of the Board of Trustees of the V & A)

Elizabeth's elder brother, Henry, Prince of Wales: Isaac Oliver (The Royal Collection © 2003 Her Majesty the Queen)

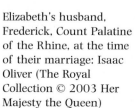

Elizabeth's husband, Frederick, Count Palatine of the Rhine, at the time of their marriage: Isaac Oliver (The Royal Collection © 2003 Her Majesty the Queen)

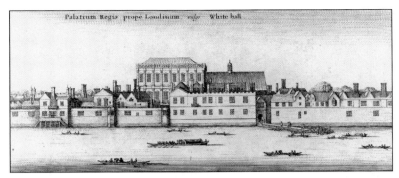

Whitehall, principal London home of the Stuart family, from the River
Thames: John Webb after Inigo Jones, c. 1637–9 (© British Museum)

Design by Inigo Jones for the Prince's Barriers, the tournament held on
Twelfth Night 1610 to celebrate the Prince of Wales's sixteenth birthday
(Devonshire Collection, Chatsworth. Reproduced by permission of the
Chatsworth Settlement Trustees. Photograph Courtauld Institute of Art)

Charles I as a child, c. 1613:
miniature by Nicholas Hilliard
(Courtesy of the Board of
Trustees of the V & A)

Queen Henrietta Maria
by Van Dyck (The Royal
Collection © 2003 Her
Majesty the Queen)

Charles I while a prisoner at Hampton Court in 1647: John Hoskins (By courtesy of the National Portrait Gallery, London)

James, Duke of York, Elizabeth and Henry, Duke of Gloucester, the three children who visited their father at Hampton Court: John Hoskins (Reproduced by permission of the Syndics of the Fitzwilliam Museum, Cambridge)

Charles Louis, Elector Palatine and Prince Rupert of the Rhine: Van Dyck
(Louvre, Réunion des Musées Nationaux, Paris)

Elizabeth, Queen of Bohemia: Gerald Honthorst (Ashdown House,
National Trust: photograph Courtauld Institute of Art)

Princess Mary, daughter of Charles I, and Prince William of Orange at the time of their marriage in 1641: Van Dyck (Rijksmuseum, Amsterdam)

Princess Mary as Princess of Orange: Van der Holst (Rijksmuseum, Amsterdam)

Princess Henrietta Anne as a child, Henrietta Maria's enfant de bénédiction: Claude Mellan (National Museum of Stockholm)

The men in Minette's life: her brother Charles II (above) in Garter robes by Peter Lely (The Royal Collection © 2003 Her Majesty the Queen); and (right) her husband, Philippe, Duc d'Orleans, Monsieur de France, by Pierre Mignard (Réunion des Musées Nationaux, Paris)

'The Exeter woman': Henrietta Anne, Duchesse d'Orleans and Madame de France, pet-named 'Minette' by Charles II (© Exeter City Museums, Royal Albert Memorial Museum, Exeter)

Princess Anne aged four, while staying in France with her aunt Minette:
unknown French artist (The Royal Collection © 2003 Her Majesty the
Queen)

Mary II as Princess of Orange in 1685: William Wissing (The Royal Collection © 2003 Her Majesty the Queen)

William III, Prince of Orange, at the time of his marriage in 1677: Peter Lely (By courtesy of the National Portrait Gallery, London)

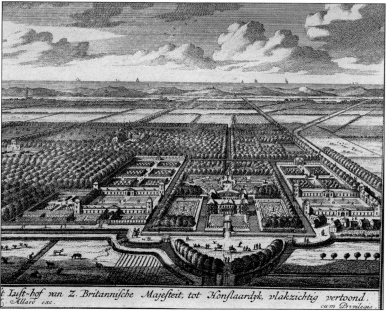

't Luft-hof van Z. Britannische Majefteit, tot Honflaardyk, vlakzichtig vertoond.
Allard exc.   cum Privilegio.

The Palace of Honselaersdijck near the Hague, where William and Mary spent the first months of their marriage (Rijksmuseum, Amsterdam)

Princess Anne aged eighteen: William Wissing and Van der Vaart
(Scottish National Portrait Gallery)

soon be seeing Monsieur in a trailing violet mantle. 'He is enchanted to hear of your father's death so as to have the pleasure of wearing one.'

From a worldly point of view it was a splendid match for a fatherless princess who had once had to stay in bed to keep warm in an unheated palace and who, until very recently, had possessed no value in the matrimonial market. 'You will marry the princess of England', Louis had told his brother, 'for nobody else wants her.' As the king's brother, Philippe bore the courtesy title of Monsieur and his wife would become Madame de France, the first lady in the land after the queen. Like her brothers and sisters, Minette had a strong sense of family pride, and rank and social status were important to her, but other considerations probably carried equal weight just then. She did not love the odd little creature who was to be her husband, but the marriage meant she would be able to remain among friends in familiar surroundings. She would not even be parted from her mother, for Henrietta Maria intended to return to France at least for the time being. Besides this, she was going to be useful to her brother. It was to be her mission to unite England and France so that Charles would be strong and independent and, unlike their father of blessed memory, able to withstand any future attacks from the enemy within. Meanwhile Minette, like any young girl, was enjoying a holiday in new, exciting surroundings which for her held no poignant memories.

Everyone was being very kind. Parliament voted her a dowry of £40,000 and the House of Commons added congratulations and the promise of the gift of an additional £10,000 which the princess acknowledged with affectionate gratitude, excusing herself that she could not do it so well in the English tongue, but desiring to supply the defect with an English heart.[22]

Everyone was anxious to catch a glimpse of her, though Mr Pepys was a trifle disappointed. 'The Princess Henriette is very pretty, but much below my expectations.' He disapproved of the way her hair was frizzed short up to her ears and thought his own wife, dressed in her best and wearing two or three black patches, looked much handsomer. But the French ambassador's secretary, who saw the princess playing cards with her sister Mary and the Duke of York, in a little mob cap and a multi-coloured cotton shawl, thought her lovely as an angel.

The French were beginning to agitate for the return of their bride, but Christmas was approaching and the royal family were planning to spend it together. Under the Commonwealth Christmas had been abolished but, as Father Cyprien recorded, the festival was always observed in England, especially in the king's palaces, 'with greater pomp than in any other realm in Europe', and this year it seemed that all the good old customs were to be revived. But once again tragedy was waiting to strike.

Unlike her younger sister, the Princess of Orange was not enjoying herself. She had been unwell ever since her arrival in London, complaining of 'an oppression at her chest' caused by the smoky atmosphere of the city, and, apart from a trip to Hampton Court, had scarcely left the precincts of Whitehall. A week before Christmas she became seriously ill and on 21 December Lord Craven wrote to the Queen of Bohemia to tell her of the 'hot alarum of the princess royal's being in great danger of death . . . but because your majesty should not be frighted at what news perchance you may hear, I have just now been with her and, God be praised, she is much better. The doctors do not yet know whether it is the pox or the measles, but I fear it will prove the smallpox.'[23]

Smallpox it was, but although the appearance of the rash was generally considered a hopeful sign, the improvement did not last. The doctors who had attended the Duke of Gloucester had been blamed for not bleeding him enough and were determined not to repeat their mistake with Mary, thus ensuring that she had no strength left to fight the infection. But it seemed she had little will to fight. Her aunt Elizabeth heard that 'as soon as she fell sick, she said she should die, but was not at all afraid of it and rather seemed willing to die'.[24] She remained fully conscious and on the morning of Christmas Eve she made her will, leaving her son to the care of her brother the king and the queen her royal mother, 'as the best parents and friends I can commend him unto', and entreating his majesty 'most especially to be a protector and tutor unto him'.

Mary had received the sacrament, 'of which she partook with great devotion and perfect confidence in her salvation' and, when the king burst into tears, had spoken of death 'without fear or emotion'. But still the physicians would not leave her in peace.

They pronounced it necessary to bleed the patient again and insisted on opening a vein in her foot. 'The operation was scarcely concluded', wrote her friend Lady Balcarres, 'when her eyes did look so dim that it was obvious to all she was dying. After that she had no signs of great pain, but every instant did visibly decay, till she lost all her senses, and about twelve or half an hour past it, the Lord took her to Himself.'[25]

In the twenty-nine years of her life the second Mary Stuart had known little personal happiness and made no lasting impression on the history of her times. Two months after her death Lord Craven remarked bitterly that the Princess Royal was as much forgotten in London as if she had never been; but that Christmas Eve of 1660 she left behind a shocked and darkened court and a sorrowing family. Charles had defied the risk of infection to stay beside her throughout her illness, remembering perhaps those long-ago holidays in Germany – the carefree interludes snatched out of the anxiety and penury of exile, when he and Mary had sailed down the Rhine, their whole party eating together without state or distinction 'to make the more merry', had gone sight-seeing and danced, even when the musicians could not tell the difference between a hymn and a coranto.

Mary had never been much liked in Holland, but the news of her death was received with respectful sympathy. 'All here from the highest to the lowest are very sorry for her, all the officers are commanded by the State to mourn.' The Queen of Bohemia went in person to Leiden to comfort the ten-year-old Prince of Orange, who had surprised his household by the intensity of his grief, and was herself 'so sad I fear I write nonsense'. At the end of January her affliction over the loss of her dearest niece was still very great. 'I shall never forget her memory. We lived almost twenty years together and always loved one another.'[26]

Mary was buried beside her brother Harry in the family vault in Westminster Abbey on 29 December, and three days later the queen and Princess Henriette set out on the first stage of their journey back to France. Minette had been hastily removed to St James's as soon as Mary's illness was diagnosed, but frantic appeals were now arriving from Monsieur who, fearing the loss or – worse – disfigurement of his bride, was imploring the queen to bring her out of the danger zone without delay.

Mother and daughter embarked at Portsmouth but were almost immediately overtaken by Henrietta Maria's proverbial bad luck at sea. A storm blew up and their vessel ran aground on the Horse Sand, so that the royal party was obliged to return to harbour. To add to their troubles, the princess had fallen ill with a high fever and for a few dreadful days it looked as if she, too, might have been struck down by the smallpox epidemic which was raging at the Court. 'This news do make people think something indeed', remarked Mr Pepys, 'that three of the Royal Family should fall sick of the same disease, one after another.' Fortunately, it was decided that Minette was suffering from no more than a bad attack of measles, but some of her people were of the opinion that she owed her recovery to her sensible refusal to allow the physicians to bleed her to excess.

At last, on 25 January, the travellers were able to set out again and this time reached their destination at Le Havre without mishap. They were met at Pontoise by the French royal family, and Father Cyprien, who had accompanied the queen and princess on their visit to England, described the reunion between the engaged couple in glowing colours. Monsieur, it seemed, 'fancied himself in Paradise on seeing Madame Henriette . . . looking steadfastly at her, he scarcely knew whether he ought to believe his eyes, so delighted was he to behold her again, and so overcome that he could hardly speak when he kissed her'.[27]

There was still some unavoidable delay before the wedding date could be fixed. The papal dispensation necessary for a marriage between first cousins did not arrive until the beginning of March. Then Cardinal Mazarin died and the court went into mourning for a fortnight. Monsieur grew increasingly restless and impatient and was further exasperated by the antics of the Duke of Buckingham, who had insisted on attaching himself to the party in England. This optimistic individual, son of the assassinated first duke, had caused a brief scandal in the family ten years earlier by his pursuit of the newly widowed Princess of Orange, and was now declaring himself hopelessly in love with the Princess Henriette. None of the English took him seriously, but Monsieur was not amused. He sulked and complained to his mother. Representations were made to London and Buckingham departed, still dolefully protesting his undying devotion. It was not usual to celebrate marriages in Lent and the bride's family was still in mourning but, in view of the bridegroom's state of nervous agitation, the two queen mothers agreed that it would perhaps be wiser not to wait any longer, and the wedding took place very quietly on 31 March in Henrietta Maria's private chapel in the Palais Royal.

The Court public relations machine greeted this auspicious union of rank, youth and beauty, of the lilies of France and the English rose, with an expectable outburst of enthusiasm. Praise was lavished on the grace and loveliness of the bride, the blue blood and virtue of the groom, and years of infinite happiness were promised to 'ce couple royal d'amoureux'. The poet La Fontaine recalled the bride's romantic history, her birth in the midst of war and tumult, her fortunate escape to become the darling of the Sun King's Court, and he too foretold a future of unalloyed bliss for the newly wedded pair.

> O couple aussi beau qu'heureux,
> Vous serez toujours aimables;
> Soyez toujours amoureux!

Minette herself, making her debut in society as a married woman, scored an immediate and triumphant personal success. Never, wrote her contemporary, the accomplished courtier and man of the world the Abbé de Choisy, 'never has France had a princess as attractive as Henriette d'Angleterre, when she became the wife of Monsieur. Never was there a princess so fascinating, and so ready to please all who approached her. . . . Her whole person seemed full of charm. You felt interested in her, you loved her without being able to help yourself.'[28] Another courtier who knew her well at this time spoke of the sweetness and gentleness 'which no one can resist. When she speaks to you, she seems to ask for your heart at once, however trifling are the words that she has to say. Young as she is, her mind is vigorous and cultivated, her sentiments are great and noble, and the result of so many fine qualities is, that she seems rather an angel than a mortal creature.'[29]

Her mother's old friend Madame de Motteville, describing the sixteen-year-old Minette, had remarked that although her beauty was not of the most perfect kind – her face was too long and her extreme thinness threatened early decay – 'she was so lovable in herself that she could not fail to please'. She might not have been able to become queen, but, 'to make up for this disappointment, she wished to reign in the hearts of all good people by the charm of her person, and the real beauty of her soul'.[30] Even La Grande Mademoiselle, who had been accustomed to regard the young princess of England with rather condescending pity and was not pleased by her sudden elevation, admitted that she was extremely amiable. 'There was a peculiar grace in all her actions and she was so courteous that everyone who approached her was charmed.'

Everyone, that is, except her husband, whose ardour had been more that of an avid collector of desirable objects than a genuine human emotion, and who was later to confess that his love for his wife had lasted exactly a fortnight. But then, as another contemporary observed, 'the miracle of inflaming his heart was not in the power of any woman in the world'. All the same, during that first brilliant summer, the novelty of marriage had not yet entirely worn off. Monsieur could still derive satisfaction from the admiration his bride was attracting, which he regarded as a compliment to his own good taste, and congratulate himself on his perspicacity in discovering and acquiring such a treasure before the rest of the world had learned to appreciate her.

After a few weeks at St Cloud, the delightful country house on the banks of the Seine which was to become Minette's favourite retreat, Monsieur and Madame joined the king and queen who were holidaying at Fontainebleau. They were all very young – Louis still only twenty-three, Philippe twenty-one, Minette barely seventeen – and although Louis, free at last from the tutelage of Mazarin, fully intended to become a great king, he also intended to enjoy himself. 'Never', wrote Madame de Motteville, 'had the Court of France witnessed festivities of so varied a kind as were seen at Fontainebleau that summertime.' The days were filled with hunting parties and rides in the forest, with bathing parties and picnics and *fêtes-champêtres*, the nights with banquets and balls and ballets, masquerades and theatricals, and always in the thick of the fun was Madame, with her delicate pink and white complexion, her sparkling dark eyes and rich auburn hair, dazzling everyone with her wit and gaiety and radiant charm, and quite eclipsing the king's dull, lethargic Spanish wife who thought of nothing but eating and going to church and playing cards.

In July a ballet was staged before the whole Court on a stretch of lawn beside the lake in the gardens of the palace. The surrounding avenues of trees were illuminated by thousands of torches and the lake shimmered with coloured lights. In this romantic setting Madame appeared as Diana the huntress, chaste and fair, with a silver crescent moon in her hair, while the king, representing Spring and followed by a troop of lovers, knelt at her feet and hailed her as Queen of Beauty.

Like most people, Louis had been taken aback by the startling transformation of the shy, skinny little girl he had once refused to dance with, but it was not long before the Court began to notice that the king admired Madame and that the understanding which had sprung up between them seemed rather closer than was suitable for a brother- and sister-in-law. It was always Madame who rode or drove beside the king on excursions abroad, Madame who was singled out for his gallantry, Madame who accompanied his Majesty on long moonlight walks in the forest. They exchanged witty little notes in verse and planned the next day's entertainment together. Suggestions have been made of a possible romance and Louis was certainly a man of strong physical appetites, but there is really no evidence that this affair was ever anything more than the sentimental pleasure of two mismatched young people finding congenial companionship in one another – a pleasure spiced, of course, with the flavour of sexual attraction and forbidden fruit.

But people were talking. Louis's wife might have been dull, but she was not stupid and was quite capable of jealousy. His mother, too, felt neglected and resented the amount of time the king was spending with Madame and the influence she appeared to be exerting over him. Henrietta Maria, out at Colombes, heard enough to make her uneasy and Madame de Motteville was encouraged to drop a hint to the princess that it would be wiser at least to give up those midnight promenades. Minette listened with her usual good grace, but 'her natural sentiments were opposed to prudence'. She 'heard with the ear the counsels I gave her', wrote de Motteville, 'but the impulses of her heart rejected them'.[31] Minette, in short, could see nothing wrong in her friendship with the king, and is said later to have told one of her confidantes that although constantly teased about Louis's attachment to her, she had never believed it to be warmer than was justified by their family relationship. Louis, though, had scented danger and began to transfer his attentions to Madame's maid of honour, Louise de la Vallière. Madame confessed to a certain amount of pique over the favours being heaped on her maid, but was soon finding consolation in the barely concealed devotion of the Comte de Guiche, a handsome soldier and courtier and a favoured member of Monsieur's circle.

By late autumn Monsieur and Madame were back in Paris and Madame was not at all well. Never very strong, she may have been suffering from general exhaustion after all the excitement and party-going of the summer. She was thinner than ever, suffering from a persistent cough and unable to sleep without the help of sedatives. She was also pregnant and the doctors, fearing a miscarriage, ordered her to stay in bed. She obeyed but, apparently unable to relax, continued to hold court till late in the evening – her bedroom becoming a salon for the cream of Paris society.

In England King Charles had been disturbed by reports of Minette's illness and wrote just before Christmas: 'For God's sake, my dearest sister, have a care of yourself, and believe that I am more concerned in your health than I am in my own, which I hope you do me the justice to be confident of, since you know how much I love you. . . . I am very glad to find that the King of France does still continue his confidence and kindness to you, which I am so sensible of, that if I had no other reason to ground my kindness to him but that, he may be most assured of my friendship as long as I live, and pray upon all occasions assure him of this.'[32]

As he wrote to his dearest sister, Charles was also concerned for the welfare of his aunt. Ever since the departure of the English exiles from the Hague and the death of her 'dearest niece', the Queen of Bohemia had grown increasingly restless. In the early months of 1661 the question of her return to the Palatinate was raised again, but as Elizabeth refused to stay under her son's roof, 'for seldom many families agree together and I love to live in quiet', and Charles Louis was not prepared to offer her separate accommodation – 'when your majesty is here, it will be but one family, for nobody will dare to contest against anything that shall be for your service and convenience' – the idea came to nothing, no doubt to the elector's relief.[33]

Elizabeth always insisted that she would have been willing to consider going back to Germany if her creditors in Holland could have been satisfied and a proper home provided for her, as laid down in her marriage contract; but she realized now that the son who had once been her favourite child had no intention of ever rebuilding Frankenthal for her, or of making any real effort to pay her anything like the income due from her dower revenues. Besides, she was determined not to appear to give any recognition to his irregular matrimonial arrangements. 'There are such accidents fallen out in your domestic affairs', she wrote sadly, 'that I thank God I am not there.' As the weeks passed, her thoughts turned more and more towards England. A little money had filtered through – just enough to pay off her most pressing debts and redeem a few precious pieces of jewellery – but her friends in London and her principal creditors were all of the opinion that her best chance of getting her affairs settled would be to go over in person, preferably soon, while parliament was still in session.

The queen had been hoping for a renewal of the invitation handed out so light-heartedly on board the *Royal Charles*. But it had not come, and as soon as the king's coronation was 'happily passed', she decided not to wait any longer. Lord Craven had offered to lend her his town house, the Dutch were providing her with ships and she assured the Duke of Ormonde rather pathetically that she would give very little trouble. She would be bringing no more than twenty-six or twenty-seven people with her, and was resolved to put herself wholly into her nephew's hands and 'obey him in all things'.[34]

It was a big upheaval and quite an undertaking for a lady approaching her sixty-fifth birthday, and her final weeks at the Wassenaer Hof were spent in an exhausting bustle of packing and receiving farewell visits. Elizabeth talked of returning to the Hague, but few of the dignitaries who came to pay their respects to the venerable princess who had lived among them for the past forty years can seriously have expected to see her back again. The only members of her own family to see her off were Sophie and her husband, who had been on a visit to Heidelberg and reached Holland, bringing young Liselotte with them, just in time to accompany her down to Helvoetsluys and wish her *bon voyage*. Elizabeth was in a state of some agitation, her pleasure in setting out on this great adventure having been more than somewhat spoilt by the arrival at the very last moment of a letter from King Charles asking his aunt to postpone her visit until he chose to send for her. But it was too late. She had said her goodbyes, her boxes were packed, all her arrangements made. It would be impossible to cancel now without making it look as if the king were offering her a deliberate slight.

'I go with a resolution to suffer all things constantly', she wrote to her son Rupert, *en route* between Delft and Delftshaven. 'I thank God He has given me courage.' Certainly this was a quality she had never lacked and the French ambassador at the Hague, who knew her well and admired her greatly, told King Louis that he thought she would be very useful to her nephew:

being a good creature, of a temper very civil and always equal, one who has never disobliged anybody, and who is thus capable in her own person of securing affection for the whole royal family. . . . Although here she is in debt more than 200,000 crowns to a number of poor creditors and tradespeople, who have furnished her subsistence during the disgraces of her house, nevertheless, from the friendship they have for her person, they let her go without a murmur, and without any other assurance of their payment than the high opinion they have of her goodness and generosity, and that, as soon as she shall have means to give them satisfaction, she will not, although absent and distant, fail to do it.[35]

The Queen of Bohemia reached Gravesend on 26 May by the English calendar and slipped very quietly into the city she had left as a bride almost half a century before. It was true that the Court was in mourning for the infant son of the Duke and Duchess of York, but gossip said the lack of any official reception was because the king's aunt had come contrary to his will, that that was why she had not been given apartments at Whitehall or Somerset House, and that her stay would not be of long duration.

In fact, Elizabeth was very cosily installed at Lord Craven's residence in Drury Lane where, unlike the Wassenaer Hof, she was surrounded with all the luxury of comfortably furnished rooms, well-cooked meals and well-trained, attentive servants. As for the king, while he would probably rather not have had the additional responsibility of entertaining his elderly aunt, he was far too much of a gentleman to make her feel unwelcome now that she had arrived. He did not invite her to his Court, where he may well have felt she would be a trifle out of place, but he went dutifully to visit her, and soon she was leading quite a busy social life. 'All goes still very well here', she told Charles Louis in July. 'Yesterday the king and I were at Kensington feasted by the Duke of Ormonde . . . there was very good company. Every week I march to one place or other with the king; the next week we go to my Lady Herbert's at a house she has taken at Hampton Court.'[36] All goes still very well here. . . . Everyone, in short, was being perfectly charming and the only unpleasantness the Queen of Bohemia was to encounter during her time in England emanated from Charles Louis himself.

Her Majesty was no longer talking about returning to Holland, but after some weeks under Lord Craven's roof she evidently felt she could not impose on her old friend's generosity indefinitely and began to look round for a house to rent. Her first choice belonged to the Earl of Leicester, but his lordship was unwilling to let, so she settled on Exeter House in the Strand, currently being occupied by the Dutch ambassador. In anticipation of the move she sent instructions to the Hague that all her remaining furniture and household effects from the Wassenaer Hof and Rhenen should be packed up and shipped to London, and was outraged when she heard that her son had given orders to have her stuff 'stayed' at Rotterdam. Even more insulting, it seemed that his agent had tried to get her creditors to arrest her goods as being their only security. Fortunately they had refused, preferring to trust to her promise, 'in which they shall not be deceived, for by the grace of God they shall be justly paid'. Elizabeth was not appeased by Charles Louis's explanation that he had only sought to delay the shipment temporarily while he made sure nothing belonging to him as his father's heir had been removed by his mother's servants, and an acrimonious correspondence between London and Heidelberg ensued.

The queen had every right to send for her own stuff for her own use. 'I am not altogether so weak as you think me, but I have wit enough to know what is good for myself', and her people at the Hague had done no more than their duty, 'which I will maintain them in'. All the old grievances about the non-payment of her jointure came up again. 'I am sorry for it, for your sake because people censure you for it.' Her son owed her far more than her shabby bits and pieces of furniture were worth, and if she had as much means as Lord Craven had to buy hangings, she might not have been so rigorous to take what was her right; but, unanswerably, 'I may claim to have some part in the Palatine house, else I am not your mother.'[37]

When the elector insinuated that he was surprised the King of England could not afford to furnish a house for his guest, he earned another stinging maternal rebuke. The king was not bound to do anything for her, 'but he is kinder than many nephews would be . . . and I am sure he will not see me want, though all that cannot excuse you to give me my due'.[38] Charles was, in fact, allowing his aunt a thousand pounds a month, and had promised to do his best to persuade parliament to pay all the arrears of the pension settled on her under the Great Seal at the time of her marriage.

The row with Charles Louis rumbled on inconclusively but, that apart, Elizabeth was enjoying herself. The king took her to the theatre to see *The Siege of Rhodes* by William Davenant and she was invited to the House of Lords, where 'they were all in their robes, the king had his robes and crown, it was a very handsome sight'.[39] The Queen of Bohemia was the only lady of the blood royal in England that summer and had begun to assume almost the role of honorary queen mother. The king's forthcoming marriage to the Portuguese princess Catherine of Braganza had now been publicly announced and Elizabeth wrote a kind letter of congratulation and welcome to her nephew's fiancée, who replied that she would look upon her Majesty as her mother in England and would wish to perform a daughter's part towards her.

A Genoese diplomat visited Elizabeth at Drury House some time in the autumn and was impressed, finding her

in her cabinet, where she had assembled many ladies, to receive me with the greater decorum. She sent attendants to welcome me as I alighted from my coach, and at the head of the stairs I was met by Lord Craven, proprietor of the house where she lives and the principal director of her court. It is incredible the pleasure which her majesty showed at this my office, and the familiar courtesy with which she discoursed with me for a very long time upon the state of the most serene republic and other various matters, even inviting me to come sometimes to see her. This princess has learned from nature, and continued through the changes of her fortune, an incomparable goodness. . . . Now she is restored to some authority, and thus is heightened the lustre of that affable manner with which she wonderfully conciliates the esteem and love of the court.[40]

Christmas came and went and the Queen of Bohemia was still at Drury House. She had not been well, and in January wrote to Charles Louis to wish him a happy new year and tell him that she had been 'forced or persuaded' by her doctors 'to take physic to be quite rid of my cold. . . . It made me sick as a dog, but I think it did me good, yet my own physic did me most good, which was letting of blood, for now I am very well. It is so hot weather here as I have felt it colder in May.'[41]

Since the Dutch ambassador still lingered irritatingly at Exeter House, the Earl of Leicester had finally been obliged to let the queen have a lease on his house in Leicester Fields, now Leicester Square. She moved in on 29 January, but the chronic bronchitis, legacy of years of colds and coughs in the damp chill Dutch winters and the icy draughts of the Wassenaer Hof, had turned to pneumonia and this time her heart was affected. Rupert, now back in London from Vienna, was with his mother when, on 10 February, she had a haemorrhage from the lungs and asked him to arrange to bring her two nephews to see her. On the following day she communicated according to the Anglican rite and gave her last instructions, asking Charles especially to make sure that her long-suffering creditors were all paid in full. The king suggested that she should come back to Whitehall where she could be nursed in greater comfort, but it was too late. She no longer had the strength to be moved, and so they left her by her fireside, propped up in a chair to ease her laboured breathing.

What memories crowded in on the Winter Queen as the

shadows closed round her? Did she see the little girl in the palace at Linlithgow, listening enthralled to her nurse's tales of her fabulous grandmother the Queen of Scots; or the schoolroom at Combe Abbey, its ordered routine disturbed by the sudden alarms of the great Gunpowder Treason? Was she riding again with Henry in the Surrey woods, or standing beside her mother in the Banqueting House at Whitehall, watching under her lashes as the dark, good-looking boy who was to be her husband approached through the crowd? Perhaps she was back at Heidelberg, the happy-go-lucky young bride out hunting all day in the hills above the castle, overspending her dress allowance and driving poor Colonel Schomberg to distraction. Or was she reliving that amazing day when she had been crowned a queen in the cathedral at Prague? It had been a very long journey uphill which was ending now with a tired old woman gasping for breath in a rented house in Leicester Fields.

Elizabeth died soon after midnight on 13 February 1662, the eve of her forty-ninth wedding anniversary. 'My royal tenant is departed', wrote Lord Leicester to his brother-in-law the Earl of Northumberland. 'It seems the fates did not think it fit that I should have the honour, which indeed I never much desired, to be the landlord of a Queen. It is a pity she did not live a few hours more, to die upon her wedding day.'[42]

The Queen of Bohemia's death caused very little public stir, for only a handful of older Londoners could now remember the beautiful blonde princess of half a century ago, of the days of ruffs and farthingales and Will Shakespeare – there is a persistent tradition that *The Tempest* was written, or at any rate revived, in honour of her wedding. But a great deal had happened since then, and in 1662 Elizabeth's chief, if not her only, claim to fame was as the mother of Rupert of the Rhine, Rupert le Diable, the legendary Cavalier general. So perhaps it was especially fitting that Rupert should have been the only one of her sons to follow the solemn funeral procession which escorted her coffin to Westminster Abbey on the night of 17 February. There, by her own express desire, the mortal remains of 'the most serene and powerful Princess Elizabeth, Queen of Bohemia, relict of Frederick, by the grace of God King of Bohemia and prince elector of the Holy Roman Empire' were laid to rest among her ancestors and close to her 'late elder brother Prince Henry', while outside the unseasonably warm and humid weather of the past few weeks broke in 'such a storm of hail, thunder and lightning as never was seen the like in any man's memory'.[43]

John Evelyn, who recorded the event in his diary, referred respectfully to the late queen's many sorrows and afflictions, and certainly they were enough to have destroyed a lesser woman. But Elizabeth was never defeated. Through all those weary years of exile and poverty, disappointment and heartache and fading hope, she never lost her zest for living, her 'wild humour' to be merry, or her capacity for taking an informed and intelligent interest in people and politics. Hers was a valiant spirit and everyone who knew her was enriched by the experience.

She was survived by six of her thirteen children. Her eldest daughter the Princess Elizabeth Palatine, nicknamed La Grecque in the family, had followed her sister Louise's example of entering a convent, but fortunately in her case a Lutheran one. 'I think you and I have cause to be glad to have her so settled', the queen had written to Charles Louis in December 1660, 'for then she will trouble nobody.'[44] The learned La Grecque had never been a favourite with her mother who had once described her as 'a hippocrit to the Root'. Also like Louise, Elizabeth later became the abbess of her community, dying in 1680 after a long illness. Charles Louis, too, died that year. Although in many ways an unsympathetic character, he was an able administrator and ruler who worked wonders in restoring the war-ravaged Rhineland Palatinate to prosperity. Edward, whose controversial marriage had turned out very successfully, and whose daughters married into royal and noble houses, survived his mother by only two years, dying in 1664 at the age of thirty-nine. Rupert never married, though he left an illegitimate daughter. He stayed on at his cousin's court, developing an interest in science and becoming a founder member of the Royal Society. He died in 1682. The youngest member of the family lived on until 1714, by which time she had become Duchess and Electress of Hanover and, in fact, Sophie only missed her chance of becoming Queen of England by a margin of two months.

As for Liselotte, her grandmother's little favourite, she was doomed to become the second wife of Philippe d'Orleans, the infamous Monsieur. She outlasted him, though, by more than twenty years, living on at the French court 'a lady of the Old Regime, German to the last drop of her blood, with the figure of a Swiss Guard'. Liselotte's gift to posterity lies in the letters that she wrote obsessively throughout her married life and her widowhood, which provide an incomparably vivid picture of the closing years of the Sun King's reign. Her memory was amazing, and it was Liselotte who finally nailed an old slander. 'Historians are liars, too', she wrote in March 1718. 'In the history of my grandfather, the King of Bohemia, they say that my grandmother, the Queen of Bohemia, was so ambitious that she gave her husband no peace until he became king; there's not a word of truth in the story. The Prince of Orange, the King's uncle, started the whole thing, the Queen knew nothing of it and in those days thought only of plays, ballets and reading romances.'[45]

Liselotte's information would have come from her aunt Sophie to whom she was devoted and Sophie, of course, would have had every opportunity to hear it at first hand. But perhaps Henry Wotton said it all and said it best:

> So, when my mistress shall be seen
> In form and beauty of her mind
> By virtue first, then choice, a Queen
> Tell me, if she were not design'd
> Th'eclipse and glory of her kind.

Six

Madame de France

. . . only remember there is no one in the world who would so willingly serve you, or who wishes for your welfare as heartily as I do.

(Henrietta Anne (Minette) to Charles II)

The death of the Queen of Bohemia robbed the little boy in Holland of his last personal contact with his mother's family. The Wassenaer Hof with all its noisy fantastical life of quarrelling servants and clamorous creditors, its dogs and monkeys and parrots so fascinating to a child, stood silent and deserted, and gone was the warm-hearted, sometimes formidable but always exhilarating old lady, the only person who could talk to him about his mother or tell him stories of that magical island across the North Sea to which his future destiny was bound.

His uncle Charles did little to fulfil the charge laid upon him by the dying Mary. He said later that he had stayed aloof because he felt too much interference might do William more harm than good, and delegated his powers of guardianship to the dowager princess on the understanding that he could be asked for help or advice if the need arose. As a result William fell more and more under the control of John de Witt and the Dutch republican party, known as the Loevesteiners, who regarded the prince's English connections with deep suspicion and were openly hostile to the pro-Orangeists.

William's contact with his mother's French kin was equally distant, when not actually unfriendly. Ever since Mary's ill-advised approach to Louis XIV his Orange principality had been effectively annexed by France, its city's fortifications destroyed, its revenues expropriated and the predominantly Protestant Orangeois oppressed by the French garrison. After vigorous protests by the prince's guardians and protracted negotiations with Paris, a new governor, approved by Louis, had been installed and the occupying force withdrawn, but it was not a good omen for future relations between the cousins. Although a portrait was painted for Henrietta Maria in 1664 when William was fourteen, he never met his maternal grandmother and there does not appear to be any evidence that she ever took any interest in his welfare. Nor did he ever get to make the acquaintance of his mother's only surviving sister, his delightful aunt Henrietta Anne.

Minette was continuing to enjoy her social success at the French court. Her 'sweet and animated conversation' was much admired and she could also talk intelligently, her 'fine and delicate taste' having been formed by study and reading good books. 'Madame', commented a contemporary historian, 'had all the wit of her brother Charles II, heightened by the charm of her sex and the gift of pleasing. Her example inspired others with a taste for letters and introduced a refinement and grace in the pleasures of the Court which were altogether new.'[1] Unfortunately, though, her marriage was already falling apart. 'Rumour says that Monsieur is very jealous of Madame, and that he makes her a very bad husband', wrote Lady Derby to her sister-in-law before the end of that first summer.

Monsieur's jealousy had been aroused by the affair of the Comte de Guiche, 'the most handsome and elegant man at court . . . gallant, dauntless and brave'. Although a close friend of Philippe d'Orleans since childhood, Armand de Guiche was not overtly homosexual and his romantic good looks and carefully cultivated air of scornful indifference made him very attractive to women. His pursuit of Madame began while they were rehearsing together for the celebrated *Ballet des Saisons* performed beside the lake at Fontainebleau, and one day 'he took the liberty to ask her for tidings of her heart, as to whether, as yet, anything had touched it'. Receiving some light-hearted inconsequential reply, he rushed out of the room, exclaiming that he was in the gravest peril.

Minette, who was becoming used to theatrical gestures of this kind from would-be admirers, thought it merely 'a matter of gallantry' and took no particular notice, but as it became clear that the king's attentions were being transferred from his sister-in-law to Mademoiselle de La Vallière, de Guiche grew bolder and 'showed so plainly what was in his heart' that gossip started to buzz. Monsieur soon got to hear of it and the result was a quarrel between the two young men which ended in de Guiche leaving the Court. When Madame heard that the Comte had been openly declaring his passion for her, she, too, took offence and let it be known that she would not receive him. There the matter might have rested but for the intervention of Anne-Constance de Montalais, one of Madame's maids of honour with an unfortunate talent for mischief-making. Whether prompted by thoughts of blackmail, or a simple desire to meddle, this girl determined to set herself up as a go-between and, having persuaded de Guiche to trust her, went to Madame with pathetic stories of his despair. 'Such discourses as these', observed Madame de la Fayette, who later had the whole story from Minette herself, 'are naturally not displeasing enough for young people to have the strength to reject them. Madame, moreover, had a certain shyness in speaking, so that half in embarrassment and half in condescension, she gave Montalais great cause for hope.'[2]

Shortly after this Minette was taken ill and returned to Paris, travelling by litter. Just as she was setting out, Montalais contrived to smuggle her a packet of letters from de Guiche. 'Madame read them on the road', says Madame de la Fayette, 'and then confessed to Montalais that she had done so. In brief, the youth of Madame, the charm of the Comte de Guiche, and, most of all, the services of Montalais, involved this princess in an affair of gallantry which brought her nothing but considerable vexation.'[3]

The affair of gallantry inevitably progressed from letters to clandestine meetings in Madame's apartments, arranged by Montalais. On one occasion de Guiche was introduced disguised as a female fortune-teller, and even told the fortunes of Madame's women, who saw him every day and did not recognize him. Other schemes were devised, and these highly perilous meetings, says Madame de la Fayette, were spent in making fun of Monsieur 'and other such raillery'.

It all had more an air of youthful bravado than a serious affair and it seems most unlikely that Minette was ever actually unfaithful to her husband. Apart from the obvious practical difficulties –

constantly surrounded by prying eyes, she was also quite seriously unwell and six months pregnant – she was not passionate by nature. Another contemporary who knew her well described her as a coquette who loved to be loved, yet believed her entirely virtuous. But in what appears to have been a teenage girl's desire for excitement and admiration, she was taking an unacceptable risk. Gossip continued to link her name with de Guiche and it was not long before the details of their relationship began to leak out.

De Guiche himself had already confided in his friend the Marquis de Vardes, while Montalais and Louise de La Vallière, who was still in Madame's service, were also old friends who told each other everything. It was from La Vallière that the king heard the story, after a lovers' quarrel when Louise had run away from the Tuileries 'like a mad woman' and sought shelter in a convent. Louis confronted his sister-in-law and made her promise to break with de Guiche, promising in return not to banish the Comte if Minette would agree to take La Vallière back, which she did, though reluctantly.

Minette was now about to retire to her mother's residence in the Palais Royal to prepare for the birth of her first child, which arrived prematurely but safely on 27 March 1662. Greatly to the disappointment of both parents the baby was a girl and, on being told its sex, Minette is reputed to have said, 'Then throw her into the river.' Greatly scandalized, her mother-in-law pointed out that the infant might grow up to be a queen, and in England, where the news was received with pleasure and relief, it was being said that Madame was young enough to have many sons and daughters.

The de Guiche affair was now beginning to resemble the plot of a rather below average soap opera. No sooner had Minette emerged from her lying-in chamber than she heard that the Comte would soon be leaving Paris to take up command of the garrison at Nancy. The king told her that de Guiche's father, the Maréchal de Gramont, had asked him for the post 'as a thing which his son most ardently desired', and that the Comte de Guiche had thanked him for it. What had actually happened was that de Guiche's supposed friend, the Marquis de Vardes, had also fallen under Madame's spell, and either from 'a sentiment of love, or one merely of ambition and intrigue, wished to gain sole mastery over her'. He was therefore plotting to separate her from de Guiche and had gone to the Comte's father, telling the Maréchal some part of what was going on and strongly advising him to arrange to send his son out of harm's way.

Minette was naturally distressed and offended that de Guiche should have been planning to run away in this fashion and de Guiche, in despair that she should be angry with him, wrote swearing that he had never asked for the post in Lorraine and saying he would refuse to go. But de Vardes went to see Madame and persuaded her that the hot-headed de Guiche would be ruined if he turned down such a senior command, and in the end it was agreed that he must go but that Madame would see him once more to say goodbye.

The farewell interview was, of course, stage-managed by Montalais and, taking advantage of a day when Monsieur would be absent, she brought the Comte into the Tuileries by a secret stair and shut him in the chapel. When Madame had dined she pretended to be sleepy, but instead went to meet de Guiche in one of the galleries. While they were still talking Monsieur returned unexpectedly and Montalais had to hide the Comte in the chimney. According to one account, Monsieur started to eat an orange and was just about to throw the peel into the grate when the ever-resourceful Montalais sprang forward and asked him to give it to her, as it was the part of the fruit that she liked best.[4]

Unfortunately all this ingenuity was wasted, for another of the maids of honour with reason to be jealous of Montalais's privileged position had seen the Comte being smuggled into Madame's rooms and gone straight to the queen mother with the story. Queen Anne, who had not forgiven her daughter-in-law for flirting with the king, went in turn to Monsieur to tell him that his wife had been seeing Armand de Guiche in secret.

Monsieur reacted less violently than might have been expected. He took his complaints to his mother-in-law at the Palais Royal, and Henrietta Maria came to see her daughter 'and scolded her a little, telling her all that Monsieur knew for certain, so that she might confess to him just this much and no more'. Monsieur and Madame then had 'a great explanation' and, says Madame de la Fayette, 'Monsieur took such pleasure in his position of authority, having Madame confess to him things that he knew already, that his acrimony melted away; he embraced her and retained but a slight grudge against her'.[5] He does not appear to have blamed de Guiche for his part in the affair, though admittedly he had not been told the whole of it, and his rancour was reserved for Montalais, who was summarily dismissed, though she still contrived to take with her all de Guiche's letters which had been entrusted to her for safe-keeping.

After the Comte's departure Minette had to face the prospect of separation from her mother, for Henrietta was about to return to England with some idea of making a permanent home there. But in any case she wanted to see Charles again and make the acquaintance of her new daughter-in-law. Catherine of Braganza had arrived from Portugal in May, bringing a dowry of £500,000, with Bombay, Tangier and the right of free trade with the Portuguese colonies. This was the new queen's principal attraction, for she was a plain, shy little creature, quite unequipped to compete with the rapacious flock of mistresses surrounding the king. However, a royal marriage was always an excuse for celebration and in the general merry-making the birth of a daughter to the Duke and Duchess of York on 30 April had passed almost unnoticed. The baby was named Mary in memory of the Princess of Orange and baptized in the chapel at St James's Palace with her cousin Prince Rupert among the godparents, but there is no mention of the event in any of King Charles's surviving letters to Minette.

Brother and sister were regular correspondents and as early as October 1662 Charles was writing of his plan to make use of her as an intermediary in promoting his friendship with the King of France. 'And if it pleases you to propose to him that we may communicate our thoughts to each other in our own hands by this private channel, I shall be very glad.'[6]

Charles liked to tease his sister about her conquests, but for Minette the reality of being a *femme fatale* was becoming more burdensome than amusing. The Prince de Marsillac, eldest son of the Duke de la Rochefoucauld, had recently begun to make sheep's eyes at her, reawakening Monsieur's jealousy to such an extent that the young man's father was obliged to send him away from the Court, although Madame, according to Madeleine de la Fayette, showed no signs of reciprocating his passion, being fully occupied with her growing friendship for the Marquis de Vardes.

De Vardes was a far more dangerous proposition than poor, romantic, headstrong de Guiche. Able, ambitious, unscrupulous and with an unsavoury reputation as a womanizer, he now set himself to consolidate his influence over Madame and she 'did not wholly repulse him', for, commented Madame de la Fayette, 'it is hard to ill-treat an agreeable confidant when the lover is away'. In his role of confidant, de Vardes offered to help Minette retrieve the letters which Montalais had stolen, thus giving himself useful opportunities to see her in private and 'make some progress in her affections'. At the same time he was writing to de Guiche, telling him that Madame was having an affair with Marsillac, while telling Madame that de Guiche believed her to be unfaithful and that he had betrayed secrets of their relationship to King Louis, who joined the army in Lorraine in the autumn of 1663. This annoyed Minette so much that she wrote angrily to her former friend, finally breaking off with him and forbidding him ever to breathe her name again.

The unhappy de Guiche, driven to despair, went off to Poland to fight the Russians, hoping he might be killed; but, in fact, his expedition was very successful and he distinguished himself by performing many deeds of 'singular valour', in the course of which he received a wound which would certainly have been fatal had he not been carrying next to his heart a case containing a portrait of Madame which deflected the bullet! When news of his heroic exploits reached Paris, Madame was much moved and told de Vardes that she now saw she must love the Comte de Guiche more deeply than she knew. This unwise confession infuriated de Vardes and he began to try to ruin her with the king. Minette had been indiscreet enough to show him some of her brother's private letters and de Vardes hinted to Louis that she was a dangerous intrigante and trouble-maker.

The next act in the drama featured de Vardes's mistress, the Comtesse de Soissons, who, not unnaturally, had for a long time been acutely jealous of Madame, although they remained on friendly terms. Then the Comtesse fell seriously ill. She asked Madame to come and see her and begged to be told the true state of her feelings for de Vardes. Anxious to set the invalid's mind at rest, Madame hastened to assure her that nothing had passed between them which could give her cause for concern, but the

Comtesse was not entirely convinced. She saw de Vardes again and managed to extract a confession from him, even getting him to admit that he had been hoping to discard her for Madame. So now, at last, the truth began to come out. Furious at her lover's treachery, the Comtesse de Soissons proceeded to reveal the full extent of his villainy to Madame, how he had cheated and lied and actually made copies of her brother's letters to show to King Louis. At first Minette was reluctant to accept that she could have been so taken in, but as the two women compared their facts, 'they brought to light deceptions that would baffle the imagination'.[7]

It was at about this point that de Guiche returned from the wars. He was allowed to come to Court on condition that he did not attempt to see Madame, but of course he did see her now and then from a distance and, in spite of everything, fell in love with her all over again. He soon realized that he had somehow been duped but was so confused, as well he might be, that he did not know what to believe. Desperate to have 'an explanation' with Madame, he tried every way he knew to reach her, but Minette was seeing nobody just then as she was awaiting the birth of her second child. The baby was born at Fontainebleau on 16 July 1664 and this time, to everyone's delight, it was a boy, to be named Philippe Charles and given the title Duc de Valois. Madame, according to a hurried note sent off to England that night, 'had but an hour's labour, and is exceeding well, as any in her case, so newly brought to bed, can be. God be praised for it!'[8]

Madame was still lying-in when the Marquis de Vardes insisted on seeing her. He flung himself on his knees, wept and raved and begged for mercy, promising to conceal, if only she would cooperate, 'all the commerce that had existed between them'. But Minette declared that she wanted the Comte de Guiche to know the truth. In fact, she wanted everybody to know the truth, 'through which her good intentions alone would shine'. De Vardes then attempted to deliver a letter from de Guiche. 'But', says Madame de la Fayette, 'Madame refused it, and it was well that she did so; for Vardes had already showed the letter to the king, telling him that Madame was deceiving him.'[9]

When de Vardes had gone, Louis arrived and Minette at once told him the whole story, 'and it was to this perfect sincerity that she owed the king's friendship'. She also wrote a detailed account of the affair to her mother in England, which Henrietta Maria showed to Charles, for he wrote sympathetically on 22 July to say that he could see she had been very badly used, but was glad to hear Louis was being so kind and just. 'I did not think it possible', he went on, 'that some persons could have had so ill a part in the matter as I see they have had by your letter. I shall have by this a better opinion of my devotion for the time to come, for I am one of those bigots who think that malice is a much greater sin than a poor frailty of nature.'[10]

Early in August Madame accompanied the king and queen to Vincennes, and the English ambassador reported that she was looking as well as ever he saw her and was grown quite fat. But Denzil Holles was being rather more diplomatic than accurate, for a French physician who saw her in September described her as frail and delicate and quite possibly consumptive. Certainly Minette was ailing again that autumn, but a month in the country at Villers-Cotterets and the diet of asses' milk prescribed by her doctors seem to have done her good, and she returned to Paris for the winter in better health.

She was still refusing to see de Guiche, but chance was about to bring them together. Monsieur and Madame had gone incognito in a borrowed coach to a masked ball, where they fell in with another party of masks. Giving her hand to one of the gentlemen, Minette recognized the Comte by his three missing fingers, lost on the field of battle, while he knew her by the carnation perfume she always used on her hair. They managed a hurried conversation under cover of the crowd and then Minette, in her agitation, tripped and would have fallen down the stairs had not de Guiche saved her by catching her in his arms. 'Everything combined to help them to be reconciled', wrote Madame de la Fayette, 'and so they were.'[11]

Before the end of the year Minette was finally able to rid herself of de Vardes, now her bitter enemy. One of Monsieur's young men was having an affair with one of Madame's maids of honour and some of the courtiers were teasing him about it when de Vardes was heard to say, in front of a roomful of people, that he wondered why the Chevalier de Lorraine bothered with the maid when he might easily have her mistress. This was a deadly insult which could not be allowed to go unavenged and Minette begged

Louis to banish de Vardes from the Court. Louis agreed, though reluctantly. He seems to have had rather a soft spot for the wicked marquis, who was one of his gentlemen of the bedchamber and an amusing companion.

Lord Holles informed King Charles that 'the Marquis de Vardes has been ordered to surrender himself to the Bastille, to expiate some unbecoming words of which it is said that Madame had complained to his Majesty'. But it seems that de Vardes had staged something of a pre-emptive strike, going of his own accord to the gates of the fortress and asking the embarrassed governor to imprison him. His friends all went to visit him and boasted that the king was most unwilling to proceed against him and Madame had been unable to procure his banishment.

Angry and humiliated, Minette went again to Louis to demand satisfaction. She also appealed to her brother in a letter dated 17 December. 'It is a thing of such importance to me', she wrote, 'that the whole of the rest of my life may be affected by it. If it is not settled as I wish it to be, it will be a scandal that any private citizen should have been able to defy me and have the king's support.' De Vardes must be exiled, she went on, as a warning to everyone in future not to dare to attack her, otherwise the consequences might be terrible. She begged Charles to intervene and help to extricate her from this wretched business.[12]

As it turned out, his intervention was not needed, for Louis had become irritated by the marquis and his claque and ordered him to return to his native town of Aigues-Mortes in the far south. Minette's honour had been vindicated and de Vardes's power broken, but it was still not quite the end of the affair. Olympe de Soissons, who had made up her quarrel with her former lover and was furious at being deprived of his company, now began to make trouble, telling Louis that de Guiche had written disrespectfully about him in letters to Madame and had conspired with her to oppose France's recent purchase of the port of Dunkirk from the English.

Minette had been keeping in discreet touch with the Comte through his father, so was able to warn him of this latest danger and counsel him to be completely frank with the king, 'having herself discovered that in all such tangles, the truth alone can save the situation'. It was good advice and Madame de la Fayette thought de Guiche would not have been banished had he stood his ground. But the old Maréchal de Gramont took fright and, feeling that his son would be safer on the battlefield than at Court, decided to send him off to Holland, where he was presently to serve with distinction in the naval war with England.

This time there were to be no goodbyes. Minette knew she was being watched and besides 'was no longer of an age when the most perilous things alone seem pleasant'. But de Guiche could not bear to go without at least seeing her. He had had a suit of Louise de La Vallière's livery made for him and one day, when Madame was being carried in her chair to the Louvre, he found a chance to speak to her. On the day of his departure, he went out into the street in his usual disguise to see her pass, but when it came to the final leave-taking his strength failed him and he fell down in a faint. Minette could do nothing for him and was left with the distress 'of seeing him thus in danger of being recognized or of lying there unsuccoured'.[13] They never met again.

The whole rather foolish episode had extended over a period of three years and had undoubtedly given the participants more pain than pleasure, though Madame de la Fayette thought the Comte's vanity had probably prevented him from suffering too severely. As for Madame, her friends believed that her feelings for de Guiche had never gone very deep, while her successor was always of the opinion that she had been guilty of nothing worse than naïveté and was very unfortunate in being surrounded by the greatest intriguers in the world, who had set out to deceive her. 'Young, gentle and full of grace, she had no idea how wicked they were', remarked Liselotte years later and out of similar bitter experience.

The twenty-year-old Minette had yet to learn the full extent of the depravity of which some of the people around her were capable. In the mean time, respectable matrons like Madame de Motteville noticed with approval that she seemed to be settling down, living on better terms with her mother-in-law and taking her part in the diversions of the Court 'with no wish but to make herself pleasant to all'. One of the principal diversions enjoyed by the Court that winter was an ambitious ballet, *The Birth of Venus*, in which Madame appeared as the goddess of beauty herself. The production was received with the usual critical acclaim and performed several times, but Minette was taken suddenly ill before the end of the run and had to delegate her part to an understudy.

'I am very glad to hear that your indisposition of health is turned into a great belly', Charles wrote on 9 February. He hoped she would have better luck than the Duchess of York, who had just given birth to another girl, but 'one part I shall wish you to have, which is that you may have as easy a labour, for she dispatched her business in little more than an hour. I am afraid your shape is not so advantageously made for that convenience as hers is, however a boy will recompense for two grunts more.'[14] The King of England made no mention of the fact that after three years of marriage his own wife showed no sign of producing either boys or girls, and that in consequence the two surviving York children, Mary and the new-born Princess Anne, were beginning to assume a greater degree of importance. Charles was not as yet much concerned about the succession and was, in any case, preoccupied just then with the impending outbreak of war with Holland.

Anglo-Dutch relations had been growing increasingly strained during 1664, as the rivalry between the two expanding colonial powers competing world-wide for trade and territory became fierce. 'You will have heard of our taking of New Amsterdam which lies just by New England', Charles had written to Minette on 24 October. ''Tis a place of great importance to trade, and a very good town. It did belong to England heretofore but the Dutch by degrees drove our people out of it, and built a very good town, but we have got the better of it, and 'tis now called New York.'[15] The English had thus succeeded in dislodging the Hollanders from their foothold in North America, but sporadic clashes continued on the Guinea coast of Africa and in the islands of the East Indies, as the merchants and colonists of the two nations raided one another's settlements and each attacked the other's shipping. Clearly a trial of strength at sea could not long be postponed, and there was 'a great appetite' for war in England, especially among the 'Parliament men'. Charles himself had some old scores to settle with the Dutch republicans, but he was worried about Louis's attitude, as France had a defensive treaty with Holland, and his letters to Minette frequently refer to his desire for 'a strict friendship' with France – something which, he felt sure, would be best achieved through his sister's good offices. 'There can be nobody so fit to make a good correspondence and friendship between us as yourself', he wrote towards the end of August 1664; and again, in September, 'If the King my brother desires to have a strict friendship with me, there is nobody so proper to make it as yourself, and I am sure I will put all my interest into your hands.'[16]

In November Louis despatched the Marquis de Ruvigny on a special mission to London and Minette seized the opportunity to use him as her courier to Charles. 'I could not let Ruvigny leave without this letter to assure you again, what he will also tell you, how much your friendship is wished for here, and how necessary it is to France. Profit by this, in God's name, and lose no time in obtaining the King's secret promise that he will not help the Dutch. You understand that he cannot bind himself publicly, owing to his engagements with them, although we all know these are only worth what he chooses to make them.'[17]

In fact, Louis, who had designs on the Spanish Netherlands, was anxious to keep out of the approaching conflict for as long as possible, and the following April Minette wrote again to Charles suggesting that he could ensure French neutrality 'by giving a pledge that you would help in the business he will soon have in Flanders, now the King of Spain is ill, and which will certainly be opposed by the Dutch, but will not be contrary to your interests. Think this over well, I beg of you, but never let anyone know that I was the first to mention it to you, only remember there is no one in the world who would so willingly serve you, or who wishes for your welfare as heartily as I do. My enemies here look so suspiciously on all I do, that soon I shall hardly venture to speak of your affairs!'[18]

England declared war on Holland in March 1665 but nothing very much happened until early June, when the English fleet under the command of the Duke of York encountered the Dutch off Lowestoft. The result was a considerable victory for the English, although the first reports reaching Paris were of such an alarming nature that Minette became quite ill with anxiety and Lord Holles told Charles that he seriously believed Madame would have died if things had gone badly at sea. Fortunately better news arrived and Madame was quite overwhelmed by the warmth of the congratulations she and Monsieur received from all the Court and nobility.

So much nervous strain was not good for her just then and a few weeks later, while on a visit to Versailles, she went into premature labour. A midwife was hastily summoned from St Cloud but the baby, a girl, was born dead. Minette made a good recovery, although she continued to be worried about the political situation, urging her brother more than once to bring the war to an end as soon as possible. 'Since you have shown, not only what your power is and how dangerous it is to have you for an enemy, but have also made your subjects see how well you can defend their interests and greatness; you may now show the world that your true desire is for peace, and triumph by clemency as well as by force. This is what gains hearts . . . besides being a surer thing than trusting to the chances of war.' Charles would never be in a better position to gain advantage from his success than now, 'when you might win over people, who, I can assure you, ardently desire your friendship and are in despair at feeling that their word is already pledged. I have spoken of this several times and always find the King most reasonable.'[19]

Henrietta Maria had returned to France that summer on her doctors' advice, and mother and daughter joined forces to try to bring about a satisfactory peace. Early in August they had a private conference with the king from which the ambassador, Lord Holles, was excluded. Holles later saw the queen and 'took the boldness to ask her how she found things. She said they had been all the time within talking over these businesses of Holland and that Louis XIV told her he had made King Charles some propositions which were very fair ones, which, if he refused, he must take part with the Hollanders.'[20]

In September the King of Spain died and Louis at once proceeded to make a formal claim to the Spanish Netherlands in his wife's name on complicated and somewhat dubious legal grounds, this being the 'business' in Flanders hinted at by Minette. In October the English parliament met at Oxford, where it had been forced to take refuge from the Great Plague still raging in London, but the Commons were in belligerent mood and needed no encouragement to vote supplies for the continuation of the war. In November Charles informed the French ambassadors that he could not accept Louis's propositions and they thankfully prepared to leave the pestilence-stricken island.

The year 1666 began badly. The French queen mother, who had been mortally ill for some time, died of cancer on 20 January and a few days later Louis declared war on England, protesting that he did so reluctantly and only because he was bound by his treaty obligations. Charles, who had become resigned to this development, was not unduly cast down, but he was distressed by the prospect of having to break off relations with his sister. 'I cannot tell what kind of correspondence we must keep with letters now that France declares war with us', he wrote to her at the end of the month; 'you must direct me in it, and I shall observe what you judge convenient for you, but nothing can make me lessen in the least degree, of that kindness I always have had for you, which I assure you is so rooted in my heart, as it will continue to the last moment of my life.'[21]

In fact the break was never very complete. Charles continued to get regular news of Minette from fat old Henry Jermyn, now Earl of St Albans, who remained in France with Henrietta Maria, and in May he was able to send her a letter by her equerry, Bonnefonds, who had been buying horses for her in England, telling her that he was just going to inspect the fleet, 'which will be ready very speedily and I do assure you 'tis much better in all respects than it was last year'. The first week of June saw the so-called Four Days' Battle off the North Foreland. This was an epic fight with heavy losses on both sides, but both fleets quickly refitted and at the end of July were engaged once more. This time the Dutch decidedly got the worst of it, losing over twenty ships, and were obliged to return to harbour to lick their wounds. A French fleet made a rather tentative appearance in the Channel towards the end of August, but bad weather forced it back into Brest and more storms put an end to any further naval activity for the rest of the year.

Minette and her mother had not given up hope of arranging a negotiated peace, but Minette had recently been distracted by an unwelcome reminder of the de Guiche affair. A scurrilous pamphlet, printed in Holland and purporting to give a true account of Madame's liaison with the Comte de Guiche, had come to the notice of the King of France. Louis showed it privately to his sister-in-law, strongly advising her to keep it away from Monsieur, and, much alarmed, she sought the help of Daniel de Cosnac, Bishop of Valence, her husband's almoner and the most trustworthy member of his household. The bishop rose nobly to the occasion, buying up and burning the whole edition and bribing the publisher not to reprint. 'The whole affair', he remarked, 'cost me a great deal of trouble and money, but far from regretting this, I was only too well paid by the thanks which Madame bestowed upon me.'

De Cosnac had a reputation for honesty and plain speaking, and he made no secret of his admiration for Madame. While admitting a certain amount of 'natural indolence' and impatience with ordinary duties, she had, he wrote, 'a clear and strong intellect. She was full of good sense, and gifted with fine perception. . . . Her whole conversation was filled with a sweetness which made her unlike all other royal personages. It was not that she had less majesty, but she was simpler and touched you more easily, for she was the most human creature in the world.'[22]

Madame's circle included virtually everyone who was anyone in the France of the *grand siècle*, from soldiers such as Condé and Turenne to the poets Nicolas Boileau and Jean de La Fontaine. Her closest woman friend was the novelist Madeleine de la Fayette, through whom she came to know La Rochefoucauld and Madame de Sévigné. Her 'excellent judgement in art and letters' was respected by serious scholars and literary men, and she became a generous and discriminating patron of the rising young playwrights Molière and Jean Racine, who dedicated his tragedy *Andromaque* to her, knowing that she would judge its merits 'not alone by the heart, but by the light of an intellect which cannot be deceived'. She had, according to the Comte de Bussy, 'more greatness and delicacy of taste, in things of the mind, than all the ladies of the Court put together'.

The Bishop of Valence declared that Madame danced better than any woman he had ever seen, and in November 1666 she was again rehearsing for a ballet in which she was to appear as a shepherdess, carrying her pet spaniel Mimi in her arms. The first performance of the *Ballet des Muses* took place at St Germain on 2 December, but on the very next day Madame was called back to Paris, where her little son was gravely ill. A week later the two-year-old Duc de Valois died of a feverish cold and convulsions, caused, it was said, by teething.

Thus the year which had begun with a death ended with a death and it was a sorrowful Christmas for Minette. However, she did have the consolation of knowing that the war was at last coming to an end. Louis was impatient to clear the ground for his invasion of the Spanish Netherlands and Charles was ready now to come to terms. He had very little choice in the matter, for the nation's appetite for war had faded and the king had no means of financing another campaign. Indeed, the corruption and inefficiency endemic in the system had brought the navy to the brink of ruin. The ships were having to be mothballed and their unpaid crews – those of them, that is, who had not already deserted to the enemy – were rioting in the streets. The Dutch, too, by and large had had enough, four out of the seven provinces having come out in favour of peace. But they still hankered for some measure of revenge for past defeats and in June Michiel de Ruyter led a daring raid up the Medway as far as Chatham, burning or capturing more than sixteen ships of the line, including the *Royal Charles* in which the king had made his triumphant return home seven years before.

The French, meanwhile, had begun their advance into Flanders. Louis himself joined the army on 16 May and was followed a few days later by his brother. Monsieur was much excited by the prospect of military glory and the Bishop of Valence, who had great hopes that the experience might make a man of him, gave him copious advice on how to behave while on active service. He must never appear to be bored; he must be lavish with praise and reward to the troops and give the appearance of great valour without actually exposing himself to serious danger. Monsieur absorbed all this eagerly. He staged a dramatic farewell scene with his wife and reminded Valence that he, too, was a grandson of that noted warrior Henri IV, exclaiming: 'Follow me to the camp, and you will see how well I can fight!'

To do him justice, Philippe d'Orleans did not lack physical courage and his coolness under fire made a good impression when he visited the trenches at Tournai and Douai. But Louis, who did not welcome competition from any quarter, especially not from his brother, viewed this sudden access of martial enthusiasm with suspicion and was careful to give it no encouragement. As a result, Monsieur soon lost interest and, to the disappointment of the Bishop of Valence, returned to more characteristic occupations, such as embellishing his quarters with mirrors and crystal chandeliers. When news arrived that Madame had had a miscarriage and was seriously ill, he seized the opportunity to return to St Cloud and on 12 July was telling King Charles that 'Madame begs me to ask Your Majesty's pardon for not writing by this post, but she has not the strength to sit up, since the accident which happened to her a week ago'. Minette had, in fact, been so ill that for the space of a quarter of an hour she was thought to be actually dead.[23]

Louis was now parading his wife and assorted mistresses on a victory promenade through southern Flanders. 'All you have heard of the glory of Solomon and of the Emperor of China is not to be compared with the pomp and warlike array which surrounds the King', wrote an excited eye-witness. 'The streets are full of cloth of gold, of waving plumes, of chariots and superbly harnessed mules.' Monsieur joined the royal caravan at Arras and soon afterwards had the pleasure of renewing his friendship with the Chevalier de Lorraine, who rode into the camp at Tournai. Philippe de Lorraine, a penniless younger son of a cadet branch of the ancient ducal house of Guise, was an outstandingly handsome young man. He was also, as quickly became apparent to everybody except Philippe d'Orleans, an outstandingly nasty piece of work, manipulative, greedy and vicious. Madame de la Fayette believed that Monsieur's vanity would always prevent him from feeling affection for anyone but himself. Nevertheless, so far as he was capable of such an emotion, he had fallen in love with the Chevalier de Lorraine, and told the horrified Valence that in future he meant to keep his favourite always with him and to have no secrets from him. When he returned home at the end of the campaigning season, the Chevalier followed and was greeted with 'transports of joy'.

Madame was still far from well, and in October Monsieur was again sending Charles her excuses for not writing: 'but for six days she has had headaches so violent that she had her shutters always closed; she has been bled in the foot, and has tried many other remedies, but they have not relieved her at all.'[24] However, she recovered in time to join a great stag hunt at Versailles to celebrate the feast of St Hubert, and in January 1668 was looking forward to a visit from Charles's illegitimate son, James, Duke of Monmouth. 'I believe you may easily guess', Charles had written, 'that I am something concerned for this bearer James, and therefore I put him into your hands to be directed by you in all things, and pray use that authority over him, as you ought to do in kindness to me.'[25]

Monmouth, an engaging youth of nineteen, had for some time been granted semi-royal status. He had come to Paris to acquire a little extra social polish and his aunt was delighted to welcome him and introduce him to the French Court. In fact, they got on so well that Monsieur's jealousy was once more aroused and he made himself disagreeable about the amount of attention Madame was devoting to her young relative, even over the fact that they spoke English to one another. Madame, for her part, was increasingly disturbed by the baneful influence being exerted by the Chevalier de Lorraine, who had become 'more absolute in Monsieur's household than was allowable, unless one desired to be taken for the master of the family'. When Louis got to hear something of what was going on, he attempted to remonstrate with his brother, but Monsieur took offence and carried his wife and the Chevalier off to Villers-Cotterets, his estate near Laon, where for several weeks that winter Minette was obliged to endure the undiluted society of a bad-tempered husband and a triumphant favourite.

Worse was to follow. Madame had come to depend heavily on the support and robust good sense of the Bishop of Valence, but again Monsieur, encouraged by Lorraine, was grumbling that she spent too much time closeted with the bishop and accused them of having secrets together. Then, some time in the spring, he found out about the Chevalier's affair with Madame's maid of honour, Mademoiselle de Fiennes, and at once dismissed the girl in a jealous fury, without having the courtesy to inform his wife. De Fiennes, however, had left behind a casket containing a number of highly indiscreet letters from her lover. These were found by Minette, who passed them on to Valence. But before he could make any use of them, Lorraine had contrived to twist the facts in such a way as to direct Monsieur's wrath against the bishop, representing him as a mischief-maker who had induced Madame to turn against her husband's dear friend. After an unsuccessful appeal to the king, who refused to intervene, Valence was obliged to resign his office and leave Paris, much to Madame's distress. 'I hope you will regard these events as a trick of destiny', she wrote to him, 'and understand that the fatality which has cost you Monsieur's favour, does not extend to me, for I shall ever retain the same esteem I have always felt for you, and shall do my utmost to prove this by my actions.' But from that moment she came to fear and loathe the Chevalier de Lorraine, and would undoubtedly have shared the opinion, freely expressed by her successor, that he was indeed 'one of Lucifer's subjects'.[26]

In spite of her domestic difficulties, Minette was still taking a keen interest in the international situation, as it affected her brother and brother-in-law. The ease and speed of Louis's conquests in Flanders had taken even that monarch by surprise, and had put the fear of God into his fellow rulers. The present King of Spain was a frail, mentally retarded child of six, not expected to reach maturity, and if the King of France had been able to annex the Spanish Netherlands for his wife almost without firing a shot, what was to prevent him from laying claim to Spain itself in the all too likely event of her half-brother's death? The nightmare vision of Louis as master of a Franco-Spanish empire stretching from Brussels to Cadiz, incorporating sizeable chunks of Italy and capable of cutting their trade routes and absorbing their colonies, was to haunt the European powers for the rest of the century.

Most immediately affected were the Dutch, who faced the disappearance of the buffer state between themselves and a predatory France. They had hastened to ratify the peace with England at Breda the previous July and were now actively engaged in mending fences with their former enemy. The English, too, had been sufficiently unnerved by the recent turn of events to consider taking precautionary measures, and in January 1668 signed an offensive and defensive treaty with the United Provinces. This arrangement, presently joined by Sweden, became known as the Triple Alliance and was clearly intended to discourage French expansionist tendencies.

Charles, who was adept at this kind of agile diplomatic footwork, maintained that his only purpose was to exert a little friendly persuasion on France and Spain, but he was aware that his sister might not take quite the same view of the matter and he wrote to her on 23 January: 'I believe you will be a little surprised at the treaty I have concluded with the States. The effect of it is to bring Spain to consent to the peace upon the terms the King of France hath avowed he will be content with, so as I have done nothing to prejudice France in this agreement and they cannot wonder that I provide for myself against any mischief this war may produce.'[27] Louis, understandably, was not best pleased. But he took the hint and, in April, signed a peace treaty with Spain by which he relinquished the Spanish province of Franche-Comté, seized by France during the winter, and in return was left in possession of his Flemish conquests. No one, least of all the King of England, believed he would be content with this for long, but Charles was satisfied that he had made his point and demonstrated to Louis that he was a force to be reckoned with.

His letters to Minette that summer – hers are unfortunately missing – were mostly concerned with family news and court gossip. He continued to be worried about her health – 'for God's sake have a care of your diet, and believe the plainer your diet is the better health you will have' – and was evidently aware of her marital problems, for he wrote in August: 'I am very glad that Monsieur begins to be ashamed of his ridiculous fancies; you ought undoubtedly to oversee what is past, so that, for the future, he will leave being of those fantastical humours and I think the less éclairecissement there is upon such kind of matters the better. For his friend the Chevalier, I think you have taken a very good resolution not to live so with him but that when there offers a good occasion, you may ease yourself of such a rival; and by the character I have of him there is hope he will find out the occasion himself – which for Monsieur's sake I wish may be quickly.'[28]

All seemed quiet on the diplomatic front and in July Louis had hosted a grand fête at Versailles, ostensibly to celebrate the peace with Spain but also to mark the enthronement of Madame de Montespan as the latest *maîtresse en titre*. The famous gardens of the palace, with its orangery, its aviary of exotic birds, its grotto of spouting tritons and sirens and life-size statues of Apollo and the Muses, were all thrown open to an admiring public, and in the evening there was a performance of Molière's new play *Georges*

Dandin, with music by Lully. Later there was a sumptuous banquet and a firework display said to have cost 100,000 livres. Three hundred ladies were guests at the king's table and Madame was there, dancing with the Duke of Monmouth, while Monsieur glowered in the background.

The festivities at Versailles went on for a week, but behind the scenes Louis and his ministers were busy drafting instructions for the new French ambassador to the Court of St James's. Colbert de Croissy arrived in London in August charged with the task of breaking up the Triple Alliance and negotiating an Anglo-French treaty – that 'strict friendship' which had been under discussion on and off for the past seven years and which had now become an essential part of Louis's plans for swallowing up the rest of the Spanish Netherlands and dismembering the United Provinces.

Charles was perfectly prepared to be wooed and, unlike the other Continental powers, was not particularly concerned by Louis's territorial ambitions. He was, however, very much concerned by the French king's plans to build up his naval strength, and made it clear that Britain's maritime interests must be safeguarded by a treaty of commerce before any other form of alliance could be considered. As he told Minette in September, this was 'so jealous a point to us here, who can be only considerable by our trade and power by sea', that it would be impossible for him to contemplate making an entire league 'till first the great and principal interest of this nation be secured, which is trade'.[29] He returned to the subject twelve days later. 'The reason why I begin with the treaty of commerce is because I must enter first upon those matters which will render the rest more plausible here, for you know that the thing which is nearest the heart of the nation is trade and all that belongs to it.'[30]

Negotiations proceeded through the autumn, and by December were sufficiently advanced for Charles to tell his sister that he would be sending her a cipher by the first safe occasion. Security was becoming very important. 'I am now thinking of the way how to proceed in this whole matter, which must be carried on with all secrecy imaginable, till the particulars are farther agreed upon', he wrote on 20 January 1669. 'I send you here enclosed my letter to the King my brother, desiring that this matter might pass through your hands as the person in the world I have most confidence in.' He assured Minette that she would be kept fully informed, but 'we must have a great care what we write by the post, lest it fall into hands which may hinder our design, for I must again conjure you that the whole matter be an absolute secret, otherwise we shall never compass the end we aim at'.[31]

It was obviously desirable that the Dutch should not get wind of the planned *rapprochement* between England and France, but there was another, more compelling reason for secrecy. Towards the end of January, at a very private gathering in the Duke of York's lodgings, the king broke the news to his brother and Lord Arlington, Sir Thomas Clifford and Lord Arundell of Wardour that he intended to convert to Roman Catholicism, and asked for their advice 'about the ways and methods fittest to be taken for the settling of the Catholic religion in his kingdoms and to consider of the time most proper to declare himself'. He spoke 'with great earnestness, and even with tears in his eyes; and added that they were to go about it as wise men and good Catholics ought to do'.[32]

This was the 'great secret', known only to a trusted handful of friends and councillors, and which had at all costs to be guarded. In March Charles sent Lord Arundell over to Paris with certain propositions for Louis's consideration, but told Minette, using their cipher for the first time, 'pray take no notice of his having any commission from me, for he pretends to go only upon his own score to attend the Queen'. Arundell, a Catholic of unimpeachable loyalty, was Henrietta Maria's Master of the Horse.

These precautions were understandable, for Charles was playing a very dangerous game, and had the terms of the treaty, now gradually taking shape, become known prematurely in Protestant London, he might well have come to share his father's fate. The King of England, it was agreed, would make a public declaration of his conversion to the Catholic faith as soon as he was able, and would receive from the King of France the sum of two million livres to assist him in making that declaration. The King of France also agreed that, if necessary, he would provide and pay for 6,000 troops to help suppress any resulting civil unrest. The King of England, for his part, undertook to join with France in declaring war on the United Provinces. He was to be responsible for the conduct of the war at sea, and would receive an annual subsidy of three million livres for the duration of hostilities. He would also be granted a share of the spoils, if any.

The negotiations for the conclusion of the treaty of commerce, which were, of course, being carried on quite openly through the usual diplomatic channels, provided a useful cover, but even so it was becoming increasingly difficult to conceal the existence of the 'main business'. Ralph Montagu, the new English ambassador in Paris, certainly suspected that something was going on behind his back, as did Lord St Albans; while the Duke of Buckingham had had to be cajoled by Madame into believing that he was fully in everyone's confidence.

Madame herself still remained the vital channel of communication between the two principals, but now Louis wanted to bring de Croissy into the secret. Charles was reluctant. 'There will be a time', he wrote on 6 June, 'when both he and Montagu may have a share in part of the matter, but for the great secret, if it be not kept so till all things be ready to begin, we shall never go through with it, and destroy the whole business. I have seen your letter to Buckingham and what you write to him is as it ought to be. He shall be brought into all the business before he can suspect anything, except that which concerns religion which he must not be trusted with. You will do well to write but seldom to him, for fear something may slip from your pen which may make him jealous that there is something more than what he knows of.'[33]

Charles continued to be hypersensitive about security. 'Remember how much the secret in this matter imports and take care that no new body be acquainted with it, till I see what Arundell brings', he wrote again on 7 June. He was becoming impatient for Lord Arundell's return. 'The sooner you despatch Arundell the more clearly we shall be able to judge of the whole matter'; and on 24 June, in his last surviving letter to his 'dearest sister', 'it will be very difficult for me to say anything to you upon the propositions till Arundell return hither.' He was aware that there could still be problems, but 'I am confident when we have heard the reasons of all sides we shall not differ in the main, having the same interest and inclinations'.[34]

For Minette the interest and excitement provided by her share in helping to negotiate the secret treaty must surely have been a welcome distraction from the wretchedness of her private life.

Monsieur's infatuation for the detestable Chevalier de Lorraine showed no sign of abating and now the favourite, whose position seemed unassailable, treated Madame with barely concealed insolence. It did not help that she was pregnant again and had been unwell on and off throughout the spring and summer, often having to stay in bed for several days at a time. In July she retired to St Cloud where the baby – another girl, to the undisguised annoyance of its father – was born on 27 August. She was still lying-in when she received the news of her mother's death. Henrietta Maria's health had been failing ever since her return from England and she had spent the last few years living very quietly at Colombes. For Minette, who had always been particularly close to her mother, it was a great sadness, and left her feeling more isolated than ever. Even Louis, whose friendship and support were so necessary, had been a little distant towards her lately.

Louis had written to Charles at the beginning of September speaking kindly of Madame as 'the natural bond of union between us'; but Madame herself perceived 'a coldness in the feelings of the King of France', and it looks as if Louis had begun to suspect that she was putting her brother's interests before his own. This suspicion may not have been entirely without foundation. Ralph Montagu, who had quickly conceived a high opinion of Madame's discretion and judgement, told Lord Arlington that no one in England ought ever to disregard 'any advices that come from her, because she is so truly and passionately concerned for the King her brother'.[35]

Charles had once teased Minette that she must not forget she was 'an Exeter woman' and she, for so long a Frenchwoman, never had forgotten it. If she had found fulfilment in her marriage things might have been different, but as it was all the force of her warmly affectionate nature was concentrated on the brother who loved and trusted her. In September she wrote him a long, closely reasoned letter, 'following the promise I made to you to let you know my opinion and what I have been able to see in this important business' – the treaty of course. Although some people, 'who do not know the inside of things', might think it unwise for England to ally herself against Holland, Charles must remember that he needed France to ensure the success of the design about religion, 'and there is very little likelihood of your obtaining what you desire from the King except on condition that you enter into a league with him against Holland. I think you must take this resolution, and when you have thought it well over, you will find that besides the intention of religion, your glory and your profit will coincide in this design. Indeed, what is there more glorious and more profitable than to extend the confines of your kingdom beyond the sea and to become supreme in commerce, which is what your people most passionately desire and what will probably never occur so long as the Republic of Holland exists?'[36]

Madame was spending September at St Cloud in the company of Madame de la Fayette, and the two friends returned to a project begun several years before, at the the time of the Comte de Guiche's final departure from the scene. One day, while describing some 'quite extraordinary instances of his passion for her', Madame had said, 'Do you not think that if all that has happened to me were written down, it would make a fine story?' And she went on, 'You write so well. Write this and I will give you all the details.' Madame de la Fayette was naturally enchanted by the idea and for a time, whenever they were alone together, Madame would continue with her tale. But 'the whim soon left her' and the work was laid aside. Now she had remembered it, and Madame de la Fayette again set herself to the task of 'showing her each morning what I had written upon her recollections of the previous night'.[37]

Those few weeks in the idyllic surroundings of St Cloud – Monsieur was mercifully absent with the king at Chambord – were to be the last peaceful, comparatively happy period in Minette's life. In October her personal problems reached some kind of crisis. Exactly what had caused it remains a mystery, but in the circumstances it seems reasonable to assume that it involved the Chevalier de Lorraine. She had always kept in touch with her old friend the Bishop of Valence through Madame de St Chaumont, her children's governess and a trusted confidante, and now she begged him either to send or bring her the most damaging letters written by the Chevalier to Mademoiselle de Fiennes, which were still in his possession. Valence hesitated. He dared not entrust such letters to the post, and he himself had been forbidden by royal decree to return to Paris. But Madame continued to send him urgent messages and finally wrote herself: 'You no longer care for me, my dear bishop, since you refuse to give me a consolation which I cannot do without.' This was too much for Daniel de Cosnac and, against his better judgement, he agreed to a meeting. He reached Paris by a roundabout route and in disguise, but unfortunately fell seriously ill in lodgings in the rue St Denis. He was able to send his nephew to deliver the dangerous letters to Madame de St Chaumont, and hardly had he done so than the police arrived to arrest him on the pretext that he was a notorious criminal they had long been looking for. In fact he had been betrayed to the authorities by his doctor.

The news quickly reached the Palais Royal, and Francis Vernon, a secretary at the English embassy, writing home on 27 November, described the chilling little scene which followed. 'They say that Monsieur, in dressing himself before he went to St Germain, broke the business to Madame, and said: 'Madame, ne savez-vous pas que M. l'Evêque de Valence est à Paris?' She answered that she thought he would not be so indiscreet as to come contrary to the King's order. So he combed his head, and a little while after, he said: 'Oui, Madame, il est vrai, il est à Paris, il est encore en prison.' Whereupon she expressed a passion, and said she hoped they would consider his character and use him with respect.'[38]

After an uncomfortable night in gaol, Valence was released and promptly sent into exile, but for Madame there was worse to come. Although the bishop had had the presence of mind at the moment of his arrest to dispose of any letters from either Madame or Madame de St Chaumont – he had them taken away in the basin of his commode and emptied down the privy – a brief note from Madame de St Chaumont had been overlooked and was seized by the police. Louis had been waiting for an excuse to get rid of Madame de St Chaumont, whom he distrusted, and he now gave orders that she was to be dismissed from her position forthwith. Madame was distraught at the prospect of losing a dear friend and one of the few remaining members of her household whom she could trust not to spy for the Chevalier de Lorraine, but the king refused to listen to her appeals or the protests of Ralph Montagu, who hinted that King Charles would take a serious view of the lack of consideration being shown to his sister.

Madame herself firmly believed that the Chevalier would not rest until he had driven away every last one of her friends –

indeed he was boasting that he had contrived the disgrace of both the Bishop of Valence and Madame de St Chaumont. Montagu, too, believed he was the principal cause of Madame's troubles, and said so in a long indignant letter to Charles. 'The King here', he wrote, 'is sufficiently convinced of all the impertinences and insolencies of the Chevalier de Lorraine, and doth at this time both desire and stand in need so much of your friendship that I believe in a little time he may be brought to remove him from about Monsieur, if he sees it is a thing your Majesty really insists upon.'[39] Charles had already summoned the French ambassador and made it very clear how much he resented the way Madame was being treated, adding that he knew the Chevalier was at the bottom of it all. De Croissy did his best to smooth things over and Louis, who was beginning to regret his high-handed action – 'I believe the King is now sorry that he has done this', wrote Montagu, 'though he be of a humour not to own it' – sent profuse apologies and promised to deal suitably with the Chevalier as soon as an opportunity presented itself.

Madame remained unimpressed and unconvinced. Writing to Valence in his exile near Toulouse at the end of December, she remarked sadly that Monsieur 'has long since lost the use of his native tongue, and can only speak in the language which has been taught him by the Chevalier de Lorraine, whose will he follows blindly, and the worst is, I have no hope that he will ever mend his ways. . . . If the King keeps the promises which he daily repeats to me, I shall in future have less cause for annoyance, but you know how little I have learned to trust such words.'[40]

Nemesis was, however, about to strike the Chevalier de Lorraine, who was not only publicly flaunting his power over Monsieur, but advising him how he could obtain a separation from his wife, and spreading rumours that they were about to be divorced. In January Monsieur wanted to bestow the revenues of two abbeys in the gift of the Orleans dukedom on his favourite, but Louis vetoed the idea. The Chevalier, he told his brother, was no fit person to be given church benefices. Monsieur flew into a rage, screaming that he was never allowed to do anything 'but still he was crosst', and the Chevalier was unwise enough, or over-confident enough, to make some very offensive remarks about the king. These, of course, were quickly repeated back to Louis, who ordered his arrest.

Monsieur is said to have fainted when he heard the news, and he grovelled at the king's feet, imploring him to relent. Again Louis refused and the favourite was removed to prison near Lyons. Monsieur now became 'so transported with choler' that he announced his intention of leaving the Court at once and never looking on his brother's face again – if he had a house a thousand leagues away he would go there. As it was, he had to be content with Villers-Cotterets and two days later, still in a furious temper, he stormed off, dragging his unfortunate wife with him.

The scandal of the Chevalier's arrest and the quarrel between Monsieur and the king caused an immense sensation in court circles, and there was widespread sympathy for Madame. She had told the Vicomte de Turenne, in a brief note scribbled before her departure, of the pain Monsieur's violent behaviour caused her, but despite 'the unpleasantness of his company in his present mood' and the dreariness of Villers-Cotterets in the depth of winter, her only real regret was having to leave her friends, and the fear that the king would forget her.

There was not much danger of her being forgotten by her friends. 'We are too sad here even to try to be agreeable, and since Madame left us, joy is no longer to be seen at St Germain', lamented one lady. 'Nobody thinks of anything else but of writing to her, and the ladies of the Court are to be seen, pen in hand, at all hours of the day.'[41] The king, too, was unlikely to forget Madame. The negotiations over the secret treaty had reached a critical stage and her presence would be essential for their successful completion. The plan, which had first been tentatively suggested more than a year ago, was for her to pay a visit to England, and in January 1670 de Croissy told the king that Charles passionately desired to see and converse with his sister.

It was already known that Louis intended to go on a tour of inspection to Flanders in the spring, and while the Court was on a progress so close to the Channel ports, it would seem perfectly natural for Madame to seize the opportunity of crossing over to see her brother – not even the Dutch would suspect an ulterior motive. There were still a few important points to be settled before the treaty could be concluded, and it was felt on the French side that a little of Madame's persuasive influence at this stage would achieve more than months of conventional diplomacy. The problem now would be to get Monsieur to give permission for his wife to leave the country, but nothing could be done while he continued to nurse his grievances at Villers-Cotterets. Fortunately he was becoming very bored with his self-imposed exile and at the end of February allowed himself to be persuaded to return to civilization.

Everyone was delighted to see Madame again. The king showered her with expensive presents and Lord Fauconbridge, an English diplomat on his way through France, was impressed by her obvious popularity. 'To say the truth, I find she has a very great influence in this Court, where they all adore her, as she deserves, being a princess of extraordinary address and conduct.' But while everyone was making a special fuss of Madame, who looked frighteningly thin and pale, everyone was also shocked by the extremely disagreeable way her husband was behaving towards her, either publicly insulting her or refusing to speak to her. The malign influence of the Chevalier de Lorraine remained only too apparent. 'The bad impression which he left on Monsieur's mind still lasts', Madame wrote to Madame de St Chaumont, 'and he never sees me without reproaches. . . . He sulks in my presence, and hopes that by ill-treating me, he will make me wish for the Chevalier's return.'[42]

Louis had now broached the delicate matter of Madame's visit to England, telling his brother something, though not very much, of the reason for it. But Monsieur, an inveterate gossip, had smelled secrets, and the suspicion that he was being excluded from important affairs of state further increased his sense of ill-usage. He reacted angrily, saying he would not even allow his wife to go to Flanders, and Madame told Madame de St Chaumont that 'the king has worked hard to bring him to reason, but all in vain, for his only object in treating me so ill is to force me to ask favours for the Chevalier, and I am determined not to give in. . . . This state of affairs does not admit of any reconciliation, and Monsieur now refuses to come near me, and hardly ever speaks to me, which, in all the quarrels we have had, has never happened before. . . . As for my journey to England, I do not despair that it may yet take place. If it does, it will be a great happiness for me.'[43]

The battle of Madame's journey to England continued to rage during March and April, until Louis finally lost patience, telling

Monsieur that it was for the good of the kingdom and he must give his consent. Monsieur gave in with a very bad grace. 'Never has anything been more wrangled over', wrote Madame on 28 April, 'and even now Monsieur refuses to let me stay more than three days with the king, my brother. This is better than nothing, but it is a very short time for all that two people, who love one another as well as he and I do, have to say'.[44]

Later that same day the royal cavalcade set out, Madame travelling in the state coach with the king and queen and Madame de Montespan. Unfortunately the weather was atrocious. Rain fell in torrents and the roads became quagmires, so that the journey, intended as a triumphal progress, turned into a miserable, muddy ordeal. Near Landrecies the River Sambre had burst its banks and carried the bridge away. The fords were all impassable and the royal family was faced with the novel experience of having to doss down for the night on the floor of a nearby barn. The only food generally available was tough chickens and thin soup, but Madame, who was exhausted at the end of each day's journey, could seldom touch anything but a little milk. Monsieur continued to be in a vile mood, not helped by the fact that his cosmetics had gone astray somewhere along the road, and missed no opportunity of being unpleasant to his wife. An astrologer had told him he would be married several times, he remarked chattily on one occasion and, glancing at her wan countenance, added that the prophecy seemed likely to be fulfilled, since it was plain Madame would not last long. The other ladies present were horrified and showed what they thought by their disapproving silence.

The travellers reached Lille on 23 May and the French ambassador at the Hague, who had come to pay his respects, was able to have a long conversation with Madame. M. de Pomponne soon discovered that she was fully briefed on Louis's plans for bringing the King of England back to his interests, while keeping the Dutch amused with meaningless negotiations, and was amazed to find 'such grasp of mind and capacity for business in a princess who seemed only born for the graces which are the ornament of her sex'. It was not difficult to guess that the purpose of her voyage to England would not be confined 'to the simple pleasure of seeing the King, her brother'.[45]

On the following day Madame left for Dunkirk, where an English fleet was waiting for her, and on the evening of 26 May she was being greeted off Dover by the royal barge containing the king himself, the Dukes of York and Monmouth and Prince Rupert, now an admiral in his cousin's navy. A joyful reunion took place on board the flagship and then Madame was escorted ashore to medieval Dover Castle, which had been made as comfortable as possible for her and her ladies.

Charles got straight down to business, although, in fact, virtually all the detailed hard bargaining had been completed by this time, and it really only remained for Madame to persuade her brother to agree to putting the declaration of war with Holland before the announcement of his conversion to Rome – Louis being a good deal more interested in the former than the latter. Charles proved easily persuadable, and there must be considerable uncertainty as to whether he ever did seriously mean to take the enormous risk of actually making such a public announcement. But neither Louis nor Madame seems to have doubted his sincerity, and if anyone else privy to the 'great secret' suspected that the King of England was merely using his promised conversion as a ploy intended to extract as much hard cash and political advantage as possible from the alliance with France, they were keeping quiet about it.

So the treaty was signed on 1 June, ready for ratification by the two monarchs under their private seals, and everyone relaxed and prepared to enjoy the rest of Madame's visit, for a message had now arrived from Louis giving her permission to stay on for another ten or twelve days. The queen and the Duchess of York came down from London and there was quite a family party to celebrate the tenth anniversary of the Restoration and the king's fortieth birthday. It was Minette's first meeting with her Portuguese sister-in-law, who was not handsome, but so kind and good that you could not help loving her. She found the Duchess of York grown stout and self-important, but was pleased to be able to give her news of her younger daughter. Princess Anne of York, who suffered from eye trouble, had been sent over to her grandmother in France in order that she might be treated by a famous French specialist, and after Henrietta Maria's death Minette had welcomed the child into her own household to be brought up with her French cousins.

Charles took his sister as far inland as Canterbury, where a ballet and a play were performed for her entertainment, followed by a grand collation in the hall of St Augustine's Abbey, so that the Dutch envoy, watching nervously from a distance, could detect nothing but the feasting and rejoicing to be expected at such a family reunion. On another occasion the royal party visited the fleet. 'Many of our expeditions are on the sea', wrote a member of the French entourage, 'where Madame is as bold as she is on land, and walks fearlessly along the edge of the ships.'

All too soon the precious extra days slipped past, and it was time to go. Charles loaded Minette with presents, including 2,000 gold crowns to build a chapel at Chaillot in memory of their mother, and he and the Duke of York went on board ship with her and sailed part of the way across the Channel. But at last they had to tear themselves away. Everyone was in floods of tears, and Charles was seen to turn back three times to kiss and embrace his little sister. Even the French ambassador was affected by such a sorrowful leave-taking, and the poet Edmund Waller, who twenty-four years before had celebrated Minette's first journey to France in verse, was moved to compose another ode:

> No wind can favour us. Howe'er it blows,
> We must be wretch'd, and our dear treasure lose!
> Sighs will not let us half our sorrow tell,
> Fair, lovely, great and best of nymphs, farewell.

Back in France Madame received an enthusiastic welcome from everyone at St Germain – everyone, that is, except her husband – and the king, delighted with her success in England, gave her a generous present of money to cover her expenses. Louis wanted her to come with the Court for a fortnight's holiday at Versailles but, much to Madame's disappointment, Monsieur turned the invitation down 'out of spite', and instead they returned to Paris, which was buzzing with rumours that Madame had had secret talks with her brother and had succeeded in breaking the Triple Alliance. 'We knew, though very vaguely,' wrote Madame de la Fayette, 'that the negotiations in which she was concerned were on the point of being carried through. At twenty-six she saw herself the link between the two greatest kings of our century, and she had in her hands a treaty whereon the fate of a part of Europe depended.'[46] Certainly her prestige had never been higher and all the diplomatic corps hastened to pay visits of congratulation on her return.

On 24 June Monsieur and Madame left for St Cloud. The weather had turned very hot and although she was again feeling wretchedly ill, complaining of stomach ache and a pain in her side, Madame insisted on bathing in the Seine, much against her doctor's advice. Her husband was still doing his best to make her life a misery and on 26 June she poured out her troubles in another long letter to Madame de Chaumont. 'Since my return, the king here has been very good to me', she wrote, 'but as for Monsieur, nothing can equal his bitterness and anxiety to find fault. He does me the honour to say that I am all-powerful, and can do everything that I like, and so, if I do not bring back the Chevalier, it is because I do not wish to please him. At the same time he joins threats for the future with this kind of talk. I have once more told him how little his favourite's return depends upon me, and how little I get my own way, or you would not be where you are now.' Sadly, Madame warned the former governess not to try to keep in touch with her daughter, Marie Louise, now eight years old. 'In God's name, put that love away. The poor child cannot return your affection, and will, alas! be brought up to hate me.'[47]

Louis had now commanded his brother to bring Madame over to Versailles, but the visit was not a success. The king wanted to talk privately to his sister-in-law about her time in England, but Monsieur deliberately interrupted their conversation, making it impossible for them to continue. Then, at dinner, one of the courtiers who had been with Madame at Dover began, with astonishing tactlessness, to describe the magnificence of her reception, dwelling especially on the attentions paid to her by the Duke of Monmouth. Madame was in tears by the time they left, and both the queen and La Grande Mademoiselle commented on how very ill she looked.

On Saturday, 28 June, Ralph Montagu came down to St Cloud and Madame was able at last to let him into the secret of the treaty of Dover. In the evening Madame de la Fayette arrived to spend a few days, and the two friends walked together in the moonlit garden until midnight.

Early on Sunday morning Madame wrote to another trusted friend, Anne de Gonzague, widow of her cousin Prince Edward Palatine, and again spoke frankly of her marital unhappiness. Monsieur still persisted in blaming her for the Chevalier de Lorraine's exile, and had told her that she could expect no improvement in his treatment of her until she had given him back his favourite to make, as she had once described it, 'a third in our union'. The Chevalier had now been released from prison and was free to go where he liked, as long as he made no attempt to return to France, but nothing would convince Monsieur that his wife could not arrange that return if she wished. He even refused to believe the king, who had told him flatly that Madame had had no part in Lorraine's banishment and had no power to bring it to an end. Madame, therefore, was trying to resign herself to putting up with his unkindness as patiently as she could – unless, perhaps, Anne de Gonzague might be able to effect a reconciliation. 'For you can do more with him than any other person', she wrote, 'and I am so well persuaded that Monsieur's interest and mine are dear to you that I hope you will take pains in it.'[48] But it was a faint hope, and later that morning she told Madame de la Fayette that she felt very depressed and out of sorts. 'She was tired of all the people who surrounded her and could bear with them no longer.'

Madame went in to see her daughter, who was having her portrait painted, and begun to talk about her brother and her visit to England. This cheered her up a little, and in the afternoon she lay down on a pile of cushions on the floor and fell asleep with her head in Madame de la Fayette's lap. Watching her sleeping face, her friend was disturbed by the change that seemed to come over it. When she woke, about five o'clock, she again complained of the pain in her side and asked for a glass of iced chicory water. This was brought by one of her ladies, but no sooner had she swallowed it than she collapsed in sudden terrible pain, crying out, 'What agony! I cannot bear it!' The women hurried to help her, and Madame de la Fayette supported her while they undressed her and laid her on her bed. But immediately 'she began to cry out more loudly than before, flinging herself from side to side like a person in fearful agony'. Monsieur's doctor was summoned and diagnosed colic, but Madame exclaimed that it was more serious than they thought; she was going to die, and asked for a priest. Her husband was standing by her bed, and she kissed him and said, 'Alas, Monsieur, for a long time past you have not loved me; but that was unjust, for I have never failed you.' Monsieur appeared to be much moved and everybody in the room was in tears.

'All this', says Madame de la Fayette, 'took place in less than half an hour.' Madame was still crying that she had terrible pains in the pit of her stomach, and then: 'All at once she bade us look to the water she had drunk, saying that it was poison, that she knew she had been poisoned and should be given an antidote.' Madame de la Fayette was standing beside Monsieur, between the bed and the wall, and though she did not believe him capable of so great a crime, found herself looking carefully at him. He did not seem at all embarrassed, but suggested that some of the chicory water should be given to a dog, and agreed that Madame should take an emetic if it would relieve her mind. Madame Desbordes, her chief *femme de chambre* and most faithful servant, said she had mixed the water herself and drunk some of it. Nevertheless, an emetic was administered to the patient, but 'her vomiting was very incomplete' and gave no relief. Madame was becoming more and more exhausted, saying her sufferings were just as great but she no longer had the strength to cry out, and repeated that she knew she was dying. One of her ladies tried in vain to find her pulse and noticed with alarm that her extremities were growing cold. By this time the parish priest of St Cloud had arrived and heard her confession, which she made supported in the arms of one of her maids.

Three hours had now elapsed since the beginning of Madame's ordeal and two more doctors had arrived. She told them of her conviction that she had been poisoned, but after a lengthy conference the three medical men seemed unable or unwilling to suggest anything more helpful than a purge of senna. Madame de la Fayette was in despair over their inertia. Madame, she wrote, 'was continually wanting to be sick, but they gave her nothing to help it'. When Madame herself heard them saying she was better, she exclaimed bitterly that this was so far from the truth that were she not a Christian she would be tempted to kill herself, so great was her pain. She added that she could not help wishing somebody else could experience just for a moment what she was suffering, so they would understand how dreadful it was. Her bed was now so soiled that it was necessary to move her. Another, smaller bed was made up for her and she was able to walk to it without assistance, but when she tried to swallow some broth, the pain redoubled in intensity.

News of Madame's illness had spread rapidly and all the principal personages of the Court were gathering at St Cloud. At about eleven o'clock the king and queen arrived, accompanied by La Grande Mademoiselle. They found Madame lying on a little bed, with her nightdress unfastened and her hair loose. Her face was deathly pale and she was still trying desperately to vomit. Mademoiselle thought 'she had the air of a dead person. She said to us, "You see the condition I am in", and we began to weep.' The king was trying to galvanize the doctors into action and suggesting remedies to them, but 'they looked at each other and said not a word'. Mademoiselle was shocked to discover that nobody had spoken to Madame about God, or made arrangements for her to receive the sacrament, and after some discussion it was agreed to send for her friend, the famous preacher Abbé Bossuet, and Nicolas Feuillet, a Jansenist canon well known for his holiness. Louis now came to the bedside and Madame whispered that he was losing the truest servant he would ever have. She had never feared death, though she had been afraid of losing his favour. The king was openly in tears as he said goodbye, and she begged him not to cry or he would make her weep too.

Presently they lifted her back into the big bed. She began to hiccup and asked again when she would die. It was clear that there was no hope for her, but, says Madame de la Fayette, 'not a word did she utter of the cruelty of Fate, which was cutting short her life in its prime'. The priest Feuillet was the next arrival. He gave the dying woman no words of comfort, instead exhorting her grimly to think of her sins, her life of frivolous pleasure and forgetfulness of God. He was still at it when Ralph Montagu came in. 'She no sooner saw me than she said, "You see the sad condition I am in. I am going to die. How I pity the King, my brother, for I am sure he is losing the person that loves him best in the world."' She asked Montagu if he remembered what she had told him about the new alliance, and said, 'Pray tell my brother that I never persuaded him to it out of interest, but was convinced that both his honour and advantage were equally concerned in it; for I always loved him more than my life, and have no other regret in dying than parting with him.' The ambassador then asked if she really believed she had been poisoned. They were speaking in English, but Feuillet caught the word 'poison' and broke in, saying that Madame must not accuse anyone, but sacrifice her life to God. Montagu ignored him and repeated the question. He says she made no reply, but Madeleine de la Fayette, who had never left her friend's side, heard her say very softly that he must say nothing about it to the king, her brother. He must be spared that grief at all costs, and whatever happened he must not think of taking vengeance, for the French king was not guilty, and no blame must be laid at his door.

Yet another doctor, summoned by Louis, had now arrived and insisted on bleeding her from the foot. This was not a success, for no blood came and the pain only increased. She was receiving the last rites when Abbé Bossuet reached St Cloud, and he at least brought her the consolations of religion. She was very weak now, but having received her assurance that she died in the Catholic, Apostolic and Roman faith, Bossuet did what he could to sustain her through her last hours. Holding the crucifix before her, he cried: 'There is Christ, whose arms are stretched out to receive you. He will give you eternal life, and raise up that suffering body in the glory of His resurrection.' The few faithful friends who remained prayed with him at the bedside till Madame seemed to have fallen asleep. But within a very few minutes she suddenly roused and exclaimed 'It is all over!' 'Madame,' said Bossuet, 'you believe in God, you hope in God, you love God?' '"With all my heart", she answered, as reasonably as if she were not ill, still holding the crucifix to her lips. Death alone made her surrender it. Her strength failed her and she let it fall, losing the power of speech at almost the same moment as her life. Her agony lasted but a minute; and after one or two little convulsive movements of her mouth, she expired.'[49]

Henrietta Anne, princess of England, Madame de France, Charles II's Minette, died at half-past two in the morning of Monday, 30 June after nine hours of unremitting and excruciating torment. She was just twenty-six years old.

SEVEN

PRINCESS OF ORANGE, DAUGHTER OF YORK

> The Prince is a very fond husband, but she is a coy bride, at least before folks.
>
> (Anonymous comment)

The news of Madame's death produced a reaction of genuine grief and shock on both sides of the Channel. When Ralph Montagu's first brief account 'of the saddest story in the world' reached Whitehall, the king burst into angry tears and began to curse Monsieur for a villain. At Versailles, the King of France, too, shed tears and the Prince de Condé later remarked that he had never seen his Majesty so deeply moved. Louis told Montagu that he felt Madame's death as much as if she had been his own wife, and wrote to Charles of his sorrow 'for the loss of one who was so dear to both of us'.

The horrific circumstances of Madame's death and her own suspicions of foul play, not to mention the future of the English alliance, made it necessary to move quickly to scotch the ugly rumours which were already circulating in Paris and London. Louis instructed Montagu to assure his master that 'if there were the least imagination that her death had been caused by poison, nothing would be wanting, either towards the discovering or the punishing so horrid a fact' and a post-mortem examination took place on the evening of 30 June. This was performed by a panel of leading French physicians headed by Antoine Vallot, the king's own doctor, who had been at St Cloud the day before. Two English doctors, who happened to be in Paris, were also present, together with the English ambassador and about a hundred other witnesses. The medical men all confirmed that they could find no trace of poison in the body and gave it as their collective opinion that death was due to natural causes. It was, of course, well known that Madame's health had never been robust. For the past three years she had frequently complained of a stitch in her side and Vallot declared that, having seen the state of her liver and lungs, he was amazed she had lived so long.

A letter from Lionne, the Foreign Minister, detailing the steps taken by the French government and expressing the sincere regret of all concerned, followed by a formal visit of condolence from the Maréchal de Bellefonds, who reached London during the first week of July bringing with him the official report of the autopsy, went a long way towards satisfying opinion in Whitehall and the City. Bellefonds, who had also been among those present at St Cloud on the night of 29/30 June, was able to provide a first-hand account of Madame's last hours, and although the king told a friend that his grief was so great that he dared not allow himself to dwell on it, he assured the French ambassador that Louis could continue to count on his friendship.

Charles found it hard to forgive Monsieur for his unkind treatment of Minette, but he does not appear to have ever seriously regarded him as a murderer, or at least not after his first shocked outburst. However, the suspicion persisted in France. Ralph Montagu certainly believed that Madame had been poisoned and so did Monsieur's second wife, although she was sure it had been done without his knowledge. The Chevalier de Lorraine, now travelling in Italy, had, it was said, sent the deadly potion to the Marquis d'Effiat, one of the 'brood of fresh favourites' who had sprung up in his absence and who had seized an opportunity to smear it on the rim of the cup from which Madame would drink her chicory water. This story, often repeated with suitable embellishments, was widely believed, although no hard evidence was ever produced to support it, and the fact that the wicked Chevalier was allowed to return to France and Monsieur's household less than two years later indicates that the authorities considered there to be no case against him. The doctors at the post-mortem had given the cause of death as cholera morbus. A later suggestion was acute peritonitis following the perforation of a duodenal ulcer; while the most recent conjecture is that, like her long-dead uncle Henry, Prince of

Wales, the Princess Henrietta Anne was the victim of a fulminating attack of porphyria – and it is worth remembering that there were rumours that he, too, had been poisoned.

For three days after her death Madame's embalmed body lay in state at St Cloud and Monsieur was able to indulge his passion for ceremonial etiquette by dressing his eight-year-old daughter and her even younger cousin, Princess Anne of York, in all the trappings of trailing violet mourning mantles, although La Grand Mademoiselle remarked that he himself did not appear to be much afflicted by sorrow. Louis had decreed that his sister-in-law was to be given the sort of state funeral usually reserved for crowned heads, and Madame was laid to rest close to her mother in the abbey of St Denis on Thursday 21 August. It was, wrote Francis Vernon from the embassy in Paris, 'extraordinarily pompous and magnificent; in that kind nothing was wanting; all symptoms of a public sorrow and affection were met together'.

Everyone who was anyone had gathered to pay their last respects. All the Court was there, all the nobility and the princes and princesses of the blood. Even the queen herself was present, 'an honour altogether new and unpractised'; while among those who had travelled from England were the Duke of Buckingham, who had fallen madly in love with the sixteen-year-old Minette, and the Earl of St Albans, who could remember the shabbily dressed little refugee arriving with her governess on the Dover packet all those years ago. Abbé Bossuet preached the funeral sermon 'with an eloquence something transported beyond a usual delicacy and sweetness', and finally all the officers of the household came to cast their badges of office into the grave 'with great silence and mourning'. But, says Francis Vernon, 'as her coffin was put in, there was a general weeping, a circumstance something unusual at these great ceremonies of the interment of princes'.[1]

So Madame was gone, a flower blooming in the morning, withered and cut down by nightfall, as Bossuet put it, and for all those who had loved her the world became a sadder, greyer place. The Bishop of Valence, still in exile, felt that since men had been known to die of grief, it seemed a crime on his part to have survived, and Madame de la Fayette wrote, 'There are sorrows for which nothing can ever console one, and which leave a shadow over the whole of one's life.' Louis, who had told Colbert de Croissy, 'I yield to no one, not even the King of England himself, in my grief and love for my sister', never appeared in another ballet, and the Marquis de la Fare considered that 'in Madame the Court lost the only person of her rank capable of distinguishing true merit. Since her death', he remarked gloomily, 'all has been gambling, confusion and bad manners.'

The 'great secret' enshrined within the Treaty of Dover remained a secret for as long as it mattered. The Anglo-French alliance, signed at the end of the year, for purposes of camouflage contained no mention of religion, and although Charles continued to discuss possible ways and means of announcing his conversion with Louis whenever it seemed expedient to do so, it became increasingly obvious that it would never be more than a talking-point, and after a few years the idea was quietly allowed to drop. Perhaps it was just as well that Minette was no longer there to be disillusioned by the spectacle of her beloved brother's cynical exploitation of an issue of conscience.

After Madame's death the five-year-old Princess Anne was sent back to England. The York children spent their earliest years at St James's Palace or Hampton Court, sometimes down at Deptford, where their father had a house convenient for the naval dockyard, and sometimes at Twickenham, the home of their maternal grandparents. They saw little of their parents, the duke being occupied either with naval matters or with his mistresses, the duchess with her social life or her numerous unhealthy pregnancies, and such family life as there was came to an end when the former Anne Hyde died of cancer in March 1671, to be swiftly followed into the grave by Edgar, born in 1666, and the most recent baby, Katherine.

The Princesses Mary and Anne were now the only legitimate members of the rising generation of the House of Stuart, and as such they represented the future of the Protestant succession, which the king had promised should be assured. Mary and Anne therefore became the Children of the State, their education the responsibility of their uncle and his ministers. After their mother's death, an establishment was created for them at Richmond, the old Thames-side palace built by the first Tudor king, where they were placed in the charge of Cavalier veteran Colonel Edward

Villiers and his wife Lady Frances, a daughter of the Earl of Suffolk, who had held the position of Lady Governess to the York children since 1661. The numerous Villiers daughters were brought up with the princesses and formed the nucleus of a select little royal school. The young ladies were taught to speak and read French, they had drawing and music lessons and learned to dance – Samuel Pepys once saw the Lady Mary as a little child 'dance most finely so as almost to ravish me' – but this seems to have been about the extent of their formal education. Both princesses were, however, thoroughly grounded in the teachings of the Church of England and strict religious observance was enforced in the Richmond household.

Mary was a month short of her ninth birthday when her mother died. She was a very pretty child, typically Stuart in appearance, with big brown eyes, dark auburn curls and a delicate pink and white complexion. She was also an intelligent, sensitive child, with a warmly emotional nature and a great capacity for loving which, in her early adolescence, found an outlet in a sentimental friendship with another girl. Frances Apsley, whose father held the post of Treasurer of the Household to Charles II, was nine years older than the princess, but discrepancies of age and rank were ignored in the correspondence which began when Mary was about eleven or twelve and writing almost daily ill-spelt, breathlessly unpunctuated letters to 'dearest dearest dearest dear Aurelia'. In the romantic fantasy world of the letters, Frances was Aurelia, probably from the character in Dryden's comedy *An Evening's Love*, and is addressed as 'dear crual loved blest husban' by Mary, who is Clorine, after the eponymous Faithful Shepherdess of the play by John Fletcher.

In 1673 the Duke of York married again and presented his teenage bride, Mary Beatrice d'Este of Modena, to his daughters as a new playfellow. In spite of the religious barrier – unkind Londoners were calling the devoutly Catholic Mary Beatrice 'the Pope's daughter' – she and the princesses became good friends, although she did not come near to replacing Frances Apsley in Mary's affections and Anne was already coming under the influence of sharp-tongued, strong-minded Sarah Jennings, one of the maids of honour.

The following winter the king's nieces made their debut at Court in an ambitious theatrical production which attempted, not entirely successfully, to re-create the brilliant entertainments of pre-war days. Mary appeared in the title role of Calisto, or the Chaste Nymph, and Anne had a supporting part as her sister, Nyphe, while their cousin Monmouth danced in the ballet. This occasion seems to have marked Mary's coming out, and although still in the care of the Lady Governess, she was seen more often in public with her father and stepmother. In 1675 the whole family was present at the lord mayor's banquet and Mary was now beginning to take her place at Court functions on a regular basis.

The intimacy with Aurelia continued as passionately as ever. 'Two leters alredy you have had today dear Aurelia from me I hope you wil read the third tho you I supose are tired with them now. . . . what can I say more to perswade you that I love you with more zeal then any lover can. . . . you are loved more then can be exprest by your ever obedient wife vere afectionate friand humbel sarvent to kis the ground where on you go to be your dog in a string your fish in a net your bird in a cage your humbel trout.'[2] None of the early letters is dated (and unfortunately Aurelia's replies have not survived), but it was probably some time in 1676 that Mary Clorine, whose spelling had not improved with the years, was writing: 'I am pore in everything but love pore but content for what greater riches can I desire then love of you & I hope it is repaid by you for if you did but love me as I do you I could live & be content with a cotage in the contre & cow a stufe peticot & wastcot in sumer & cloth in winter a litel garden to live upon the fruit & herbs it yeelds.'[3]

Mary entered her sixteenth year on 30 April 1677. Childhood and make-believe were coming to an end and her future was already under serious consideration. It had long been accepted that the sad little Portuguese queen would never bear a child and the Duchess of York had not yet managed to produce a son. So far, in four years of marriage, there had been two miscarriages, one short-lived daughter and one living, but ominously fragile, daughter. In any case, the duke's Catholic marriage and his own avowed conversion to Roman Catholicism had raised so many Protestant hackles that the exclusion of his second family from the succession seemed by no means out of the question. Mary's marriage, therefore, was assuming an unexpectedly urgent dynastic importance.

The obvious choice of bridegroom from the Protestant viewpoint had always been her cousin William, Prince of Orange, and indeed the match had been talked of at intervals over a number of years, but it was not until the spring of 1676 that William himself had raised the matter with Sir William Temple, English ambassador at the Hague. For some time now, he said, his friends had been urging him to get married. He knew it was a thing to be done 'at one time or other', and he had now begun to think seriously about taking a wife. Of the various candidates who had been suggested to him, the English princess seemed the most promising, but before he went any further there were two points on which he wanted to ask Temple's advice. Some of his English friends were against the idea of his marrying into the royal family because they believed it would not be long before there was some great disturbance in England, 'especially upon the point of religion', and they feared the prince would risk losing 'all the esteem and interest' he had with the people if he became too closely identified with the crypto-Catholic Court. Then there was the 'person and dispositions of the young lady'. William knew that princes were not supposed to concern themselves too closely with personal details, but they mattered to him 'and in such a degree that no circumstances of fortune or interest would engage him, without those of the person, especially those of humour and disposition'. So, if Temple knew anything particular about the Lady Mary in these points, he begged him to speak freely.

The ambassador was, of course, delighted to hear that the prince was considering an English marriage, which he thought would be entirely in his interest, and would bring him one degree nearer the crown, which, contrary to report, 'stood upon surer foundations than ever it had done in former times, and the more for what had passed in the last reign'. As for the Lady Mary, Temple could not speak from personal knowledge, but his wife and sister both thought very highly of her and were friendly with her governess who, they felt sure, had taken great pains over her bringing up.[4]

Thus encouraged, William made up his mind to 'enter upon this pursuit', and the necessary letters were despatched to London. But it would be another eighteen months before William was able to come and do his courting in person.

The joint attack on the United Provinces plotted by Charles and Louis and begun in April 1672 had resulted in a revolution which broke the power of the republican party in Holland and finally emancipated the 21-year-old William from the oppressive regime of the Loevesteiners. That summer John de Witt and his brother were murdered by the mob in an uncontrollable explosion of popular rage and panic and the prince, made Captain General and Stadtholder by popular acclaim, was called upon to save his country from an apparently irresistible enemy, much as his great-grandfather had been called upon a century earlier. William was thus launched on his lifelong, life-and-death struggle against the might of French imperialism, just as the first William had struggled all his life against the might of Spanish imperialism, and, like him, by sheer stubborn refusal to admit defeat and often very little else, contrived to hold disaster at bay.

The emergence of the young Prince of Orange as war leader and statesman came as a most unwelcome surprise to his kinsmen, who had so confidently planned the carve-up of the Low Countries. Contrary to all expectations William clung with grim loyalty to his 'Dutch blockheads', fully prepared if necessary to die on the last dyke in their defence, and defiantly rejected his designated role of puppet prince dependent on the patronage of France and England.

England's part in the war had been inglorious, consisting of little more than two unsuccessful naval excursions, and by the beginning of 1674 the strength of anti-French, anti-Catholic feeling in parliament had forced the king to make a separate peace. The war dragged on without him, but it was becoming depressingly clear that, even with the assistance of Spain and the Hapsburgs, the United Provinces would never be strong enough to force a decision on the battlefield. Sooner or later they would have to accept a negotiated peace, and although William had learned not to trust his uncle further than he could see him, he clung to the hope that a solution to his problems might be found across the North Sea. His English friends were keeping him informed on the situation there and, despite Temple's assurances, he knew that Charles's pro-French policy was intensely unpopular in the country. Parliament, indeed, was agitating for war with France, while angry suspicions about the king's religious sympathies were being fuelled by the Duke of York's recent refusal to continue to attend Anglican services.

For his part, Charles had no desire to put his 'strict friendship' with France at risk – not, at any rate, while there was still any financial gain to be wrung from it – but, encouraged by Temple and the Lord Treasurer Danby, he could see definite advantages in coming to an understanding with his nephew. There would be no more certain way to soothe the general Protestant disquiet than by a marriage between his niece and such a famous Protestant champion as the Prince of Orange. It would also serve to attach William to the Stuart family interest away from the opposition party, which was growing dangerously in self-confidence and organization. Added to that, if the prince could be parted from his European allies and persuaded to agree to a sensible composition with France, then perhaps everyone would be satisfied. So, in the autumn of 1677 an invitation was finally issued. William landed at Harwich in October and went straight to join his uncles who were at Newmarket for the autumn meeting.

He seemed like an impatient lover, but William had not come as a suppliant and soon made it clear that he had his own agenda, refusing, politely but firmly, to talk business until he had seen the princess for himself. Charles was not best pleased, as he had been hoping to use his niece as a prize to be withheld until his nephew came to heel. But, realizing that the young man meant what he said, he abandoned the races and brought the Court back to town sooner than expected.

There is no description of the cousins' first meeting, but William at least was more than satisfied by what he saw. Mary at fifteen was a very pretty girl, tall, slender and graceful, with charming manners and an appealing air of gentleness about her. She looked, in fact, to be everything a reasonable man could wish for and the prince 'was so pleased with her person, and all those signs of such a humour as had been described to him upon former inquiries, that he immediately made his suit to the King and the Duke'.[5] But if he had expected an immediate acceptance, he was to be disappointed. Charles had not given up his plan to use the marriage as a weapon, and now that William was so plainly taken by his prospective bride the king's hand would appear to have been strengthened. Yes, he would be delighted to give the young people his blessing, but the peace with France must be settled before any betrothal could be announced. Again William refused to cooperate. He would get married first and talk peace afterwards. He was very well aware that he and his allies could expect to get hard terms from the French whatever happened, but he would not have it said that he had sold his honour for a wife and from that position he was not to be budged.

After a few days' apparent deadlock, the prince asked Temple to come and see him in his lodgings at Whitehall. He was in a thoroughly gloomy mood and told the ambassador he very much regretted ever having come to England and intended to go home in two days' time. But before he left, the king must choose how they were to live in future. 'I am sure', he said, 'it must be either like the greatest friends – or the greatest enemies.' Temple, remembering William's numerous influential contacts among the opposition, took the hint, and next day he went to see the king and repeated his nephew's ultimatum. It was time to stop playing games and Charles gave way with every appearance of spontaneity. He had never yet been mistaken in judging a man's honesty, 'and if I am not deceived in the Prince's face, he is the honestest man in the world, and I will trust him and he shall have his wife'. Temple was now instructed to go and break the news to the Duke of York and to tell him 'that it is a thing I am resolved on'. James had been hoping very much that the marriage was off, but since his whole philosophy was based on a belief in the absolute authority of the monarch, he had no choice but to accept the situation, albeit reluctantly. Telling William was a pleasanter task. Once he had been convinced that there were no strings attached to the king's sudden surrender, the prince hugged his friend in an unusually demonstrative gesture, exclaiming that he was a very happy man – and very unexpectedly so.[6]

But if the prince was happy, the princess was in floods of tears. According to the diary entry of her chaplain Edward Lake for 21 October: 'the Duke of York din'd at Whitehall: after dinner return'd to Saint James', took Lady Mary into her closet, and told her of the marriage designed between her and the Prince of Orange; whereupon her highness wept all that afternoon and the following day.'[7]

The violence of her reaction is a little surprising, for the news can hardly have come as a total shock. Like every daughter of a royal house, Mary had always known that her marriage would be an affair of state and she must also surely have guessed that the Prince of Orange was the most likely candidate for her hand. The prospect of the match had been common gossip at Court for months. She may, of course, have been seriously disappointed by her first sight of William. To begin with, he was nearly a whole head shorter than herself and more than ten years older, a thin, unremarkable man with melancholy dark eyes and a long nose. He was also almost comically unfashionable in appearance, wearing his own thick dark brown hair in preference to the now ubiquitous periwig. The prince was, as he described himself, a plain man, his public manner was stiff and reserved and he was certainly not given to making pretty speeches, or displaying the sort of extravagant gallantry which Mary's favourite reading of romantic plays and novels had led her to expect in a suitor. That he possessed many sterling qualities is not in question, but courage, integrity and steadfastness of purpose were not the sort of qualities calculated to make an immediate appeal to an immature, over-emotional teenage girl.

That Mary should have shed tears at the thought of leaving home, family and friends for life among strangers in a strange land is perfectly understandable – especially as she would have been accustomed to hearing Holland and the Hollanders ridiculed and reviled by the Court party, most of whom were being bankrolled by the French – but her distress was probably aggravated by her father's attitude. James, who had been cherishing dreams of a Catholic husband for his eldest and favourite daughter, detested William's Calvinism and all it stood for. He may well have taken a perverse pleasure in painting a deeply discouraging picture of Mary's future in a joyless Dutch desert inhabited by ill-bred, boorish dissenters who hated royalty – the Stuart brothers never forgot or forgave the inhospitable treatment they had received from the States during their years of exile.

But however bleak the outlook, there was no appeal. Father and daughter both knew that the king must be obeyed, that Mary must dry her tears and get ready to play her part in the coming celebrations just as if her heart was not breaking. Perhaps it was as well that the next two weeks would be fully occupied and Clorine had scarcely a moment to scribble a note to Aurelia – 'if you do not come to me some time today dear husban that I may have my bely full of discours with you I shal take it very ile' – before she had to face her first formal encounter with her real-life husband-to-be, and prepare to accept the congratulations of the Council, the judiciary and the lord mayor and aldermen. News of the engagement was being rapturously received throughout the country and on 29 October the City entertained the royal family to an immense banquet at the Guildhall. 'If I were to describe to you the number of the dishes and how they were built up in pyramids, as also the amount of venison and pies, you would not believe it', wrote an awestruck Dutch visitor.[8]

Meanwhile, details of the marriage contract and the numbers of Mary's English household were being settled, with the usual scramble for places among 'the old ladies and young beggarly bitches'. The king and his nephew had also been doing some serious talking. William refused point-blank to consider the idea of a separate peace, insisting that only a treaty agreeable to his allies and guaranteeing a strong frontier in Flanders would contain French aggession. Nevertheless, Charles believed they had arrived at a workable formula, declaring with his usual easy optimism that it was only a matter of one town more or less in Flanders and peace would be made.

The wedding day was now fixed for 4 November, William's twenty-seventh birthday, and the private ceremony, conducted by the Bishop of London, took place in Mary's apartments at St James's Palace at nine o'clock in the evening. It could not be said to have been a festive occasion. The bridegroom was ill at ease, the bride woebegone, the bride's father morose and the bride's sister sickening for smallpox, which was once more rife in the Court. Only the king appeared relentlessly cheerful and did his best to enliven the proceedings, urging the bishop to make haste in case the heavily pregnant Duchess of York should be delivered of a son before he had finished, 'and so the marriage be disappointed' – a dig at the prince which no doubt found its mark. When William endowed Mary with all his worldly goods, laying a handful of gold coins on the prayer book, Charles intervened again, telling his niece 'to put it all up in her pocket, for 'twas clear gain'. After the blessing the traditional sack posset and sweetmeats were handed round and Mary withdrew to be undressed and put to bed by the queen, her stepmother and the Duchess of Monmouth. Then William was brought in to join her and the king drew the bedcurtains with a flourish, exclaiming, 'Now, nephew, to your work! Hey, St George for England!'[9]

Next day London rejoiced with bells and bonfires, and William Bentinck, the prince's close friend and best man, came to St James's bearing William's official wedding present, a small chest full of jewels valued at £40,000, the exact amount of Mary's dowry as specified in the marriage contract. A few days later William gave his bride a more personal present of a ruby and diamond ring, 'the first thing he ever did give me', which she came to value more than her kingdom. But in the hectic round of social events which followed the wedding there was little opportunity for the newly married pair to become better acquainted, and it was noticed that while the prince seemed a very fond husband, 'she is a very coy bride, at least before folks'.

It was, of course, a horribly difficult situation for both of them and circumstances were conspiring to make it worse. Mary Beatrice was indeed delivered of a son two days after the wedding, much to the Duke of York's delight and the discomfiture of all those who feared for the future of the Protestant succession. The infant was said to be 'sprightly and like to live', but he died a month later of the prevalent smallpox, which also claimed the life of Mary's governess, Frances Villiers. By 10 November Princess Anne was known to have the disease, and William and Mary had their first quarrel. William, not unnaturally, wanted his wife to leave the infected surroundings of St James's, but 'the princess would by no means be persuaded'. It was a pathetic gesture of defiance and when her chaplain, Edward Lake, went to say goodbye to her, he found her tearful and very disconsolate, 'not only for her sister's illness, but also for some discontent occasioned by the prince's urging her to remove her lodgings to Whitehall'.[10]

William, who never felt well or comfortable in England, was longing to get away. Their departure date was to be 15 November, immediately after the queen's birthday ball, at which Mary appeared decked out in all her wedding-present jewels. But at the last moment an easterly gale blew up and they were delayed in town for another four interminable days. The strain was showing by this time and 'the court began to whisper the prince's sullenness, or clownishness, that he took no notice of his princess . . . nor came to see her at St James's'.[11]

Mary had had a last snatched meeting with Frances Apsley late one evening, but had been so tired out and overwrought that she had scarcely known what she was saying. Frances had then had to go away in a hurry because her father was ill, so they were not able to have a proper leave-taking and Mary could only write miserably, 'I hope you will keep your word to me and not forget your pore Clorine that loves you better then can be exprest.'[12]

At last, on Monday 19 November, the wind changed. Mary, once more dissolved in tears, begged the Duchess of Monmouth to look after her little sister, and said her last goodbyes to the queen and to Mary Beatrice. Catherine tried to comfort the weeping girl by reminding her that when she had first arrived to be married she had not even seen her future husband. 'But, madam,' replied Mary unanswerably, 'you came into England; but I am going out of England.'[13]

The king and the Duke of York accompanied the Prince and Princess of Orange downriver in the royal barge as far as Erith, where they all had dinner. The weather was still very stormy and the travellers got no further than Sheerness before the wind changed again. Although pressed to do so, William was determined not to return to London. Whatever happened he was not going to risk 'a second scene of grief', and decided to make for Canterbury – familiar staging-post on such journeys over the years. It was a full week before conditions began to improve a little, but on the morning of 28 November they were finally able to set sail from Margate. The sea was still horribly rough and by the time the little convoy came within sight of the Dutch coast twenty-four terrifying hours later, everyone on board was soaked to the skin and prostrate with seasickness or exhaustion or both. Ice-floes in the River Maas made their planned disembarkation at Rotterdam impossible and instead they had to go ashore at Terheyde, a tiny fishing village lurking behind the sand dunes. Mary's first glimpse of Holland under a lowering grey sky, with icy waves crashing on to a deserted beach and not a tree or a house to be seen anywhere, can have done nothing to raise her spirits.

Nor was the ordeal over even now, for the shivering, bedraggled company had to walk several miles over frostbound, rutted lanes before the hurriedly summoned carriages could pick them up, and it was well after noon before they came at last to the lighted windows and blessed warmth of the palace at Honselaersdijck.

A fortnight later the Prince and Princess of Orange rode in state in a golden coach to the Hague, where the townsfolk were waiting to give their Stadtholder and his bride a guard of honour. Troops of young girls dressed in white strewed sweet herbs along the way, and the streets were decorated with garlands and triumphal arches and lined with cheering crowds. In the evening William and Mary stood together at a window in the Binnenhof to watch a spectacular firework display, and next day the States General laid on a formal reception for them. Mary, 'beautiful, young and good', made an excellent impression and was generally pronounced to be a great improvement on the previous Stuart Princess of Orange.

After two days of official engagements the couple resumed their interrupted honeymoon at Honselaersdijck – an elegant mansion house built in the Dutch renaissance style of pale red brick with stone facings under a mansard roof and surrounded by gardens – which was to become their principal residence. In contrast to the faded grandeurs of Whitehall, Honselaersdijck was furnished in the best modern taste and boasted such up-to-the-minute conveniences as sash windows and marble bathrooms plentifully supplied with running hot water. Everything, of course, gleamed with cleanliness. The Dutch had been seriously shocked by the unhygienic conditions they had encountered in England.

Reports reaching London in February suggested that the princess was well and settling down happily in her new home, growing 'somewhat fatt but very beautiful withal'. But outside the peaceful precincts of Honselaersdijck the war was still going on, and with the opening of the spring campaigning season news arrived that the French were once more on the move in Flanders. At the beginning of March 1678 William was obliged to leave hurriedly for the front 'after a very tender parting on both sides', and for the first time Mary had leisure to write a long letter home to Frances Apsley. But this was a very different Mary Clorine. Three months of marriage had transformed the tearstained rebellious child into a young woman very much in love with her husband. She who had once thought that 'coming out my own contry parting with my friends and relations' the greatest trouble that could happen to her, now realized her mistake. 'Now I find till this time I never knew sorow for what can be more cruall in the world then parting with what on loves . . . and nott ondly comon parting but parting so as maybe never to meet again to be perpetually in fear for god knows when I may see him or wethere he is nott now at this instant in a batell i recon him now never in safety ever in danger.' The parting was not, in fact, so very dramatic. Mary was able to join William in Antwerp for two weeks at the end of March, and again at Breda for a short visit early in April, 'for that is so neer the Army he can live in the town and go to it at any time at a quarter of an hour warning when I am there if I dont ritt dont wonder for may be I shant have time or twenty things may happen'.[14]

What did happen, around the middle of April, was a miscarriage in the third month of pregnancy. This was a serious disappointment and Mary was ill for several weeks afterwards. Another event which took place that summer was the signing of a Franco-Dutch peace treaty at the insistence of the States General. William remained deeply dissatisfied by the terms of the treaty, which left France in possession of the Franche Comté and a dozen key towns in the Spanish Netherlands, but the States overruled him.

Mary, though, was thankful to have him home again and not 'to be perpetually in fear' about his safety, especially as she now believed herself to be pregnant again. On 9 August she confided her hopes to Frances Apsley, whom she was still addressing as 'dear dear husban', in terms which would have surprised those who only knew the demure exterior of the Princess of Orange. After apologizing for not having written since her illness, she went on:

if any thing in the world can make amend for such a faut I hope trusting you with a secrett will . . . tho I have reason to fear becaus the sea parts us you may belive it is a bastard but yett I think upon a time of need I may make you own it . . . you ought to keep this a secrett since if it shoul be known you might get a pair of horns and nothing else by the bargain but dearest Aurelia you may be very well assured tho I have played the whore a littell I love you of all things in the world tho I have spoke as you may think in jest all this while yett for god sake if you love me dont tell it becaus I would nott have it known yett for all the world since it cannott be above 6 or 7 weeks att most.[15]

A month later the secret was out and the Duke of York wrote to his son-in-law that he was glad to know his daughter continued so well and hoped she would go out her full time, adding: 'I have written to her to be careful of herself, and she would do well not to stand too much, for that is very ill for a young breeding woman.'[16]

At the beginning of October Mary had the pleasure of seeing her sister and stepmother, who came over for a brief private visit and were lavishly entertained by William. It was a happy reunion for them both; Anne had been too ill even to know when Mary left the year before. The duchess, too, was delighted to find her dear 'Lemon', her pet name for Mary, whom she had last seen dissolved in tears and misery, now apparently in good health and spirits, and James wrote again after their return thanking the prince for his hospitality. Mary Beatrice had been 'so satisfied with her journey and with you as I never saw anybody; and I must give you a thousand thanks from her and from myself for her kind usage by you'. Sadly Mary miscarried for the second time shortly after the visitors departed. She was never to conceive again.

The winter of 1678 saw the beginnings of the so-called Popish Plot which was to plunge England into a frenzy of anti-Catholic hysteria and political uproar which effectively prevented the sensible conduct of affairs for the next three years. Among the first victims of the general paranoia were, inevitably, the Catholic heir to the throne and his Catholic wife and in March 1679 the king was forced to send his brother out of the country for a cooling-off period. The Yorks settled in Brussels and in August they were joined by the Princess Anne and her frail little half-sister Isabella. Fourteen-year-old Anne recorded her impressions of Brussels in letters to Frances Apsley and her mother. She had been to see a grand firework display to celebrate the King of Spain's wedding and found that 'all the people heare are very sivil'. As for the town, 'it is a great & fine town methinks tho the streets are not so cleane as they are in Holland yet they are not so dirty as ours they are very well paved & very easy they only have od kinds of smells'.[17] 'The Park heare is very pretty', she wrote on 22 September, 'but not so fine as ours at St. Jameses. I saw a ball at court which far surpasde my expectations for it was very well there we had Limonade cinemont [cinnamon] water & chocolate sweet meats all very good.'

The princess's Protestant entourage were zealously protecting her from any possible Popish contamination. 'All the fine churches & monasterys you know I must not see', she told Frances, 'so can give you no good account of them, but those things which I must needs see as theire images which are in every shope & corner of the street the more I see of those foolerys & the more I heare of that Religeon the more I dislike it.'[18] Young Anne soon became rather bored with Brussels – 'this place affords no news' – and really there was nothing much to do but 'going to fine places to walk'. However, her stay was to be brief. In the late autumn the family returned to England. The duke and duchess then left for Scotland while their daughters remained in London.

Mary had seen her family briefly on two occasions in 1679, when it was plain to her stepmother's sympathetic eye that all was not well. The Princess of Orange had been ailing ever since her second miscarriage, suffering from recurrent bouts of a malarial-type fever throughout the winter and spring. She spent a month at Aix during the summer taking the waters and seemed much better on her return, but in March 1680 she fell seriously ill with a high fever and for a few days her life was thought to be in danger. She recovered slowly but this was an unhappy time for her, caused in part no doubt by her failure to conceive and also by the dawning realization that her husband was having an affair with one of her maids of honour.

Elizabeth Villiers, one of the three Villiers sisters who had grown up with the princesses at Richmond and had come to Holland with Mary, was no voluptuous sex symbol. On the contrary, she was rather a plain girl with a cast in one eye which earned her the nickname of Squinting Betty, but she was highly intelligent, a witty conversationalist and, one suspects, a good listener. William was genuinely attached to his wife, but he was reserved by nature, always finding it difficult to express his deepest feelings, and he may, at this time of mutual disappointment, have found her emotionalism and ready tears rather too much to take, turning for comfort instead to the undemanding companionship of a woman who could talk sensibly about other things.

Much of this is speculation, for the whole Betty Villiers affair remains obscure. Unlike his uncles, the Prince of Orange conducted his one extra-marital relationship with almost obsessive discretion and Mary at least never had to endure the sort of public humiliation routinely suffered by so many women in her position. Years before, in one of her earliest letters to Frances Apsley, she had commented with childish worldly wisdom on the well-known fact that men always wearied of their wives and looked for mistresses 'as sone as thay can gett them'. Now, facing the reality of betrayal, however discreet, seems to have had a temporarily devastating effect. Unable or perhaps afraid to have it out with her actual husband, Mary Clorine turned back to Frances and the Aurelia fantasy as a familiar safety-valve. 'I do not now mourn a dead lovere but a false on . . . oh love what plesure canst thou have to torment a pore creature. . . . Oh dearest dearest dearest dearest dear husband send me a letter on kind word will give me ease.'[19] She begs Frances 'not to show my leters for that I think you ware allways kind enough to hid them', but 'I must ritt or dy for my heart is so full if I did not give itt some vent itt must of necessity break . . . tis you has raised this tempest in my brest tis you oh cruall dear had maid me all most dispare of your love by nott ritting thus long . . . if it ware dagers darts or poisond arow from you I coud indure all for on kind word if I had butt on kind look from you I shoud dy happy.'[20]

The tempest slowly subsided but the presence of Betty Villiers and her acknowledged status cast a shadow over the next five years. Not that Mary was always unhappy, far from it. She was never one of those sophisticates who found it amusing to mock the sober bourgeois virtues of the Dutch and by her own admission appreciated the serene domestic atmosphere of Holland, where she was able to lead a life 'so suitable to my humour' and had 'the esteem of the inhabitants'.[21] She was an intensely feminine woman, made for an affectionate family life and the motherhood which sadly was denied her. But there were compensations and Mary had plenty to occupy her time. Apart from her religious duties, and the private prayer and meditation which became increasingly important to her as time went on, there were charitable works and the supervision of her several households. As well as Honselaersdijck and the Binnenhof, there was Soestdijk between Amsterdam and Amersfoort, described as 'a pretty box', with good gardens, fine walks and rows of trees about it; Dieren, William's hunting lodge in Gelderland; Het Huis ten Bosch, the House in the Wood, a charming little summer palace near the Hague which the prince had inherited from his grandmother Amalia and which often became Mary's retreat when he was away; and later on the ambitious new building at Het Loo. There was always plenty of official entertaining and visiting, and for recreation theatre-going, card-playing – Mary's old chaplain Dr Lake had been dismayed to hear that the princess was in the habit of playing cards on Sundays – needlework, music and painting. Mary was also an energetic walker and liked to make little journeys by barge along the canals.

She and William shared a number of interests, especially the furnishing and embellishing of their various homes and the laying-out of gardens. Mary loved flowers and the Prince and Princess of Orange were both passionate gardeners. Husband and wife usually spent their evenings together, and this was a time to relax and unwind. 'I have ever used my self not to trouble the king about bussiness since I was married to him', Mary wrote in later years, 'for I saw him so full of it that I thought, and he has told me so himself, that when he could get from it he was glad to come to me to have his thoughts diverted by other discourse.'[22]

Certainly William had more than enough 'bussiness' to trouble him during the early 1680s. Ever since the end of the war in 1678 he had been fighting a losing battle with the peace-at-any-price element in the States General, especially the Amsterdammers, who stubbornly refused to recognize the continuing threat of French aggression. Encouraged by the French ambassador, they consistently blocked their Stadtholder's efforts to strengthen the country's defences and maintain the essential buffer of the Spanish Netherlands, preferring to believe that it would be much more useful for the States to live in peace with Louis 'without defiance or alarm', than to ruin themselves by keeping up armies which might be used against them by the Prince of Orange. The prince, as the servant of the republic, thus found himself in the unenviable position of responsibility without power and was frequently driven to near desperation by his masters' apparently wilful blindness and paranoia. He also needed to keep a weather eye on the situation across the North Sea. By the spring of 1682 the excesses of the Popish Plot had abated and the attempts by the opposition party – the Whigs as they were becoming known – to exclude the Duke of York from the succession having failed, James and Mary Beatrice had been able to return from their exile in Scotland and were warmly welcomed by the Court.

The Princess Anne, who had joined her parents in Edinburgh the previous summer, returned with them and her marriage was now being considered. At Christmas 1680 her aunt Sophie's son, the twenty-year-old George of Hanover, had come over to England on purpose, so it was thought, to see the Lady Anne, 'but not liking her person he left the Kingdom without making any motion to the King or the Duke of York for their consent to marry her'. It was also said that the Hanoverian family were against the match, considering the daughter of plebeian Anne Hyde not good enough for their prince. Whatever the reason, the project came to nothing and left Anne with an abiding dislike of her German cousin.

Although never approaching beauty, Anne at seventeen was not unattractive, pleasantly plump, with curling reddish brown hair, pretty hands and a particularly well-produced musical speaking voice – as a child she had received elocution lessons from the actress Mrs Betterton. She continued to suffer from a 'defluxion' or watering from her weak eyes but had been lucky enough to escape any disfigurement from the smallpox. In the summer after her return from Scotland she was pursued by a well-known philanderer, John Sheffield, Earl of Mulgrave, whose attentions caused a minor scandal at Court. It was the one romantic episode of Anne's life, and although some people maintained that Mulgrave did no more than 'ogle' her, the family were taking no chances and the amorous earl was hurriedly despatched to Tangier in a leaky frigate. Mary heard the gossip at the Hague and wrote anxiously to Frances: 'Not but that I believe my sister very innocent however I am so nice upon the point of reputation that it makes me mad she should be exposed to such reports . . . oh my dear Aurelia tis not to be imagined in what conserne I am that

I should ever live to see the ondly sister I have in the world, the sister I love like my own life thus abussed and wronged.'[23]

Mary went on worrying about Anne's reputation, 'for I think nothing more prejudicciell to a young woman then ill company', but negotiations were now in progress with the Danish ambassador and towards the end of May 1683 the princess was informed that a marriage had been arranged for her with Prince George of Denmark, brother of King Christian V. George arrived in England on 19 July and the wedding took place at St James's Palace ten days later. It was a more cheerful occasion than the last royal wedding. Anne at least shed no tears at the sight of her bridegroom – a big, blond, bovine man of thirty of whom Charles II famously remarked that he had tried him drunk and tried him sober but found there was nothing in him. The prince had, in fact, had quite a distinguished military career fighting against the Swedes, but now seemed perfectly content to melt into the background, an amiable nonentity occupying his time by making model ships, over-eating and getting peacefully drunk. He became, inevitably, the butt of many unkind jokes. It was said, among other things, that his bouts of asthma were caused by the fact that he had to breathe hard in case he were taken for dead and removed for burial. But Anne, shy, withdrawn and painfully lacking self-confidence, found him a perfectly satisfactory partner and became devoted to him, defending him loyally and nursing him through his numerous illnesses. It had been agreed that the couple would live in England and they settled down at Whitehall in a range of apartments known as the Cockpit, where Anne began her tragic childbearing marathon with a stillborn girl in May 1684.

At the end of January 1685 King Charles suffered a stroke and four days later he was dead, having at the very last moment kept his promise to Minette and been received into the Catholic Church by the priest who had helped in his escape from Worcester all those years ago. The Merry Monarch, that cheerfully raffish figure with his mistresses, his spaniels, his cynical outlook and his genius for survival, was gone. His brother James was king after all, and his niece Mary became heiress presumptive.

The Duke of Monmouth was staying at the Hague that winter. Mary had always had a soft spot for her handsome cousin – most people fell for Monmouth who possessed more than his share of persuasive Stuart charm – and she and William had gone out of their way to entertain him with a round of balls, parties, theatre-going and informal dances. There was sledging on the ice and the French ambassador had been scandalized to observe the normally sedate Princess of Orange 'with very short skirts partly tucked up, and iron skates on her feet, learning to slide now on one foot and now on the other'.

All this gaiety came to an abrupt end when news of the king's death arrived and Monmouth's presence, however charming, became an embarrassment. Ever since the days of the Popish Plot there had been a strong movement in the Protestant Whig party which wanted James set aside in favour of Monmouth. Undeterred by repeated denials, rumours were deliberately spread that the king was planning to legitimize his eldest son, rumours that he was indeed legitimate, that Charles had been married secretly to Lucy Walter. But although Charles loved his son and treated him with often undeserved indulgence, he had never at any time shown any sign of preferring his bastard before his brother. Casual though he might have been about a lot of things, he had held immovably strong views about the true line of the succession. Now that James had actually succeeded, William could no longer be seen to appear to be harbouring his possible competitor. Monmouth was therefore sent on his way, with enough money for his immediate needs and some good advice about not getting involved in conspiracies against his uncle. Sadly it was advice wasted. That summer Monmouth, spoilt, vain, ambitious and fatally suggestible, set out on the road leading to Sedgemoor, the Bloody Assizes and his own traitor's death. 'Thus ended this quondam Duke, darling of his father and the ladies', wrote John Evelyn. 'A favourite of the people, of an easy nature, debauch'd by lust, seduc'd by crafty knaves. . . . He fail'd, and perish'd. He was a lovely person.'[24] For Mary his death snapped another link with childhood and made her see her father in a new and shocking light. The merciless revenge taken by James on the hapless West Country peasants who had followed Monmouth turned stronger stomachs than hers.

Towards the end of the summer an extraordinary rumour began to circulate at the Hague that the King of England was planning to kidnap his daughter and marry her to the widowed King of France. This, of course, was fantasy, but it is possible that James, never noted for his pragmatic approach, may have been cherishing dreams of being able to dissolve a partnership he was finding increasingly threatening, both politically and dynastically. Certainly there was a deliberate attempt about this time, involving the ambassador Bevil Skelton and Mary's chaplain Dr Covell, and presumably approved by London, to stir up trouble between the Prince and Princess of Orange.

The story depends to some extent on an unreliable source, but it appears that certain members of Mary's household had been trying to inflame her jealousy of her husband's mistress – to the extent that she lay in wait for him one night at the foot of the staircase which led to the sleeping quarters of the maids of honour. When the prince finally descended, at two o'clock in the morning, there was a scene of tears and reproaches, followed by a period of noticeable marital coldness. But William, knowing his wife's usual 'sweetness and good nature', felt certain that someone had been making mischief. He therefore took steps to have the outgoing mail intercepted and, having obtained the evidence he needed, summoned Mary to an interview in his private cabinet, locked the door and told her that her servants were plotting to sow dissension between them. He swore a sacred oath that 'what had caused her pain' was simply a distraction. There was no crime involved and his feelings for her remained the same as ever. Thus reassured, Mary burst into tears, threw herself into his arms and 'from that day on lived with him as she had always been wont to do'.

Taking away the imaginative detail, supplied by one Daniel de Bourdon, a hanger-on around the fringes of the Court who claimed to be a particular friend of a friend of Betty Villiers, it does seem as though William and Mary had at last been able to bring the Villiers affair into the open and talk about it. Also William now had the proof he needed to clear out a nest of spies and trouble-makers, which included not merely the unpleasant gossiping Covell, but Mary's old nurse Mrs Langford and Anne Trelawney, another of the maids of honour. 'You will be very much surprised to hear of the changes which have been happening in our Court', wrote William Bentinck to an English friend. 'His Highness, having seen by chance a letter which made clear that Dr Covell had for a long time been the malicious spy of the house, who reported many things invented to be hurtful, Madame the princess dismissed him with no other punishment on account of his position; and as it was evident that Mrs Langford and Miss Trelawny were acting in concert with him, Madame sent them off this morning as well.'[25]

Covell had represented Mary as being broken-hearted, but in fact, she seems to have taken the whole thing very coolly, and there were no hectic appeals to Aurelia, who was married herself now. The two friends were still corresponding, but these days the letters were concerned with everyday matters – Mary's sore eyes, which had prevented her from writing; the weather, 'we have the coldest Easter I think that ever was'; Frances's pregnancy, 'I long very much to hear you are brought to bed'; and shopping commissions. In October Mary was asking her dear Aurelia to send her enough black brocaded satin for a gown, 'you must leave a border round about plain to be embroidered that I can have done heer very well'; and it was not until December 1685, towards the end of a letter asking for '2 cotten petticotes' and a pair of sleeves to be sent by post, that the princess first mentions the departure of her 'Mam', that is Mrs Langford, 'my Mam haveing put her self out of a conditione of ever doing any thing more for me'. Mary had been sorry about it at first, 'remembring what she had bin to me . . . but her behaviour has bin such as has given me but just cause to forget that. I will say no more upon this subject. . . . When what is past cant be recaled the lesse one thinks of it the beter.'[26] Another departure which Mary cannot have regretted was that of Betty Villiers. Now that the scandal of her position had become public, Betty could no longer remain under the prince's roof and she seems to have found a home with her married sister, Katherine de Puisars.

Mary and William had other, more serious preoccupations that winter. The Revocation of the Edict of Nantes had brought a fresh influx of desperate Huguenot refugees to the United Provinces, and the Prince and Princess of Orange were both greatly distressed by the atrocity stories coming out of France – especially the persecution being visited on the people of Orange, now finally swallowed up by Louis. By the following summer, events in

England were causing the Protestant heiress and her husband further concern. Emboldened by his success in defeating the Monmouth rebellion, James was now pushing ahead with his plans for restoring the Catholic religion in England. Mass was being openly celebrated in the capital and Catholic propaganda freely disseminated. Catholics were being appointed to influential civil and military posts in open defiance of the law, and, ominously, the army raised to meet the threat from the West Country was still under arms and camped on Hounslow Heath. In April 1686 the king began to undermine the authority of the Church of England. The Bishop of London was suspended for refusing to take action against an Anglican clergyman who had preached an anti-Catholic sermon, while vacant sees were either left empty or filled by men of suitably Roman inclinations.

Disturbed by the trend of her father's policy and aware of a persistent undercurrent of rumour that he had not given up hope of finding some way of passing the crown to a Catholic successor, Mary evidently felt it prudent to write to her sister on the subject of her faith. The response was reassuring. 'I hope you dont doubt but that I will ever be firm to my religion whatever happens', declared the Princess of Denmark. 'However . . . I must tell you that I abhor the principles of the Church of Rome as much as it is possible for any to do. . . . God be thanked we were not bred up in that communion, but are of a Church that is pious and sincere, and conformable in all its principles to the Scriptures.'[27]

Anne had given birth to a living daughter in the summer of 1685 and in January 1687 wrote to thank Mary 'for the plaything you sent my girl. It is the prettiest thing I ever saw and too good for her yet, so I keep it locked up and only let her look on it when she comes to see me. She is the most delighted with it in the world and in her own language gives you abundance of thanks.'[28]

But less than a month later the little girl, named Marie after her aunt, was dead at the age of twenty months, and in the same week a second baby, Anne Sophia, also died aged eight months to the great grief of both parents. 'I never heard any relation more touching than seeing them together', wrote one of the Court ladies; 'sometimes they wept, sometimes they mourned in words, but hand-in-hand.' It would be three miscarriages and two and a half years later before Anne bore another living child.

It was about this time that the Prince and Princess of Orange first made the acquaintance of Gilbert Burnet, a Scottish refugee clergyman who came to live at the Hague in 1686. Burnet, talkative, kindhearted and outspoken, quickly became devoted to Mary, 'the most wonderfull person that I ever knew. . . . She has a modesty, a sweetness, and a humility in her that cannot be enough admired.' He also noted that she had a good understanding and knew a great deal. However, she knew very little about English affairs – a gap which Burnet felt himself called upon to fill. 'I began to lay before her the state of our Court, and the intrigues in it, ever since the Restoration, which she received with great satisfaction and shewed true judgement . . . in all the reflections that she made.'[29]

According to Burnet, he asked the princess in the course of one of their conversations if she had given any thought to the position the prince would fill when she became Queen of England. Mary, who had apparently always assumed that William would automatically become king, was astonished and dismayed to discover that this was not the case. He would simply become the queen's husband, unless, Burnet explained, she were content to be his wife and give him the real authority as soon as it came into her hands. He advised her to think the matter over carefully before coming to a decision, but Mary did not hesitate. 'She would take no time to consider of anything by which she could express her regard and affection to the Prince.' Next day, in Burnet's presence, she told William, 'in a very frank manner', that she had not realized the laws of England were so contrary to the laws of God. 'She did not think that the husband was ever to be obedient to the wife; she promised him he should always bear rule; and she asked only, that he would obey the command of, Husbands love your wives, as she should do that, Wives be obedient to your husbands in all things.'[30] William seems to have said nothing at the time, but he later told William Bentinck that Burnet had, in a few minutes, settled a question he had felt unable to raise in nine years of married life.

It was a question which was about to become of more than academic interest. In April 1687 James issued his Declaration of Indulgence, giving freedom of worship to all Dissenters and Catholics, and suspending the laws that debarred them from holding public office, and on 9 May Anne wrote from Richmond: 'By this one may easily guess what one is to hope for henceforward, since the priests have so much power with the King as to make him do things so directly against the laws of the land. . . . It is a melancholy prospect that all we of the Church of England have. . . . Every one has the free exercise of their religion, on purpose no doubt to ruin us.'[31]

Even the Catholic powers were disconcerted by James's zeal. 'The King seems determined to push on in religious matters as far as he possibly can', commented the Imperial ambassador. There were now four avowed Catholics on the Privy Council, Father Petre, the king's Jesuit confessor, was always at the king's elbow, and Catholic influence was being flaunted at Court. Even the Pope thought James was overdoing it, but James was becoming a man in the grip of an obsession – convinced that he had only to act boldly, and show the resolution his father and brother had lacked, to succeed where they had failed and establish himself as an absolute monarch on the French pattern.

In the autumn of 1687 the king made a pilgrimage to St Winefrede's Well to pray for a son and it appeared that the saint was listening, for at Christmas it was announced the the queen was pregnant. Isabella, the only one of Mary Beatrice's children to survive babyhood, had died in 1681 and since then there had been one other short-lived daughter and two miscarriages. It was three years since she had last conceived and the news was greeted with a sharply contrasting mixture of triumph and horror. The king and his Catholic kitchen cabinet were naturally cock-a-hoop. The Protestant majority was appalled. The nation which had been enduring James's antics with sullen resignation seems on the whole to have been prepared to go on putting up with him as long as they had the comforting prospect of a Protestant successor to look forward to. The prospect of a papist son of James on the throne was something else altogether and rumours that the queen's 'great belly' was false and a wicked papist plot in the making were soon in circulation.

Mary had first heard the news from her stepmother, who had mentioned the subject in her letters but only 'in very dubious terms'. However, two or three posts later, the king referred to it also 'in another style, and', wrote the princess in her diary, 'talked of it in a manner so assured and in a time when no woman could know anything for certain that there was certainly cause enough to raise a small suspicion'.[32] Anne, too, was more than a little sceptical and confided her fears that 'there may be foul play intended'. She promised to do all she could to find it out, and to pass on any discoveries to her sister. Her efforts were unsuccessful, but her suspicions increased that it was indeed 'a false belly', for if it were not, she wrote in a letter to Mary on 20 March, 'there having been so many stories and jests made about it, she [the queen] should, to convince the world, make either me or some of my friends feel her belly; but quite contrary, whenever one talks of her being with child, she looks as if she were afraid one should touch her. And whenever I happen to be in the room as she has been undressing, she has always gone into the next room to put on her smock.'[33] Mary Beatrice's desire to avoid the prying hostile eyes of the Protestant ladies was understandable, but perhaps in the circumstances not very wise.

At the end of April, James, whose conduct was neither understandable nor wise, issued a second Declaration of Indulgence suspending the penal laws and ordered the Anglican clergy to read it from their pulpits. When seven of the English bishops, headed by the Archbishop of Canterbury himself, protested that the declaration was founded on an illegal dispensing power and petitioned the king to withdraw it, he responded by having them sent to the Tower and charged with seditious libel. In the midst of the public uproar which followed, on 10 June 1688 the queen gave birth to a healthy son at St James's Palace.

The event had not been expected for another month and Anne, to her intense annoyance, had been away, taking the waters at Bath. 'My dear sister cant imagine the concern and vexation I have been in that I should be so unfortunate to be out of town when the Queen was brought to bed, for I shall never now be satisfied whether the child be true or false. It may be it is our brother, but God only knows. . . . One cannot help having a thousand fears and melancholy thoughts; but whatever changes may happen you shall ever find me firm to my religion and faithfully yours.'[34]

Controversy over the provenance of Mary Beatrice's child continued to rage – 'where one believes it, a thousand do not.'

There had been no lack of witnesses in the delivery room, and although much was made of the absence of such key figures as the Princess Anne, the Archbishop of Canterbury, the Dutch ambassador and the Hyde brothers, maternal uncles of the princesses, it was no longer seriously disputed that the queen had indeed given birth. The favourite theory now was that the infant had been either stillborn or another girl and that a substitute had somehow been smuggled into her bed at the last moment. Thus the story of the baby in the warming pan entered the national folklore.

Serious men – the seventeenth-century equivalent of the men in suits – were, however, less concerned with the authenticity of the baby's parentage than with the threat which its mere existence posed for the future, and by the end of June a formal invitation, signed by the so-called Immortal Seven – the Earls of Devonshire, Danby and Shrewsbury, Richard Lumley, Edward Russell, Henry Sidney and Dr Compton, Bishop of London – had gone to the Hague, requesting William of Orange to come over and save England for the Protestant religion, parliamentary government and the Whig party. They assured him that 'there are nineteen parts of twenty of the people throughout the Kingdom who are desirous of a change' and promised to be waiting to support him as soon as he arrived.

For the politicians it was, of course, necessary to present the 'supposed Prince of Wales' as a changeling being falsely imposed on the nation. 'Not one in a thousand' believed otherwise. But for the Princess of Orange, pious, conscientious, hypersensitive, it was not so simple. When news of the birth first arrived she had given orders that the infant should be publicly prayed for in her chapel, 'hoping still, for the sake of the King, that it was really his son. . . . But one hears every day things so strange it is impossible to avoid having very strong suspicions.'[35]

Early in July it seemed as if the problem might be going to solve itself in the usual way, for the baby was reported to be ill. 'If he has been as bad as some people say', wrote Anne, 'I believe it will not be long before he is an Angel in Heaven.'[36] But he recovered and Mary, in an attempt to resolve some of her doubts, sent her sister a detailed obstetrical questionnaire. Anne could not add any fresh information from her own knowledge, except to say that she had never seen any milk and to repeat that she 'never heard of anybody say they felt the child stir'. But she interrogated Mrs Dawson, one of the bedchamber women, who told her that the queen had gone into labour about eight o'clock in the morning and had been delivered in the bed she lay in all night. Although the curtains at the foot of the bed were drawn, the two sides were open and there had been no screen round it. The Lord Chancellor and the rest of the council were all standing close by so that the unfortunate Mary Beatrice asked the king to hide her face with his periwig, 'for she said she could not be brought to bed and have so many men look on her'. As soon as the child was born and the cord cut, the midwife had given the baby to one of the queen's women, who was about to carry it into the little bedchamber, but the king stopped her and said to the privy councillors 'that they were witnesses there was a child born, and bid them follow it into the next room and see what it was, which they all did'.[37]

It is difficult to see how much more proof anyone could have wanted, but then Mary did not really want to be convinced. On the contrary, she desperately wanted to have her worst suspicions confirmed. It was dreadful to think that her father, who had loved her better than all the rest of his children, could be capable of so horrid a crime, but it was only by believing it that she could in conscience justify her support of the projected invasion. The dilemma was very real. It was, after all, almost equally dreadful to contemplate the thought of her husband having forcibly to turn her father off his throne in order to save the English Church and state. Mary shed many tears and prayed long and anxiously for guidance – her affliction would not have been supportable without the assistance of God – but in the last resort it was William who mattered.

In July William's cousin, Frederick Zuylestein, returned from a formal congratulatory mission to James with a comfortingly negative report, which did indeed bring 'only the confirmation of the suspicions that we already had', and by the end of the month Mary's mind was made up. A pathetically reproachful note from her stepmother – 'you have never once in your letters to me taken the least notice of my son . . . you have for him the last indifference' – received a coldly evasive reply: 'all the King's children shall ever find as much affection and kindness from me as can be expected of children of the same father.'[38]

William's preparations were now going ahead. What he believed about the parentage of the new Prince of Wales is not revealed. Most likely he did not care very much either way. But it had been clear to him for some time that England would either drift into another civil war or become a satellite of France unless he intervened to preserve the balance of power and safeguard his wife's inheritance, and now it seemed was the moment. It was not a decision to be taken lightly, for it was a massive undertaking and an immensely risky one. But the King of France, of all people, helped to make it possible. Louis had already alienated many of his Dutch friends by imposing restrictions on their vital herring trade and was succeeding, where William had often failed, in uniting the German princes against him by his threatened takeover of the Lower Palatinate. The male line having ended with Charles Louis's son, the King of France was now claiming the territory for his sister-in-law and William's old playmate, Liselotte. At the end of September the French army marched into the Rhineland, thus removing any immediate danger to the United Provinces, and the States General finally gave William their blessing.

The prince had been keeping his wife fully informed and said later that he had done nothing without her knowledge and approval. He had expected and understood her filial scruples – 'he has seen my tears and has compassion on me', she wrote in her journal – and throughout the tense and hectic summer of 1688 they spent as much time together as they could, both of them only too well aware that whatever happened in England, nothing would ever be the same again.

Early in October Mary returned to the Hague, leaving the quiet of the countryside where she had, thanks to the grace of God, found an unexpected tranquillity of spirit, 'altogether beyond that which I could hope at the time when the Prince makes preparation for a war, where his person (which is to me a thousand times dearer than my own) will be exposed to danger and that against my own father'.[39] She had been getting some upsetting letters from her father recently. James felt sure it was not in her nature to approve of anything so manifestly unjust as the prince's invasion. 'And though I know you are a good wife, and ought to be so, yet for the same reason I must believe you will be still as good a daughter to a father that has always loved you so tenderly, and that has never done the least thing to make you doubt it.'[40] The queen, too, had sent a last appeal. Mary Beatrice refused to credit the reports that her 'dear lemon' could have such a thought against the worst of fathers, much less against the best, 'that has always been kind to you'.

But it was too late now for emotional blackmail, and in Holland Mary was constantly being told how important it was for her to show approval, to appear cheerful and confident. She did her best, but as the moment of parting approached it became more and more difficult to seem cheerful, especially when William had to tell her that if he did not come back, she must marry again. There was no need for him to add that it must not be to a papist. 'He himself', wrote Mary, 'could not utter these words without shedding tears and during the whole conversation showed me all the tenderness I could wish for.' Mary was so shocked and distressed at the very idea, that it was some little time before she could collect herself to reply and she could not remember all she said. 'But I assured him that I had never loved anyone but him, and could never love anyone else. . . . I said that I prayed God that He would not let me survive him, and that if I must do so, it not having pleased God to give me a child by him, I would not wish to have one by an Angel. . . . We talked then of several other things. I asked him to pardon all my faults and he replied with so much tenderness that, if it had been possible, my love for him increased even more.'[41]

Next day, William took his leave of the States. He thanked them for their support in the past, assuring them that he had always served them faithfully and kept the welfare of the republic constantly before him. In conclusion, and visibly moved, he said: 'What God intends for me I do not know, but if I should fall, have a care for my beloved wife, who has always loved this country as her own.'[42] That afternoon he and Mary had dinner together at Honselaersdijck for the last time, and afterwards she went with him to the riverside, where he embarked in his yacht on his way to join the fleet. 'God knows if we shall ever see one another again', she wrote. The thought was so terrible that for a time she could not move or speak, but sat in her carriage frozen with silent misery watching the prince out of sight.[43]

She went back to the Hague to wait and pray. The following day, 27 October, had been set aside as an official day of prayer and fasting so universal 'that even the Jews observed it' and the Spanish envoy had a mass for the happy success of the venture. Only the French ambassador held aloof. The expedition set sail three days later, but almost immediately a storm blew up and the ships were driven back to port. In London they waited for a Protestant wind and hummed 'Lilliburlero'. Then, on 9 November, Mary got a message asking her to come down to Brill the next day. She had two precious hours with her husband, but 'the second separation was more terrible to me than the first, and when he left me it was as if someone had torn my heart out. I could not even weep as I had done the time before.'[44]

She waited at Brill that night and next morning the prince sailed from Helvoetsluys 'with a wind as favourable as he could have desired'. Mary attended public prayers in the town and then climbed to the top of the church tower hoping to be able to see the fleet, but only the masts were visible. By early afternoon all 600 sail were well out to sea 'with a following wind, very good weather and ardent hopes for their lucky success'. From the masthead of William's flagship, the *Den Briel*, streamed a banner with the motto of his house – *Je Maintiendrai* – and other vessels carried banners bearing such messages as *Pro libertate et religione* and *Pro religione protestante*, or, more simply, *The liberty of England and the Protestant religion*. The Glorious Revolution was under way.

EIGHT

THE TWO QUEENS

I had another thing troubled me extreamly, which was the
continuance of the coldness between my sister and I.

(Mary II, *Memoirs*)

Anne had spent the late summer of 1688 at Tunbridge Wells,
'which the doctors tell me is the best thing I can do to hinder me
from miscarrying when I am with child again'. She was glad of an
excuse to get out of London, 'for it is very uneasy for me to be with
people that every moment of one's life one must be dissembling
with, and the papists are all so insolent that it is unsupportable
living with them'.[1] The princess seems to have felt no sympathy for
her father, living in dread that he would try to convert her – 'I
expect it every minute, and am resolved to undergo anything rather
than change my religion.' She had also become coldly hostile
towards her stepmother. The queen was 'of a proud, haughty
humour', she had told Mary the previous spring. 'Everyone believes
that she pressed the King to be more violent than he would be of
himself . . . for she is a very great bigot in her way. . . . She pretends
to have a great deal of kindness for me, but I doubt it is not real, for
I never see proof of it, but rather the contrary. It is not for me to
complain, and as long as she does not make the King unkind to me,
I don't care what she is.'[2]

Anne was back at Whitehall by the autumn, like everyone else
waiting nervously for the east wind and news of the Dutch fleet.
William actually came ashore at Brixham on 5 November by the
English calendar, and on 18 November Anne wrote wishing him
'good success in this so just an undertaking'. She went on to
explain that although the prince (George) had gone with the king
as far as Salisbury, he intended 'to go from thence to you as soon

as his friends thought it proper'. As for her own plans: 'I am not yet certain if I shall continue here or remove into the City; that shall depend on the advice my friends shall give me.'[3]

The friends on whose advice the Prince and Princess of Denmark relied so heavily were that handsome and predatory pair, John and Sarah Churchill. John already had a considerable reputation as a professional soldier, while Sarah, who had been Sarah Jennings, was Anne's first lady of the bedchamber and bosom friend. This famous relationship went back to childhood days. 'We used to play together when she was a child', recalled Sarah, who was some four years the elder, 'and she even then expressed a particular fondness for me. This inclination increased with our years. I was often at Court and the princess always distinguished me by the pleasure she took to honour me, preferably to others, with her conversation and confidence.'[4]

John was raised to the peerage in 1683 and in a letter to Lady Churchill Anne had written: 'Let me beg of you not to call me Your Highness at every word, but to be as free with me as one friend ought to be with another.'[5] 'It was this turn of mind', according to Sarah, 'which made her one day propose to me, that whenever I should happen to be absent from her, we might in all our letters write ourselves by feigned names, such as would import nothing of distinction of rank between us. Morley and Freeman were the names her fancy hit upon, and she left me to choose by which of them I would be called. My frank, open temper naturally led me to pitch upon Freeman, and so the Princess took the other, and from this time Mrs Morley and Mrs Freeman began to converse as equals, made so by affection and friendship.'[6]

There is more than an echo of Mary Clorine's letters to Aurelia in Mrs Morley's correspondence with Mrs Freeman. Like her sister, Anne craved affection and reassurance, and she clung to strong, vital, dominant Sarah with a fiercely passionate devotion; while Gilbert Burnet noted disapprovingly that Lady Churchill had gained such an ascendancy over the princess 'that there never was a more absolute favourite in a Court. She is indeed become the mistress of her thoughts and affections, and does with her, both in her Court and in all her affairs, what she pleases.'[7]

On 23 November John Churchill, closely followed by the Prince of Denmark, rode quietly out of the king's camp to join up with

William, now advancing unopposed from the west. They were not the only deserters and James, suffering from recurrent violent nose-bleeds and a terminal loss of any sense of purpose, turned back towards London. This unexpected move put his daughter 'into a great fright'. The last thing Anne wanted was a confrontation with her father. She would, she told Sarah, rather jump out of the window. Sarah had her own reasons for wanting to get out of the way, as she put it – James had ordered her arrest – and she wasted no time in contacting the Bishop of London, who was lying low in the City waiting to hear if his help was needed. It was agreed that 'he should come about midnight in a hackney coach to the neighbourhood of the Cockpit, in order to convey the Princess to some place where she might be private and safe'.[8] That night, Sunday 25 November, Anne retired to bed as usual, 'to avoid suspicion', and when all was quiet she and Sarah, with two companions, slipped out by the back stairs to the waiting coach, taking nothing but the clothes they stood up in.

Their flight was not discovered until the next morning, when Anne's bed was found empty and cold and a great outcry went up from her women that the princess had been carried off and murdered by the priests. It was even rumoured that the queen had made away with her. By this time, however, Anne and Sarah were well on their way north, having paused at Copt Hall, where Lady Dorset supplied a change of clothes and other necessities. They travelled by way of Hitchin, stopping for refreshments at an inn, and then on through Bedfordshire to Northampton, where they stayed for two nights and the Earl of Northampton collected a troop of horse to guard the princess. This grew into quite a little army, led by gallant Bishop Compton, who had been a cornet of dragoons in his youth, riding with drawn sword and pistols on his saddle. By the time they reached Market Harborough the journey had turned into a triumphal progress, and at Leicester there were great demonstrations of joy and a banquet was provided for the princess and her escort, for which the borough paid £5 plus £7 12s 6d for wine. At Nottingham, where she arrived at the beginning of December, Anne awaited developments while being royally entertained by the Earl of Devonshire.

A fortnight later she was reunited with her husband at Oxford, after making a right royal entry into the city. The Earl of

Northampton with 500 horse led the van, with the Bishop of London, still 'in martial habit', at the head of a noble troop of gentlemen. The mayor and aldermen greeted her highness at the north gate, and 'the Vice Chancellor with the heads of the university attended in their scarlet gowns, made to her a speech in English'.[9] By Christmas week she was back at Whitehall. Mary Beatrice and her baby son had now left for France, and on 18 December, as William entered the capital from the west, James was making an ignominious exit downriver towards Rochester and subsequent exile. The next day his daughter and her friends went to the theatre wearing orange ribbons.

In Holland Mary waited and prayed anxiously for news. On 19 November she heard that the expedition had landed safely, but it was nearly six weeks before she got a letter from William. 'Though I was a long time without having letters from the Prince, which was very disagreeable to me,' she wrote in her diary, 'I had, however, thanks to God, the consolation of learning from all the world, enemies and friends, of the good success of the affair.'[10] At the beginning of the New Year she had a visit from the Elector of Brandenburg and his wife. The elector was William's cousin and ally, and Mary made a special effort to be civil to him and 'divert' the electress. 'The circumstances of the time were such we could have no public entertainments but onely treating them at my several houses, which I did and played at cards out of complaisance so late at night, that it was ever neer two before I got to bed.' Some nights there was dancing, but the princess did not take part. It would not have been suitable while her father was in such distress and her husband in possible danger, but she was pleased to find that she was not tempted, 'so that I believed I had overcome that which used to be one of my prettiest pleasures in the world, and that I feard might be a sin in me for loving it too well'.[11]

The visitors left on 10 January and Mary returned to her 'old solitary way of living'. But not for much longer, for in England events were beginning to move. The unexpectedly precipitate departure of the king had left a vacuum which had to be filled without delay, and a variety of possible solutions to this unusual and delicate constitutional problem were already under discussion. Those who clung to the hereditary principle were in favour of a regency. Another group, led by Lord Danby, held that there had been a demise of the crown and that Mary, as next heir, should therefore be proclaimed forthwith. The Whig party in the Commons wanted William as king, in effect an elected sovereign; a revolutionary notion which would have the advantage of finally killing off the old doctrine of the divine right of kings, cause of so much trouble in the recent past.

In the end the matter was settled by the Prince and Princess of Orange themselves. Mary, who had once regretted having no more than three crowns to bring to her husband, made it clear in a sharply worded letter to Danby that she had no intention of occupying the throne by herself. She was the prince's wife, she wrote, and would never be 'other than what she should be in conjunction with him and under him'. She would take it very unkindly 'if any, under a pretence of their care of her, would set up a divided interest between her and the Prince'.[12] William, who had so far maintained a dignified silence on the subject, now made his position clear. He would not be regent, nor would he be prince consort, 'his wife's gentleman usher' as one of his friends put it. He would not oppose the princess's rights and no one respected her virtues more than he did, but he would not hold any position by apron strings or in dependence on another's life. If the English cared to offer him the crown for his lifetime, he would accept. If not, he would be happy to go back to Holland and meddle no more in their affairs.[13]

After that there was not much more to be said. The Convention Parliament, which met in January 1689, agreed that William and Mary should rule jointly, but with the administration of government in William's hands. As this meant that the Princess Anne might be called upon to waive her right to succeed her sister, her consent was necessary and Sarah Churchill, according to her own account, at first thought this so unreasonable that she was prepared to do her best to promote her friend's interests. However, she quickly discovered that all the principal men – except the Jacobites, as James's supporters were already becoming known – supported William, and that the settlement would be carried in parliament whether the princess consented or not. 'So that in reality there was nothing advisable but to yield with a good grace.' Sarah added piously that, had she been in Anne's place, she would have thought it 'more for my honour to be easy in this matter than to show an impatience to get possession of a Crown that had been wrested from my father'. Nevertheless, her ladyship took the precaution of consulting 'several persons of undisputed wisdom and integrity', including Rachel Russell, widow of the Whig hero and martyr Lord William Russell, and the highly respected clergyman Dr Tillotson. She found them 'unanimous in the opinion of the expediency of the settlement as things were then situated. In conclusion, therefore, I carried Dr Tillotson to the Princess, and upon what he said to her, she took care that no disturbance should be made by her pretended friends, the Jacobites, who had pressed her earnestly to form an opposition.'[14]

The stage was now set for Mary's arrival, and on 1 February Admiral Herbert appeared at the Hague bringing 'a letter from the prince to loose no time of coming to him as fast as I could. This, tho' expected, surprised me and gave me much trouble', she wrote and she lay awake that night 'thinking how much I should suffer in leaving a place where I knew how happy I could be'. The next few weeks were full of the bustle of packing up and leave-taking. 'From 6 in the morning till night I was never alone. The great concern all persons there shewd to part with me, increased my trouble and moved me so much that I shall never forget it.' The continuall hurry and crowd' caused her to neglect her devotions and the Almighty promptly manifested his displeasure by sending contrary winds which delayed her departure until 18 February. 'That day I embarkt and left the Hague and all that was in it with a grieff I can not expresse, but the wind changing again, I was obliged to stay in the yacht, the Lord shewing by that his providence, how wholy one must rely on him, and that not the least thing can be composed without his leave.' At last, on Sunday 20 February, she was able to set sail, the sea 'like a looking glass'.[15]

Mary found it hard to describe the conflicting emotions she felt in her heart as the English coast came into sight twelve hours later. 'I looked behind and saw vast seas between me and Holland that had been my country for more then 11 years. I saw with regret that I had left it and I believed it was for ever; that was a hard thought, and I had need of much more constancy than I can bragg of, to bear with patience. Yet when I saw England, my native country, which long absence had made me a stranger to, I felt a secret joy . . . but that was soon checked with consideration of my fathers misfortunes which came immediately into my mind.'[16]

William was waiting for her at Greenwich and they had a brief time alone together. 'I had a joy greater then can be expresd to come to the prince', Mary wrote in her journal, 'but I found him in a very ill condition as to his health, he had a violent cough upon him and was grown extreamly lean. . . . We both shed tears of joy to meet, and of sorrow for meeting in England, both wishing it might have been in Holland, both bewailing the loss of the liberty we had left behind and were sensible we should never enjoy here; and in that moment we found a beginning of the constraint we were to endure here after, for we durst not let owr selves go on with those reflections, but dryed up owr tears lest it should be perceived when we went out.'[17]

Everyone was naturally curious to catch a glimpse of the new queen and the Court was thronged with sightseers. Mary was now approaching her twenty-seventh birthday, a tall, elegant figure who was generally agreed to be handsome and good-natured, her face very agreeable, her shape graceful and fine. Some people, though, were distinctly taken aback by her almost hectic air of gaiety. Poor Mary, it had been impressed upon her by William and others that whatever happened she must 'put on a cheerfulness' in public, and in her anxiety to please she rather overdid it, 'acting a part which was not very natural to her', so that John Evelyn, among others, complained that she came into Whitehall 'laughing and jolly, as to a wedding'. Sarah Churchill remarked nastily that 'she wanted bowels', meaning sensitivity, and reported that the queen ran about her apartments 'looking into every closet and conveniency, and turning up the quilts upon the bed, as people do when they come to an inn'. Sarah thought her behaviour 'strange and unbecoming' in the circumstances. 'For whatever necessity there was of deposing King James, he was still her father who had so lately been driven from that chamber and that bed; and, if she felt no tenderness, I thought she should at least have looked grave, or even pensively sad.'[18]

Mary was also criticized for playing cards, and for smiling and talking to everyone, but if she gave an uncaring impression it was certainly not an accurate reflection of her feelings. 'I was fain to force myself to more mirth then became me at that time, and was by many interpreted as ill nature, pride, and the great delight I had to be a queen. But alas they did little know me, who thought me guilty of that. . . . My heart is not made for a kingdom and my inclination leads me to a quiet life, so that I have need of all the resignation and self denial in the world to bear with such a condition as I am now in.'[19] And she wrote to her cousin the Electress Sophia of Hanover: 'You must not doubt the sincerity of my feelings when I say that I cannot forget my father, and I grieve for his misfortune.'[20]

William and Mary were crowned together in Westminster Abbey in April 1689. It was a unique occasion in that it is the only time an English king and queen have been jointly invested with equal majesty and equal ceremony. Mary was raised into the throne as William was, the Sword of State was girded on her, and she too was handed the orb and sceptre and Bible. Towards the end of the long exhausting ritual Anne is reputed to have whispered her sympathy for the queen's obvious fatigue, only to receive a snappish response: 'Sister, a crown is not so heavy as it seems.' It sounds uncharacteristic of Mary, but if true this little interchange is indicative of an already deteriorating relationship.

Mary and Anne had met again after their ten-year separation with every appearance of affection but, according to Sarah Churchill, this soon wore off and a visible coldness ensued which she believed was due partly to the influence of the king, who no longer needed the support of the Prince and Princess of Denmark, and partly to 'the different characters and humours of the two sisters. It was indeed impossible they should be very agreeable companions to each other, because Queen Mary grew weary of anybody who would not talk a great deal, and the Princess was so silent that she rarely spoke more than was necessary to answer a question.'[21]

In fact, of course, it was Sarah's influence which had most to do with the growing coolness between the sisters. There was a dispute over Anne's accommodation at Whitehall very early on, when the princess applied to exchange her lodgings in the Cockpit for the larger, more luxurious apartments once occupied by the

Duchess of Portsmouth, one of Charles II's mistresses. This was agreed, but problems arose when she asked for some more adjoining rooms for her servants, as these had already been requisitioned by the Earl of Devonshire. 'After many conversations upon the affair the Queen told the Princess that she could not let her have the lodgings she desired for her servants, till my Lord Devonshire had resolved whether he would have them or a part of the Cockpit. Upon which the Princess answered, she would then stay where she was, for she would not have my Lord Devonshire's leavings' – a riposte which sounds a good deal more like Sarah than Anne.[22]

Soon afterwards another quarrel, potentially more serious, arose over Anne's allowance. The Churchills – or rather the Marlboroughs, for John Churchill was created Earl of Marlborough in the Coronation honours – decided that the Princess of Denmark's income ought to be settled by parliament rather than left to her brother-in-law's generosity, and got the matter raised in the House of Commons without prior reference to the king and queen. This breach of good manners infuriated Mary, who asked her sister what was the meaning of such proceedings. Anne muttered something about having heard that 'her friends had a mind to make her some settlement'. 'Pray what friends have you but the King and me?' exclaimed Mary, 'with a very imperious air'. All this was promptly repeated to Sarah, who had never seen the princess show 'so much resentment as she did at this usage' and hastened to fan the flames, 'for it was unjust in her sister not to allow her a decent provision without an entire dependence on the King'.[23]

William would naturally have preferred to keep the heir to the throne dependent on him financially, but was anxious to avoid any open appearance of discord in the family. He therefore sent the Earl of Shrewsbury with an offer to give the princess an allowance of £50,000 a year out of his Privy Purse if she would agree to drop her approach to parliament. Shrewsbury was confident that his Majesty would keep his word. If he did not, he, Shrewsbury, would not serve him another hour. Lady Marlborough was unimpressed. Such a resolution might be all very well for his lordship, but it would not be of much use to the princess if his Majesty did not perform his promise. Anne herself was equally uncooperative. She had met with so little encouragement from the king that she could expect no kindness from him, and now that the affair had gone so far she thought it reasonable to see what her friends could do for her.[24]

This was too much for Mary, always quick to resent any slight to William, and when she next saw her sister she demanded an explanation. Anne evidently took refuge in one of her irritating silences. 'She could tell me no one thing in which the king had not been kind to her, and would not own herself in the wrong for not speacking to either of us, so that I found as I told her she had shewed as much want of kindness to me as respect to the king and I both. Upon this we parted ill friends.'[25] However, William was now determined to put an end to the whole unseemly squabble, thinking it 'an ungenerous thing to fall out with a woman', and by the end of the year Anne had got her £50,000 a year from the House of Commons, out of which she begged Sarah to accept an annuity of £1,000 'as an earnest of my good will'.

Anne's consequence had increased considerably when, in July 1689, she had, to everyone's surprise, been safely delivered of a son. The baby was delicate and almost died of convulsions in his first few weeks, but a change of wet-nurse brought about a wonderful improvement and he began precariously to thrive. Tactfully christened William and given the title of Duke of Gloucester, he was greeted with relief as the heir who would guarantee the future of the Protestant succession. It was an occasion for family rejoicing, but relations between the new duke's mother and aunt were still strained.

In the spring of 1690 Mary was facing the frightening prospect of William's imminent departure for Ireland, where her father had recently landed with an army supplied by King Louis. 'With this I had another thing troubled me extreamly, which was the continuance of the coldness between my sister and I, which, had there been none else concerned, I should not have scrupled speacking to her of it; but I saw plainly she was so absolutely governed by Lady Marlborough that it was to no purpose.'[26] But in April Anne came, apparently of her own accord, 'and asckt both the king and I pardon for what was past, and desired we would forget it'. Mary was only too willing to forgive and forget, although she suspected the hand of Lady

Marlborough in the affair when Anne immediately began to ask for more money, and had little hope of 'a lasting kindness, since it seems on her side to depend so much on another's humour'. However, she was thankful to be on better terms with her sister and determined to remain so.[27]

It was an acutely anxious summer for Mary, left in charge for the first time, worrying about William and agonizing over her new responsibilities – especially when a French fleet appeared in the Channel. Anne accompanied the queen when she reviewed the troops camped on Blackheath, but she was 'of a humour so reserved' that Mary, who would have enjoyed some sisterly chat, did not find her much comfort. September brought relief. William returned a hero after the Battle of the Boyne and Mary was able, temporarily at least, to return to the more congenial occupations of creating comfortable homes on the Dutch pattern at Kensington Palace and Hampton Court, where the air was so much better for William's asthma.

Outwardly the sisters continued to appear fairly amicable and there was a family party on Anne's twenty-sixth birthday in February, but given the circumstances and the personalities involved, further discord was probably unavoidable. There were, of course, faults on both sides. William disliked Anne, whom he thought stupid and greedy, and hardly bothered to hide the fact that she bored him to tears. He made no attempt at all to hide his contempt for poor Prince George, who had followed him to Ireland at his own expense and been ignored for his pains. William, it was said, had taken no more notice of the prince than if he had been a page of the back stairs and had not even invited his brother-in-law to ride in the same coach with him – open affronts to her beloved George which roused Anne to fury. Mary, for her part, had grown to detest Lady Marlborough, while Sarah, avid for mischief, missed no opportunity to stir the pot, encouraging Anne's resentment and jealousy of the queen and poking spiteful fun at the king, whom she called Caliban or the Dutch abortion.

On a more serious level, William distrusted the Marlboroughs' political affiliations with the High Church Tories and suspected the earl, with some justification, of having been in touch with James. Marlborough was a disappointed man. He had expected to be given the Garter. He had wanted the lucrative post of Master of the Ordnance. Most of all he had wanted an active military command. He bitterly resented William's preference for his Dutch friends and in this he was not alone. 'The strain of the nation almost was that the English were overlooked and the Dutch were the only persons favoured or trusted', and by the autumn of 1691, according to Gilbert Burnet, Marlborough had begun 'to set on a faction in the army and the nation against the Dutch and to lessen the King'. By the end of the year he had gone so far as to move an address in the House of Lords that the king should dismiss all foreigners from his service, which would, of course, have had the effect of depriving William of his Dutch guards. James, ever optimistic, believed this could have been the first step towards his own recall, but William, who took good care to keep himself well informed, seems to have had reason to suspect that Marlborough was planning some kind of *coup d'état* involving the army, the Tories and the Princess Anne. He moved quickly, and early in the new year his lordship found himself suddenly relieved of all his appointments and forbidden the Court.

Anne and Sarah remained and Anne defiantly brought her friend to the queen's drawing-room, in spite of the rule which decreed that no wife of a disgraced officer could appear at Court. The princess was pregnant again and Mary shrank from a public scene, but next day she wrote a stern letter of rebuke. It was very unfit that Lady Marlborough should stay with the princess, and the queen regarded Anne's bringing her to Kensington 'as the strangest thing that ever was done. . . . I must tell you', she went on, 'it was very unkind in a sister, would have been very uncivil in an equal, and I need not say I have more to claim. . . . I know what is due to me, and expect to have it from you. 'Tis upon that account, I tell you plainly, Lady Marlborough must not continue with you in the circumstances her Lord is.'[28]

But Anne thought her sister was being quite unreasonable and flatly refused to be separated from her beloved Mrs Freeman. 'I must as freely own that as I think this proceeding can be for no other intent than to give me a very sensible mortification, so there is no misery that I cannot readily resolve to suffer rather than the thoughts of parting with her.'[29] Mary's response was to order Lady Marlborough to leave the Cockpit, whereupon Anne herself flounced out of Whitehall and retired to Syon House, which she borrowed from the Duke of Somerset.

The quarrel between the sisters could no longer be concealed from the public but when, in April, Anne gave birth to a son who lived for only a few minutes and was said to be very ill, Mary went to see her at Syon. The visit does not appear to have been a success. According to Sarah's account, which she says she had from the princess, the queen never asked how her sister was, 'nor expressed the least concern for her condition, nor so much as took her by the hand. The salutation was this: "I have made the first step by coming to you, and I now expect you should make the next by removing my Lady Marlborough." The Princess answered that she had never in all her life disobeyed her except in that one particular. . . . Upon which the Queen rose up and went away.'[30] Sarah heard later that when she came home the queen had been pleased to say she was sorry for having spoken sharply to her sister, who had trembled and looked as white as the sheets. Mary might not have been thus 'touched with compassion' had she known that Anne had been writing conciliatory letters to James at a time when another Jacobite invasion attempt was threatened.

William was away again that summer, campaigning in Flanders, and the queen found herself called upon to face a grave national crisis unsupported by either husband or sister. A large and businesslike Franco-Irish expeditionary force, intended to restore James to the throne, was known to be assembling on the Normandy coast, and there were serious doubts as to the loyalty of the Admiral of the Fleet Edward Russell and many of his officers. 'We were very much unprovided', wrote Mary, 'and owr enemies seemed so sure, that I at last thought I had very good reason to believe all in great danger.' Anne, down at Syon, was being secretly urged to declare for her father who, if the wind served, might be in the country within twenty-four hours with an army at his back. At the same time, Mary was being told 'of such dreadful designs against myself' that she admitted she was frightened. 'I am naturally extreamly fearfull, and now found I had so much reason for it, that had I not been supported by God's special grace, I had dyed almost with the apprehensions.' However, trusting the Lord to preserve her husband and take care of his Church and, sadly, 'having no children to be in pain for', she committed herself once more to God and prepared, 'not without impatience', to see the end.[31]

This came in May, when the combined English and Dutch fleets, in an action lasting several days, engaged and decisively defeated the French navy at La Hogue, thus ensuring England's command of the Channel and putting paid to all danger of invasion for the foreseeable future. Proud and relieved, the English rejoiced with bonfires and bell-ringing, and the queen announced that the old royal palace at Greenwich was to be converted into a hospital for disabled seamen.

While these stirring events were taking place, the Earl of Marlborough was languishing in the Tower on what subsequently proved to be a trumped-up charge of conspiring against the king, and Anne was writing frequent anxious little notes to his lady, who had gone to London to be near him.

Though I have nothing to say to my dear Mrs Freeman, I cannot help enquiring how she and her Lord does. . . . All I desire to hear from you at such a time as this is that you and yours are well. . . . I give dear Mrs Freeman a thousand thanks for her kind letter, which gives me an account of her concerns. . . . You do not say anything of your health, which makes me hope you are well. . . . Dear Mrs Freeman [you] don't say when I can see you, if I come to town; therefore I ask what day will be most convenient to you. . . . I wish with all my soul that it may soon be in our power to enjoy one another's company more than it has been of late. . . . My dear Mrs Freeman was in so dismal a way when she went from hence, that I cannot forbear asking how she does, and if she had yet any hopes of Lord Marlborough's being soon at liberty. For God's sake have a care of your dear self, and give as little way to melancholy thoughts as you can.[32]

Lord Marlborough was, in fact, released on bail after a very few weeks in prison and Anne offered him a post in her household, which he prudently refused.

After she had recovered from her last difficult confinement, Anne wrote to Mary asking permission to come and see her. 'For whatever reason I may think in my own mind I have to complain of being hardly used, yet I still strive to hide it as much as possible. And though I will not pretend to live at the Cockpit, unless you would be so kind as to make it easy to me, yet wherever I am, I will endeavour always to give the constant marks of duty and respect which I have in my heart for your Majesty.'[33]

This letter reached the queen while she was still waiting in almost unbearable suspense for news of the fleet, 'the fate of England . . . depending on our success at sea', and her sister received short shrift. ''Tis none of my fault we live at this distance, and I have endeavoured to show my willingness to do otherwise. And I will do no more. Don't give yourself any unnecessary trouble, for be assured it is not words can make us live together as we ought. You know what I required of you. And I now tell you, if you doubted it before, that I cannot change my mind.'[34]

Anne could not change her mind either, she would rather be torn in pieces. 'Nothing but death can ever make me part with you', she told Sarah. 'For if it be possible, I am every day more and more yours.' When Sarah herself offered to leave in order to ease the situation she provoked a storm of tears and shrieks of protest. 'I hope in Christ you will never think more of leaving me. . . . Let me beg once more, for God's sake, that you would never mention parting more; no, nor so much as think of it. And if you should ever leave me, be assured it would break your faithful Mrs Morley's heart.'[35]

There had been some talk of applying financial pressure on the Prince and Princess of Denmark, and Sarah insisted that Anne should discuss the question of her leaving with the prince. Anne, of course, did as she was told, but 'we both beg you would never mention so cruel a thing any more. Can you think either of us so wretched that for the sake of twenty thousand pound . . . we should forsake those we have such obligations to. . . . Besides, can you believe we would ever truckle to that monster [William] who from the first moment of his coming used us at that rate as we are sensible he has done. . . . No, my dear Mrs Freeman, never believe your faithful Mrs Morley will ever submit. She can wait with patience for a sunshine day, and if she does not live to see it, yet she hopes England will flourish again.'[36]

So the feud smouldered on. Each sister possessed a full share of Stuart family stubbornness and both had by this time become so entrenched that neither could give ground without unacceptable loss of face. In the autumn of 1692 Anne moved with Sarah into Berkeley House in Piccadilly. She was now being subjected to a series of petty manifestations of royal displeasure. Her guards had been removed, orders were given that no public honours were to be paid to her and the courtiers were forbidden to visit her. It amounted to social ostracism and seems small-minded, but while the heir to the throne continued to defy the king and queen, maintaining a rival court frequented by known Jacobite sympathizers, 'because, as it was easy to observe, all of that interest rejoiced much at the quarrel', it is hard to see what else Mary could have done in a situation where personal animosity had become inextricably involved with national politics.

William and Mary continued to take an interest in the little Duke of Gloucester and when he was ill, which was often, the queen would send one of her bedchamber women to enquire for him. But, again according to Sarah, 'this compliment was made in so offensive a manner to the Princess that I have often wondered how any mortal could bear it with the patience she did. For whoever was sent used to come without any ceremony into the room where the Princess herself was, and passing by her, as she stood or sat, without taking more notice of her than if she were a rocker, go directly up to the Duke, and make their speech to him, or to the nurse.'[37]

In February 1693 Anne miscarried again and some time after this another attempt was made to dislodge Lady Marlborough. The Earl of Rochester, one of the sisters' maternal uncles, approached certain members of the household insinuating that if the princess would only agree to part with her friend, he was sure the queen could, after a decent interval, be persuaded to agree to her reinstatement. Lady Marlborough herself considered this to be 'altogether improbable and indeed ridiculous', because her only crime was to be Lord Marlborough's wife, something she could neither excuse nor repent of. However, being 'resolved to leave nothing undone on her part', Anne sent Lady Fitzharding, who had been Barbara Villiers and who was thought to be able to speak more freely to the queen than anybody else, to enquire if perhaps she had mistaken her Majesty's meaning and to say that if she might hope Lord Rochester had any grounds for his suggestion, she would be very ready to consider such a compromise. But Sarah's narrative records that Mary 'fell into a great passion and said her sister had not mistaken her, for she would never see her upon any other terms than parting with me, not for a time but for ever, adding that she was a Queen and would be obeyed. Which final sentence, my Lady Fitzharding confessed, the Queen repeated several times in their conversation.'[38]

The deadlock thus appeared to be complete and was indeed to be broken only by death. In the winter of 1694 smallpox was once again raging in London. A few days before Christmas Mary began to feel unwell and realized that she had contracted 'the inexorable and pitiless distemper' which had killed so many members of her own and William's family. For nearly a week she hung between life and death in the usual ghastly conditions of royal sickrooms, crowded with supernumeraries, the air foul with the stench of sweat and candle grease and human excreta. William scarcely left his wife's side, heroically suppressing his asthmatic cough in case it disturbed her, while no fewer than nine doctors disputed over whether the queen had measles or smallpox, and tormented her with bleeding and purging and blistering. On Christmas Day there seemed to be some improvement, but that evening she grew rapidly worse. The rash had turned inwards, always a bad sign, and now the diagnosis was malignant smallpox. Mary was not in pain and looking at her weeping friends, murmured, 'why are you crying? I am not very bad.'

By the morning of 26 December all hope had faded and the clergy, headed by the Archbishop of Canterbury, took over from the doctors. 'We were, God knows, a sorrowful company', wrote Gilbert Burnet, 'for we were losing her who was our chief hope and glory on earth.' Mary took the Sacrament and then 'composed herself solemnly to die' asking the Archbishop to read her 'such passages of scripture as might fix her attention'. But she was dozing most of the time, and although she tried once or twice to say something to William, the effort was too great. Some time during the following day she finally slipped into merciful unconsciousness and just before one o'clock in the morning of Friday 28 December she died 'after two or three small strugglings of nature and without such agonies as are usual'.[39] She was thirty-two years old.

Mary as queen had been greatly loved and was sincerely mourned. Large crowds had taken the road to Kensington, standing silent in the bitter cold waiting for news. 'Never was such a state of universal sorrow seen in the Court or in the town at this time', remembered Bishop Burnet; 'all people, men and women, young and old, could scarce refrain from tears.' Apart from the implacably hostile Sarah Churchill, no one had an unkind word to say of the pious, conscientious, home-loving Mary who had held the reins of government with great competence when called upon to do so, but who had never wanted to be anything but William's wife.

William himself, normally so reserved and self-contained, broke down completely and was so devastated by grief that for a time it was feared he too might die or lose his sanity. Anne, who had been excluded from the sickroom on the excuse that the queen had to be kept quiet, wrote a letter of condolence. 'I beg your Majesty's favourable acceptance of my sincere and hearty sorrow for your great affliction. . . . And I do assure your Majesty I am as sensibly touched with this sad misfortune as if I had never been so unhappy as to have fallen into displeasure.'[40] On 12 January the princess, who believed she might be pregnant again, was carried in a chair to see William at Kensington. Brother and sister-in-law had a private interview and both wept.

Neither William nor Anne was present at the funeral – William because custom thankfully did not require it; Anne, who should have been chief mourner, because of her condition. But no expense, no detail of funereal pomp and ceremony was spared. They carried the last Mary Stuart in solemn procession to Westminster in a March snowstorm and laid her among her ancestors in the Henry VII chapel, while the Tower guns boomed and the abbey choir sang her to her rest with Purcell's specially composed anthem, *O Dive Custos Auricae Domus*.

Anne was now returned to favour. In the changed circumstances it would not have done for the king and the heir apparent to have been seen to be openly at odds. The princess's guards were restored and visitors flocked to pay their respects at Berkeley House. William presented Anne with all Mary's jewels and offered her the use of St James's Palace. They never grew to like each other – Sarah continued to grumble about William's boorish bad manners – but they contrived to live harmoniously enough on the surface and Anne once more took her proper place at Court.

At the end of March the reconciliation was stretched to include the Earl of Marlborough, who was readmitted to the king's presence and kissed hands, though he was not employed again until 1698 when he was appointed Governor to the nine-year-old Duke of Gloucester. This was a prestigious and profitable position and a significant indication of returning favour, but once again a cruel tragedy was waiting to strike the unlucky Stuarts. By all accounts Gloucester was a particularly bright and attractive little boy. But he had always been delicate with an unusually large head – he appears to have suffered from hydrocephalus (water on the brain). In July 1700 his eleventh birthday was celebrated at Windsor with a firework display and a grand banquet. Next day the child woke with a fever and sore throat and four days later he was dead. This was a most dreadful blow, not only to the grief-stricken mother, who never really recovered from her loss, but to the entire nation. Since Gloucester's birth there had been ten pregnancies ending in miscarriages or stillbirths and no one now seriously believed that Anne would ever bear another living child. Certainly William and parliament did not, and in 1701 was passed the Act of Settlement which secured the succession to the Protestant descendants of Elizabeth of Bohemia, the Winter Queen – that is, to her daughter Sophie of Hanover and Sophie's children.

Two more characters left the stage in the first few days of the new century. In the autumn of 1701 Anne received a letter from her stepmother with the news of her father's death. 'He bid me find means to let you know that he forgave you all that's past from the bottom of his heart', wrote Mary Beatrice, ' . . . that he gave you his last blessing and prayed to God to convert your heart and confirm you in the resolution of repairing to his son the wrongs done to himself.'[41] His thirteen-year-old son, destined to be remembered as the Old Pretender, was recognized as king by Louis XIV, who thus helped to ensure further Stuart tragedies for succeeding generations.

The following February William was riding in the park at Hampton Court when his horse stumbled on a molehill and the king was thrown, breaking his collar bone. It was not in itself a serious injury but it proved to be the final straw for an already frail and exhausted physique. The bone would not set, pneumonia developed and at eight o'clock on the morning of Sunday 8 March 1702, clutching the hand of William Bentinck, his oldest and dearest friend, 'he expir'd with two or three soft gasps'.

Dutch William had never courted popularity in England – indeed he had never greatly liked the English, something they found hard to forgive – and consequently he was not greatly mourned. A victim of the powerful Jacobite propaganda machine, he has often been depicted as cold, callous and ill-bred, the uncouth Mr Caliban mocked by Anne and Sarah Churchill. Closer examination reveals a sensitive, thoughtful, unpretentious man; humane and tolerant in an age not noted for such attributes. William's public qualities as a soldier, statesman and diplomat are not in question, but it was the private man Mary had loved, affectionate, caring, domesticated, quite often funny, sometimes infuriating, capable of inspiring true devotion in his friends and dependants; the man in whom there remained more than a trace of the lonely little boy at Leiden who had cried so bitterly for his mother and of whom his great-aunt Elizabeth had written: 'he is a very extraordinary child and very good-natured.'

The new queen was thirty-seven years old, overweight and already middle-aged. She had long suffered from 'flying gout' which caused acute pain and weakness in her limbs and her strength had been drained by no fewer than seventeen pregnancies. Even in the seventeenth-century context Anne's obstetrical history was appalling and various possible explanations have been put forward, from inherited syphilis to, more likely, inherited porphyria, but at this distance of time any diagnosis must be a matter of conjecture. Just as it is conjecture to suggest that Mary's failure to conceive was due to William's impotence or, more likely, to an infection contracted after her second miscarriage. What is certain is that their failure to have children was a personal tragedy for both sisters.

Anne possessed none of the style and easy charm of the Stuarts – in many ways she resembled her mother's family – but after fourteen years of William's often brusque and off-putting public manner, she was welcomed as a model of dignity and queenly grace. Her attractive speaking voice was much praised and her address to parliament a few days after her accession struck exactly the right note. 'As I know my heart to be entirely English, I can very sincerely assure you that there is not one thing you can expect or desire of me which I shall not be ready to do for the happiness or prosperity of England.'[42] Anne may have been commonplace, limited and unimaginative, but she was not a stupid woman, possessing a strong vein of native common sense as well as a strong sense of duty, and, after all the upheavals of recent years, her very ordinariness had a reassuring quality about it.

It is difficult to conceive of a more unwarlike figure, and yet the stout, homely queen was to preside over that string of famous victories – Blenheim, Oudenarde, Malplaquet – with which Marlborough crowned William's life-work and finally extinguished Louis's dream of empire – the dream once innocently foreshadowed by Minette, 'the business he will soon have in Flanders', and which had dominated the European scene for fifty years.

Marlborough became a national hero and England's international reputation stood higher than at any time since the days of the Spanish Armada. But England's queen was increasingly a sad, sick, lonely woman. Her husband died in 1708 and she had quarrelled with Sarah who had become more and more impossible. By the summer of 1714 she was visibly failing and on 28 July she suffered what sounds like a stroke. The usual ferocious remedies were applied, but 'her constitutional gout flew to the brain, and she sunk into a state of stupefaction, broken by occasional fits of delirium'. She died in a coma at seven-thirty in the morning of 1 August and one of her doctors wrote to Jonathan Swift, 'I believe sleep was never more welcome to a weary traveller than death was to her.' She was the last Stuart sovereign and had, ironically enough, fulfilled the prophecy made long ago by James V on his death-bed. The house of Stuart had indeed come with a lass, when Marjorie Bruce married her father's steward, and now it was to go with poor, gouty, unromantic Anne, for, despite all the hopes and manoeuvrings of the Jacobites the succession passed peacefully to George of Hanover.

THE STUART PRINCESSES

The Winter Queen's German grandson took possession of a London very different from the one his grandmother had left almost exactly a century before. The Great Fire of 1666 had destroyed most of the medieval and Tudor city she had known and the plague was no longer an annual visitor. An even more complete break with the royal family's past had come in 1698, when a Dutch laundry maid airing some clothes accidentally started a fire which gutted the rambling, ramshackle palace village of Whitehall. But the world of the Stuart princesses was already passing into history. The monarchy retained political influence, patronage and prestige but the days of divine right and absolute rule were gone for ever. The future lay with the new dynasty, the Whigs and Tories, the Age of Reason and Reform.

NOTES

CHAPTER ONE

1   D. Calderwood, *History of the Kirk of Scotland*, ed. T. Thomson
     (Edinburgh, 1845), vol. V, p. 438
2   D. Moysie, *Memoirs of the Affairs of Scotland* (Bannatyne Club, Edinburgh,
     1830), p. 127
3   Treasurer's Accounts, published in *Letters to James VI* (Maitland Club,
     Edinburgh, 1835), p. lxxiv *et seq.*
4   ibid.
5   *Correspondence of James VI of Scotland with Sir Robert Cecil*, ed. J. Bruce
     (Camden Society lxxviii, London, 1861)
6   John Nichols, *Progresses of King James I* (London, 1828), vol. I, p. 56
7   John Manningham, *Diary*, ed. J. Bruce (Camden Society xcix, London, 1868)
8   Thomas Birch, *Life of Henry, Prince of Wales* (London, 1760), p. 29
9   M.A. Everett Green, *Elizabeth of Bohemia* (Methuen, London, 1909), p. 4
10   Nichols, *Progresses*, vol. I, p. 170
11   ibid., p. 172; and Everett Green, *Elizabeth*, p. 5, note
12   Dudley Carleton to John Chamberlain, 4 July 1603, printed in Everett
     Green, *Elizabeth*, p. 6
13   Lady Anne Clifford, *Diary*, ed. V. Sackville-West (London, 1923), p. 24
14   Everett Green, *Elizabeth*, p. 6; and Carola Oman, *Elizabeth of Bohemia*
     (London, 1938, rev. edn 1964), p. 17
15   Lodge, Illustrations, vol. III; and F. Devon, *Issues of the Exchequer during
     the Reign of James I* (London, 1836), p. 6
16   Sir John Harington, *Nugae Antiquae* (2 vols, London, 1804), vol. I, p. 371
17   Harleian MS 6986, printed in Everett Green, *Elizabeth*, p. 11
18   Nichols, *Progresses*, vol. I, p. 429
19   Sir Ralph Winwood, *Memorials of Affairs of State* (London, 1725) vol. II,
     pp. 170–3; Birch, *Court and Times of James I*, p. 38; Harington, *Nugae
     Antiquae*, vol. I, p. 373
20   Harington, *Nugae Antiquae*, vol. I, pp. 348–53
21   Nichols, *Progresses*, vol. II, p. 348
22   Everett Green, *Elizabeth*, p. 22
23   Sir Thomas Edmondes to Lord Salisbury, September 1611, printed in
     Everett Green, *Elizabeth*, p. 31
24   Nichols, *Progresses*, vol. II, pp. 463–5; Birch, *Court and Times*, p. 198; Sir
     Henry Ellis, *Original Letters Illustrative of English History*, series III, vol. 4
     (London, 1827), pp. 170–3
25   Birch, *Court and Times*, p. 203; I. Macalpine, R. Hunter and C. Rimington,

'Porphyria in the Royal Houses of Stuart, Hanover and Prussia', *British Medical Journal*, January 1968

26   Birch, *Court and Times*, p. 205
27   Nichols, *Progresses*, vol. II, p. 513; Birch, *Court and Times*, p. 216
28   Nichols, *Progresses*, vol. II, p. 515
29   Oman, *Elizabeth*, p. 78; Birch, *Court and Times*, p. 222
30   Nichols, *Progresses*, vol. II, p. 524
31   Birch, *Court and Times*, p. 224
32   Nichols, *Progresses*, vol. II, pp. 536 *et seq.*; W. Kennet, *History of England* (London, 1706), vol. II, p. 690; Birch, *Court and Times*, p. 225; *Letters of John Chamberlain*, ed. N.E. McClure (Philadelphia, 1939), no. 166
33   Printed in Everett Green, *Elizabeth*, p. 64

CHAPTER TWO

1   Winwood, *Memorials*, vol. III, p. 407
2   Public Record Office (PRO), State Papers (SP), Foreign, German States
3   ibid., Elizabeth to Winwood, 14 October 1614
4   Everett Green, *Elizabeth*, p. 95
5   SP, Foreign, Venetian, Sir Henry Wotton to James I, 23 April 1616
6   SP, Foreign, Holland, Elizabeth Apsley to Dudley Carleton, April 1618
7   S.R. Gardiner (ed.), *Letters and Other Documents Illustrating the Relations between England and Germany at the Commencement of the Thirty Years War* (London, Camden Society, 1865–1868), vol. I, p. 13
8   ibid., p. 30
9   ibid., vol. 2, p. 2
10   ibid., p. 47
11   SP, Foreign, German States, 27 June 1619
12   Harrison, *Short Relation of the Departure*, printed in Everett Green, *Elizabeth*, pp. 132–3
13   Hist. MS Commission, 10th Report, App. 1, pp. 89–90; printed in Oman, *Elizabeth*, p. 190 and in *Letters of Elizabeth, Queen of Bohemia*, ed. L.M. Baker (London, 1953), p. 50
14   Everett Green, *Elizabeth*, p. 138
15   ibid., p. 153
16   SP, Foreign, German States, Francis Nethersole to Secretary of State George Calvert, 5 September 1620
17   ibid.
18   *Letters of Queen of Bohemia*, p. 54, Elizabeth to Prince Charles, 15/25 September 1620
19   SP, Foreign, German States, Francis Nethersole, 26 October 1620
20   Sir George Bromley, *Collection of Original Royal Letters* (London, 1837), p. 10
21   Everett Green, *Elizabeth*, p. 163
22   SP, Foreign, Holland, 27 November 1620

23   Everett Green, *Elizabeth*, p. 169; and Father H. Fitz-Simon, *Diary of the Bohemian War of 1620* (Dublin, 1881), p. 103

24   SP, Foreign, Holland, 25 January 1621

25   ibid., Dudley Carleton to Calvert, 6 April 1621

26   SP, Foreign, German States, early 1621

27   Nichols, *Progresses*, vol. III, p. 751

28   Everett Green, *Elizabeth*, pp. 193–4

29   SP, Foreign, Holland, Dudley Carleton to Calvert, 28 April 1622

30   Bromley, *Royal Letters*, p. 16

31   ibid., p. 15

32   ibid., p. 18

33   SP, Foreign, Holland, Dudley Carleton to Calvert

34   *Sir Thomas Roe's Negotiations in his Embassy to the Ottoman Porte*, ed. S. Richardson (London, 1740), p. 135, and printed in Everett Green, *Elizabeth*, p. 212

35   R. Coke, *State of England* (London, 1719), p. 109; and see also C.V. Wedgwood, *The Thirty Years War* (London, 1938), p. 158

36   Roe, *Negotiations*, p. 222; and Everett Green, *Elizabeth*, p. 229

37   SP, Foreign, German States, 11 April 1625

38   Roe, *Negotiations*, p. 597

CHAPTER THREE

1   Sir Philip Warwick, *Memoirs of the Reign of Charles I* (London, 1813), p. 65; Lucy Hutchinson, *Memoirs of the Life of Colonel Hutchinson*, ed. J. Sutherland (London, 1973), p. 46

2   SP, Foreign, Holland, October 1625

3   Everett Green, *Elizabeth*, pp. 253–4; *Letters of Queen of Bohemia*, p. 74

4   Everett Green, *Elizabeth*, p. 254

5   SP, Foreign, Holland, Mr Carleton to Lord Carleton, 25 January 1627

6   SP, Foreign, German States, 1 September 1628, printed in Everett Green, *Elizabeth*, p. 264

7   Sophia, Electress of Hanover, *Memoirs*, trans. H. Forester (London, 1888), pp. 2–3

8   SP, Foreign, Holland, Sir Henry Vane's despatch, 8 August 1630

9   Everett Green, *Elizabeth*, p. 275

10   *Letters of Queen of Bohemia*, p. 82, Elizabeth to Charles, 17 October 1631

11   Everett Green, *Elizabeth*, p. 301

12   *Letters of Queen of Bohemia*, pp. 86–7, Elizabeth to Charles, 24 December 1632

13   ibid., p. 88, Elizabeth to Thomas Roe, 12 April 1633

14   Agnes Strickland, *Lives of the Last Four Princesses of the House of Stuart* (London, 1872), pp. 3–4

15   ibid., pp. 10–17

16   *Somers Tracts*, ed. W. Scott, 13 vols (London, 1809–15), vol. IV, pp. 143–6; John Rushworth, *Historical Collections*, 8 vols (London, 1680–1701), vol. IV, p. 429

17   SP, Foreign, Venetian, 1640–2, pp. 271–2

18   ibid., p. 281

19   M.A. Everett Green, *Lives of the Princesses of England*, 6 vols (London, 1855), vol. 6, pp. 124–5

20   SP, Domestic, 1641–3, p. 283

21   SP, Foreign, Venetian, 1640–2, p. 296; ibid., 1642–3, p. 5

22   Sophia of Hanover, *Memoirs*, p. 13

23   Everett Green, *Lives of the Princesses*, vol. 6, p. 128

24   SP, Foreign, Venetian, 1642–3, p. 21; Mme. de Motteville, *Memoires* (1886), vol. 1, p. 209

25   Strickland, *Last Four Princesses of Stuart*, pp. 29–30

26   Ellis, *Original Letters*, vol. IV, p. 2

27   Everett Green, *Elizabeth*, p. 357

28   *Letters of Henrietta Maria*, ed. M.A. Everett Green (London, 1857), pp. 59 and 88 n.

29   *Letters of Queen of Bohemia*, p. 155, Elizabeth to William Lenthall, 13 April 1643

30   ibid., p. 156, Elizabeth to Thomas Roe, 20 April 1643

31   ibid., p. 160, Elizabeth to Thomas Roe, 12 September 1643

32   Strickland, *Last Four Princesses of Stuart*, p. 159

33   ibid., p. 162; Everett Green, *Lives of the Princesses*, vol. 6, p. 341

34   *Letters of Henrietta Maria*, p. 249, 9 July 1644

35   Everett Green, *Lives of the Princesses*, vol. 6, pp. 407–8

36   ibid., pp. 409–10; Rushworth, *Historical Collections*, vol. VI, p. 318; diary of Père Gamache, from Thomas Birch, *Court and Times of Charles I*, 2 vols (London, 1849), vol. II, pp. 409–10

37   Everett Green, *Lives of the Princesses*, vol. 6, pp. 354–5

38   *Memoirs of Edmund Ludlow*, ed. C.H. Firth (Oxford, 1844), vol. 1, p. 156; Sir John Berkeley, *Memoirs* (1702), p. 27

39   *The Weekly Intelligencer and Perfect Occurrences*, 16 September 1647, printed in Everett Green, *Lives of the Princesses*, vol. 6, p. 359

40   Rushworth, *Historical Collections*, vol. VII, p. 841, Charles to Fairfax, 10 October 1647

41   Ellis, *Original Letters*, vol. III, p. 330

42   Francis Peck, *Desiderata Curiosa* (London, 1732) vol. II, p. 375, Colonel Whalley to William Lenthall, 15 November 1647

43   Ellis, *Original Letters*, vol. III, p. 329; Rushworth, *Historical Collections*, vol. VII, pp. 1067 and 1074

44   Ellis, *Original Letters*, vol. III, p. 331; Sir Thomas Herbert, *Memoirs of the Last Two Years of Charles I* (London, 1813), p. 47

45   *Eikon Basilike: Memoirs of the Portraiture of His Sacred Majesty in His Solitude and Sufferings* (London, 1649); also printed in Everett Green, *Lives of the Princesses*, p. 369

46   *Eikon Basilike*; Herbert, *Last Two Years*, p. 122 *et seq.*

47   ibid.

CHAPTER FOUR

1   Cardinal de Retz, *Memoirs*, printed in Everett Green, *Lives of the Princesses*, vol. 6, p. 413
2   Père Gamache, *Memoirs*, printed in Strickland, *Lives of the Queens of England*, vol. 8, Henrietta Maria, pp. 181–2
3   Bromley, *Royal Letters*, p. 151
4   ibid., pp. 133–4
5   Sophia of Hanover, *Memoirs*, pp. 14–16, 27
6   *Letters of Queen of Bohemia*, p. 178, Elizabeth to Charles Louis, 29 August 1650
7   Cary, *Memorials of the Civil War* (1842), vol. II, p. 127; also printed in Everett Green, *Lives of the Princesses*, vol. 6, pp. 372–3
8   Leicester's *Diary* and Blencowe's *Sidney Papers*, printed in Everett Green, *Lives of the Princesses*, vol. 6, p. 376
9   Everett Green, *Lives of the Princesses*, vol. 6, pp. 376–7
10   SP, Thurloe, vol. I, p. 158
11   Strickland, *Last Four Princesses of Stuart*, p. 207
12   Everett Green, *Lives of the Princesses*, vol. 6, p. 386, note
13   Diary of Père Gamache, from Birch, *Court and Times of Charles I*, vol. II, p. 397
14   Sophia of Hanover, *Memoirs*, pp. 23–4
15   *Letters of Queen of Bohemia*, p. 178, Elizabeth to Charles Louis, August 1650
16   ibid., p. 181, same to same, January 1651
17   Everett Green, *Lives of the Princesses*, vol. 6, pp. 417–18
18   Gamache, from Birch, *Court and Times of Charles I*, vol. II, p. 411 *et seq.*
19   SP, Thurloe, vol. II, p. 646
20   Everett Green, *Lives of the Princesses*, vol. 6, p. 223
21   Everett Green, *Elizabeth*, p. 384
22   SP, Cal. Clarendon, vol. II, pp. 414–38
23   *Somers Tracts*, vol. VI, p. 323
24   *Mercurius Politicus*, August 1655, printed in Everett Green, *Lives of the Princesses*, vol. 6, pp. 230–1
25   Ellis, *Original Letters*, vol. III, p. 376
26   Everett Green, *Lives of the Princesses*, vol. 6, p. 233
27   *Letters of Queen of Bohemia*, p. 178, Elizabeth to Charles Louis, August 1650
28   ibid., p. 182, same to same, 27 February 1651
29   ibid., p. 184, same to same, 24 April 1651
30   ibid., p. 189, same to same, 13 May 1652
31   Everett Green, *Elizabeth*, p. 379, same to same, 17 November 1653
32   *Letters of Queen of Bohemia*, p. 201, same to same, 23 February 1654
33   SP, Thurloe, vol. II, p. 677, Elizabeth to the States of Holland, 27 October 1654
34   Bromley, *Royal Letters*, p. 203, Elizabeth to Charles Louis, 23 August 1655

35 *Letters of Queen of Bohemia*, p. 220, Elizabeth to Edward Nicholas, 19 October 1654
36 ibid., p. 227, same to same, 10 January 1655
37 Everett Green, *Lives of the Princesses*, vol. 6, p. 247
38 Strickland, *Last Four Princesses of Stuart*, p. 97
39 Everett Green, *Lives of the Princesses*, vol. 6, p. 262
40 Everett Green, *Elizabeth*, p. 391
41 Bromley, *Royal Letters*, p. 289
42 *Letters of Queen of Bohemia*, pp. 273–4, Elizabeth to Charles Louis, 12 June 1658
43 Sophia of Hanover, *Memoirs*, p. 76
44 SP, Cal. Clarendon, vol. III, p. 412
45 *Letters of Queen of Bohemia*, p. 278, Elizabeth to Charles Louis, 30 September 1658

CHAPTER FIVE

1   SP, Cal. Clarendon, vol. III, p. 337
2   *Letters of Queen of Bohemia*, pp. 283–4, Elizabeth to Charles Louis, 21 June 1659; same to same, 30 June
3   ibid., p. 285, Elizabeth to Charles Louis, 14 July 1659
4   *Letters from Liselotte*, trans. and ed. Maria Kroll (London, 1970), pp. 229–30
5   *Letters of Queen of Bohemia*, pp. 290, 293, 296–7, Elizabeth to Charles Louis, 17 November 1659; 8 December 1659; 12 January 1660, 23 February 1660
6   Sir John Reresby, *Memoirs*, ed. A. Browning (Glasgow, 1936), printed in Strickland, *Last Four Princesses of Stuart*, p. 228
7   Madame de Bregis, printed in Julia Cartwright, *Madame: A Life of Henrietta, Daughter of Charles I and Duchess of Orleans* (London, 1894), pp. 49–50
8   Cyril Hughes Hartmann, *Charles II and Madame* (London, 1934), pp. 9–10, Charles II to Minette, December 1659
9   Cartwright, *Madame*, p. 52, Minette to Charles II
10 ibid., p. 53, Charles II to Minette, 7 February 1660
11 *Letters of Queen of Bohemia*, p. 300, Elizabeth to Charles Louis, 18 March 1660
12 Everett Green, *Lives of the Princesses*, vol. 6, p. 288
13 *Letters of Queen of Bohemia*, p. 303, Elizabeth to Charles Louis, 26 April 1660
14 Samuel Pepys, *The Shorter Pepys*, ed. R. Latham (London, 1986), p. 45
15 *Letters of Queen of Bohemia*, p. 310, Elizabeth to Charles Louis, 7 June 1660
16 Pepys, *The Shorter Pepys*, pp. 50–1
17 Everett Green, *Lives of the Princesses*, vol. 6, p. 427, Charles II to Minette, 26 May 1660
18 John Evelyn, *Diary*, ed. W. Bray, 4 vols (London, 1874), vol. III, p. 246

19   *Letters of Queen of Bohemia*, p. 332, Elizabeth to Charles Louis, 22 December 1660

20   Everett Green, *Lives of the Princesses*, vol. 6, p. 429, Henrietta Maria to Charles II, 25 August 1660

21   Cartwright, *Madame*, p. 71

22   Hartmann, *Charles II and Madame*, p. 23; Everett Green, *Lives of the Princesses*, vol. 6, pp. 434–5

23   Everett Green, *Elizabeth*, pp. 324–5, Lord Craven to Elizabeth of Bohemia

24   *Letters of Queen of Bohemia*, p. 334, Elizabeth to Charles Louis, 17 January 1661

25   Everett Green, *Elizabeth*, p. 328, Lady Balcarres to Elizabeth of Bohemia, 28 December 1660

26   *Letters of Queen of Bohemia*, p. 335, Elizabeth to Charles Louis, 31 January 1661

27   Père Gamache, in Birch, *Court and Times of Charles I*, vol. II, p. 423

28   Cartwright, *Madame*, p. 88

29   ibid., p. 89

30   Madame de Motteville, *Memoirs*, printed in Everett Green, *Lives of the Princesses*, vol. 6, pp. 446–7

31   ibid., p. 457

32   Cartwright, *Madame*, p. 110, Charles II to Madame, 16 December 1661

33   Bromley, *Royal Letters*, p. 228, Charles Louis to Elizabeth

34   *Letters of Queen of Bohemia*, p. 344, Elizabeth to the Duke of Ormonde, May 1661

35   Everett Green, *Elizabeth*, p. 403, De Thou to Louis XIV, 19 May 1661

36   *Letters of Queen of Bohemia*, p. 346, Elizabeth to Charles Louis, 15 July 1661

37   ibid., pp. 347, 349, Elizabeth to Charles Louis, 22 July 1661, 12 August 1661

38   ibid., p. 348, Elizabeth to Charles Louis, 29 July 1661

39   ibid., p. 347, Elizabeth to Charles Louis, 22 July 1661

40   Everett Green, *Elizabeth*, p. 409

41   *Letters of Queen of Bohemia*, p. 351, Elizabeth to Charles Louis, 10 January 1662

42   Sidney Papers, ed. A. Collins, vol. II, p. 723, the Earl of Leicester to the Earl of Northumberland, printed in Everett Green, *Elizabeth*, p. 410

43   Everett Green, *Elizabeth*, p. 411; Evelyn, *Diary*, vol. II, p. 188

44   *Letters of Queen of Bohemia*, p. 332, Elizabeth to Charles Louis, 22 December 1660

45   *Letters from Liselotte*, p. 194

CHAPTER SIX

1   Everett Green, *Lives of the Princesses*, vol. 6, p. 454

2   Marie Madeleine de la Fayette, *The Secret History of Henrietta, Princess of England*, trans. J.M. Shelmerdine (London, 1929), p. 47

3   ibid.

4 De la Fayette, *Secret History*, p. 58; Everett Green, *Lives of the Princesses*, vol. 6, p. 465

5 De la Fayette, *Secret History*, pp. 60–1

6 Hartmann, *Charles II and Madame*, p. 57, Charles II to Madame, 26 October 1662

7 De la Fayette, *Secret History*, pp. 80–2

8 Cartwright, *Madame*, p. 165, Denzil Holles to Charles II, 16 July 1664

9 De la Fayette, *Secret History*, pp. 84–5

10 Cartwright, *Madame*, p. 167, Charles II to Madame, 22 July 1664

11 De la Fayette, *Secret History*, pp. 86–7

12 Hartmann, *Charles II and Madame*, pp. 131–2, Madame to Charles II, 17 December 1664

13 De la Fayette, *Secret History*, pp. 90–1

14 Cartwright, *Madame*, pp. 206–7, Charles II to Madame, 9 February 1665

15 ibid., p. 176, Charles II to Madame, 24 October 1664

16 Hartmann, *Charles II and Madame*, pp. 111–12, Charles II to Madame, 23 August 1664 and 19 September 1664

17 Cartwright, *Madame*, p. 177, Madame to Charles II, 28 November 1664

18 ibid., p. 211, Madame to Charles II, 8 April 1665

19 ibid., p. 217, Madame to Charles II, 22 June 1665

20 ibid., p. 222

21 ibid., p. 227, Charles II to Madame, 29 January 1666

22 ibid., p. 234

23 ibid., p. 244, Monsieur to Charles II, 12 July 1667

24 Everett Green, *Lives of the Princesses*, vol. 6, p. 512, Monsieur to Charles II, 28 October 1667

25 Cartwright, *Madame*, p. 251, Charles II to Madame, 14 January 1668

26 ibid., p. 253

27 ibid., p. 255, Charles II to Madame, 23 January 1668

28 ibid., p. 270, Charles II to Madame, 9 August 1668

29 ibid., p. 270–1, Charles II to Madame, 2 September 1668

30 ibid., p. 272, Charles II to Madame, 14 September 1668

31 ibid., pp. 279–80, Charles II to Madame, 20 January 1669

32 Hartmann, *Charles II and Madame*, pp. 233–4

33 Everett Green, *Lives of the Princesses*, vol. 6, p. 523, Charles II to Madame, 6 June 1669

34 Cartwright, *Madame*, p. 292, Charles II to Madame, 24 June 1669

35 Hartmann, *Charles II and Madame*, pp. 274–5

36 ibid., pp. 277–8, Madame to Charles II, 21 September 1669

37 De la Fayette, *Secret History*, p. 3

38 Everett Green, *Lives of the Princesses*, vol. 6, p. 527

39 Hartmann, *Charles II and Madame*, pp. 287–8, Ralph Montagu to Charles II, 12 December 1669

40 Cartwright, *Madame*, p. 307, Madame to the Bishop of Valence, 28 December 1669

41 ibid., p. 312

42 ibid., p. 316, Madame to Madame de St Chaumont, 10 March 1670

43 ibid., pp. 318–19, Madame to Madame de St Chaumont, 26 March 1670
44 ibid., p. 327, Madame to Madame de St Chaumont, 28 April 1670
45 Everett Green, *Lives of the Princesses*, vol. 6, p. 544
46 De la Fayette, *Secret History*, p. 91
47 Cartwright, *Madame*, pp. 337–8, Madame to Madame de St Chaumont, 26 June 1670
48 ibid., pp. 340–2, Madame to Anne de Gonzague, Princess Edward Palatine, 29 June 1670
49 De la Fayette, *Secret History*, pp. 93–109; Everett Green, *Lives of the Princesses*, pp. 560–6; Cartwright, *Madame*, pp. 353–4

CHAPTER SEVEN

1 Everett Green, *Lives of the Princesses*, vol. 6, p. 582
2 *Letters of Two Queens*, ed. Lt. Col. the Hon. Benjamin Bathurst (London, 1924), letter 17, pp. 60–1
3 ibid., letter 20, p. 66
4 Sir William Temple, *Works*, 4 vols (London, 1814), vol. II, pp. 343–5
5 ibid., p. 419
6 ibid., pp. 430–3
7 Dr Edward Lake, *Diary*, Camden Miscellany I, Camden Society 39 (London, 1847), p. 5
8 Henri and Barbara van der Zee, *William and Mary* (London 1973), p. 119
9 Lake, *Diary*, p. 6
10 ibid., p. 8
11 ibid., pp. 9–10
12 *Two Queens*, letter 31, p. 81
13 Lake, *Diary*, p. 10
14 *Two Queens*, letter 34, p. 89
15 ibid., letter 35, pp. 91–2
16 SP, Domestic, 1678, 411–12; van der Zee, *William and Mary*, p. 142
17 *Two Queens*, p. 107, Anne to Lady Apsley, 20 September 1679
18 ibid., p. 109, Anne to Frances Apsley, 22 September 1679
19 ibid., letter 36, pp. 93–4
20 ibid., letter 41, pp. 99–100
21 R. Doebner, *Memoirs of Mary, Queen of England* (London, 1886), p. 4
22 ibid., p. 23
23 *Two Queens*, letter 61, pp. 154–5
24 Evelyn, *Diary*, vol. 2, pp. 471–2, 15 July 1685
25 Henry Sidney, *Diary and Correspondence*, ed. R.W. Blencowe, 2 vols (London, 1843), vol. 2, pp. 253–5, William Bentinck to Henry Sidney
26 *Two Queens*, letter 81, pp. 189–90
27 *Letters of Queen Anne*, ed. Beatrice Curtis Brown (London, 1935), p. 16, Anne to Mary, 29 April 1686
28 ibid., p. 22, Anne to Mary, 10 January 1687
29 Gilbert Burnet, *History of His Own Times*, 6 vols (London, 1833), vol. III, pp. 133–4

30   ibid., vol. III, pp. 131–9; ibid., *Supplement*, ed. H.C. Foxcroft (Oxford, 1902), pp. 308–10

31   *Letters of Queen Anne*, pp. 29–30, Anne to Mary, 9 May 1687

32   *Lettres et Mémoires de Marie II, Reine d'Angleterre*, ed. Mechtild, Comtesse Bentinck (the Hague, 1880), pp. 62–3

33   *Letters of Queen Anne*, p. 35, Anne to Mary, 20 March 1688

34   ibid., p. 37, Anne to Mary, 18 June 1688

35   *Lettres et Mémoires*, p. 71

36   *Letters of Queen Anne*, p. 38, Anne to Mary, 9 July 1688

37   ibid., pp. 39–40, Anne to Mary, 24 July 1688

38   Ellis, *Original Letters*, 1st series, vol. III, p. 348

39   *Lettres et Mémoires*, p. 78

40   Agnes Strickland, *Lives of the Queens of England*, vols 8–11 (London, 1845–7), vol. 10, p. 378

41   *Lettres et Mémoires*, pp. 80–2

42   Van der Zee, *William and Mary*, p. 249

43   *Lettres et Mémoires*, p. 82

44   ibid., pp. 85–7

CHAPTER EIGHT

1   *Letters of Queen Anne*, p. 38, Anne to Mary, 9 July 1688

2   ibid., p. 30, Anne to Mary, 9 May 1688

3   ibid., pp. 43–4, Anne to William, 18 November 1688

4   Sarah, Duchess of Marlborough, *Memoirs*, ed. W. King (London, 1930), pp. 7–8

5   *Letters of Queen Anne*, p. 12, Anne to Sarah Churchill, 20 September 1684

6   Dss of Marlborough, *Memoirs*, pp. 10–11

7   Burnet, *Supplement*, p. 293

8   Dss of Marlborough, *Memoirs*, pp. 12–13

9   Ellis, *Original Letters*, 2nd series, vol. IV, pp. 177–8

10   *Lettres et Mémoires*, p. 90

11   Doebner, *Memoirs*, pp. 4–5

12   Burnet, *History*, vol. III, p. 390

13   Van der Zee, *William and Mary*, p. 272; M. Grew, *William Bentinck and William III* (London, 1924), pp. 150–2; Nesca A. Robb, *William of Orange: A Personal Portrait* (London, 1966), vol. 2, p. 278

14   Dss of Marlborough, *Memoirs*, pp. 16–17

15   Doebner, *Memoirs*, pp. 7–9

16   ibid., pp. 9–10

17   ibid., p. 10

18   Dss of Marlborough, *Memoirs*, pp. 18–19

19   Doebner, *Memoirs*, p. 11

20   Van der Zee, *William and Mary*, p. 279

21   Dss of Marlborough, *Memoirs*, p. 18

22   ibid., pp. 19–20

23   ibid., p. 21
24   ibid., p. 24
25   Doebner, *Memoirs*, p. 18
26   ibid., p. 24
27   ibid., pp. 26–7
28   Dss of Marlborough, *Memoirs*, pp. 32–3
29   *Letters of Queen Anne*, p. 53, Anne to Mary, 6 February 1692
30   Dss of Marlborough, *Memoirs*, pp. 49–50
31   Doebner, *Memoirs*, p. 48
32   Dss of Marlborough, *Memoirs*, pp. 45–7
33   *Letters of Queen Anne*, pp. 54–5, Anne to Mary, 20 May 1692
34   Dss of Marlborough, *Memoirs*, p. 55
35   ibid., pp. 57–9
36   *Letters of Queen Anne*, pp. 60–1, Anne to Lady Marlborough, ? 1692
37   Dss of Marlborough, *Memoirs*, p. 73
38   ibid., pp. 70–1
39   Strickland, *Queens of England*, vol. 11, pp. 307–15; Marjorie Bowen, *The Third Mary Stuart* (London, 1929), pp. 271–6; Hester Chapman, *Mary II, Queen of England* (London, 1953), pp. 252–4; Van der Zee, *William and Mary*, pp. 384–6
40   *Letters of Queen Anne*, p. 63, Anne to William, 28 December 1694
41   Neville Connell, *Anne: The Last Stuart Monarch* (London, 1937), p. 104
42   ibid., p. 109

Select Bibliography

Note   Place of publication is London unless otherwise stated.

Ailesbury, Thomas, Earl of, *Memoirs*, ed. W. Buckley, 2 vols, Roxburghe Club, 1890

Aitkin, Lucy, *Memoirs of the Court of King James*, 1822

Ashley, Maurice, *The Glorious Revolution*, Hodder, 1966

—— *England in the Seventeenth Century*, Pelican History of England, no. 6, 3rd edn, revised, Harmondsworth, Penguin, 1968

Berkeley, Sir John, *Memoirs*, 1702

Bevan, Bryan, *Charles II's Minette: Princess Henriette Anne, Duchess of Orleans*, Ascent Books, 1979

Birch, Thomas, *Court and Times of James I*, 2 vols, 1849

—— *Court and Times of Charles I*, 2 vols, 1849

—— *Life of Henry, Prince of Wales*, 1760

Bone, Quentin, *Henrietta Maria, Queen of the Cavaliers*, Peter Owen, 1972

Bowen, Marjorie, *The Third Mary Stuart*, John Lane, 1929

Bromley, Sir George, *Collection of Original Royal Letters*, 1837

Bryant, Arthur, *King Charles II*, Collins, 1955

Burnet, Gilbert, *History of His Own Times*, 6 vols, 1833

—— *History of His Own Times, Supplement*, ed. H.C. Foxcroft, Oxford, 1902

Calderwood, D., *History of the Kirk of Scotland*, ed. T. Thomson, Edinburgh, 1845

Cartwright, Julia (Mrs Henry Ady), *Madame: A Life of Henrietta, Daughter of Charles I and Duchess of Orleans*, 1894

Cary, H., *Memorials of the Great Civil War*, 2 vols, 1842

Chapman, Hester, *Mary II, Queen of England*, Cape, 1953

—— *The Tragedy of Charles II*, Cape, 1964

Clark, Sir George, *The Later Stuarts*, Oxford, 1955

Clifford, Lady Anne, *Diary*, ed. V. Sackville-West, Heinemann, 1923

Coke, R., *The State of England*, 1719

Connell, Neville, *Anne: The Last Stuart Monarch*, Butterworth, 1937

Correspondence of James VI of Scotland with Sir Robert Cecil, ed. J. Bruce, Camden Society, xcix, London, 1861

Curtis, Gila, *The Life and Times of Queen Anne*, Weidenfeld, 1972

Dalrymple, Sir John, *Memoirs of Great Britain and Ireland*, 1790

Devon, F., *Issues of the Exchequer during the Reign of James I*, 1836

Doebner, Dr R. (ed.), *Memoirs of Mary, Queen of England*, 1886

Eikon Basilike: the Portraiture of His Sacred Majesty in His Solitude and Sufferings, 1649

Ellis, Sir Henry, *Original Letters Illustrative of English History*, 1st series, 1824; 2nd series, 1827

Evelyn, John, *Diary*, ed. W. Bray, 4 vols, 1874

Everett Green, M.A., *Elizabeth of Bohemia*, 1909

—— *Lives of the Princesses of England*, 6 vols, 1855

Fayette, Comtesse Marie Madeleine de la, *The Secret History of Henrietta, Princess of England*, trans. J.M. Shelmerdine, Routledge, 1929

Fitz-Simon, Father H., *Diary of the Bohemian War of 1620*, Dublin, 1881

Gardiner, S.R. (ed.), *Letters and Other Documents Illustrating the Relations between England and Germany at the Commencement of the Thirty Years War*, 2 vols, Nos 90 and 98, Camden Society, 1865–1868

Goodman, G., *Court and Times of James I*, 1839

Gorst Williams, Jessica, *Elizabeth, The Winter Queen*, Abelard, 1976

Gregg, Pauline, *King Charles I*, Dent, 1981

Grew, E. and Grew, M., *The Court of William III*, 1910

Grew, M.E., *The House of Orange*, Methuen, 1947

Grew, M., *William Bentinck and William III*, John Murray, 1924

Hamilton, Elizabeth, *William's Mary*, Hamish Hamilton, 1972

—— *Henrietta Maria*, Hamish Hamilton, 1976

Harington, Sir John, *Nugae Antiquae*, 2 vols, 1804

Hartmann, Cyril Hughes, *Charles II and Madame*, Heinemann, 1934

Herbert, Sir Thomas, *Memoirs of the Last Two Years of Charles I*, 1813

Hibbert, Christopher, *Charles I*, Weidenfeld, 1968

Hutchinson, Lucy, *Memoirs of the Life of Colonel Hutchinson*, ed. J. Sutherland, Oxford, 1973

Kennet, W., *Complete History of England*, 3 vols, 1706

Lake, Dr Edward, *Diary*, Camden Miscellany, vol. I, Camden Society 39, 1847

Letters from Liselotte, trans. and ed. Maria Kroll, Gollancz, 1970

Letters of Elizabeth, Queen of Bohemia, ed. L.M. Baker, Bodley Head, 1953

Letters of Henrietta Maria, ed. M.A. Everett Green, 1857

Letters of John Chamberlain, ed. N.E. McClure, Philadelphia, 1939

Letters of Queen Anne, ed. Beatrice Curtis Brown, Cassell, 1935

Letters of Two Queens, ed. Lt. Col. the Hon. Benjamin Bathurst, Robert Holden and Co., 1924

Letters Relating to the Mission of Sir Thomas Roe, ed. S.R. Gardiner, Camden Miscellany, vol. VII, 1865

Letters to and from Sir Dudley Carleton, ed. P. Yorke, 1757

Letters to James VI, Maitland Club, Edinburgh, 1835

Lettres et Mémoires de Marie II, Reine d'Angleterre, ed. Mechtild, Comtesse Bentinck, the Hague, 1880

Lodge, E., *Illustrations of British History*, 3 vols, London, 1791

Macalpine, I., Hunter, R. and Rimington, C., 'Porphyria in the Royal Houses of Stuart, Hanover and Prussia', *British Medical Journal* (January 1968)

Manningham, John, *Diary*, ed. J. Bruce, Camden Society, xcix, London, 1868

Marlborough, Sarah, Duchess of, *Memoirs*, ed. W. King, Routledge, 1930

Marshall, Rosalind, *Henrietta Maria, the Intrepid Queen*, HMSO, 1990

Memoirs of Edmund Ludlow, ed. C.H. Firth, Oxford, 1844

Miller, John, *Charles II*, Weidenfeld, 1991

Motteville, Mme. de, *Mémoires*, Paris, 1886

Moysie, D., *Memoirs of the Affairs of Scotland*, Bannatyne Club, Edinburgh, 1830

Nichols, John, *Progresses of King James I*, vols I and II, 1828

Nyeveldt, Baroness van, *Court Life in the Dutch Republic*, 1906

Oman, Carola, *Elizabeth of Bohemia*, 1938, rev. edn, Hodder and Stoughton, 1964

—— *Henrietta Maria*, Hodder and Stoughton, 1936

—— *Mary of Modena*, Hodder and Stoughton, 1962

Parkinson, C. Northcote, *Gunpowder Treason and Plot*, Weidenfeld, 1976

Peck, Francis, *Desiderata Curiosa*, 2 vols, 1732

Pepys, Samuel, *The Shorter Pepys*, ed. R. Latham, Bell and Hyman, 1986

Reresby, Sir John, *Memoirs*, ed. A. Browning, Jackson and Co., Glasgow, 1936

Retz, Cardinal Jean Paul de Gondi de, *Memoirs*, 1723

Robb, Nesca A., *William of Orange: A Personal Portrait*, vol. 1, 1962, vol. 2, Heinemann, 1966

Roe, Sir Thomas, see *Letters Relating to the Mission of*

—— see Sir Thomas Roe's *Negotiations in his Embassy to the Ottoman Porte*

Rowse, A.L., *The Early Churchills*, Macmillan, 1956

Rushworth, John, *Historical Collections*, 8 vols, 1680–1701

Rye, W., *England as seen by Foreigners in the Days of Elizabeth and James I*, 1865

Sidney Papers, ed. A. Collins, 2 vols, 1746

Sidney, Henry, *Diary and Correspondence*, ed. R.W. Blencowe, 2 vols, 1843

Sir Thomas Roe's Negotiations in his Embassy to the Ottoman Porte, ed. S. Richardson, 1740

Somers Tracts, ed. W. Scott, 13 vols, 1809–15

Sophia, Electress of Hanover, *Memoirs*, trans. H. Forester, 1888

Strickland, Agnes, *Lives of the Queens of England*, vols 8–11, 1845–7

—— *Lives of the Last Four Princesses of the House of Stuart*, 1872

Strong, Roy, *Henry, Prince of Wales and England's Lost Renaissance*, Thames and Hudson, 1986

Temple, Sir William, *Works*, 4 vols, 1814

Thurloe, J., *State Papers*, ed. T. Birch, 7 vols, 1742

Turner, F.C., *James II*, Eyre and Spottiswoode, 1948

Warwick, Sir Philip, *Memoirs of the Reign of Charles I*, 1813

Wedgwood, C.V., *The Thirty Years War*, Cape, 1938

—— *The King's Peace, 1637–1641*, Collins, 1955

—— *The King's War, 1641–1647*, Collins, 1958

Winwood, Sir Ralph, *Memorials of Affairs of State*, 1725

Zee, Henri and Barbara van der, *William and Mary*, Macmillan, 1973

INDEX

Amalia de Solms, Princess of
  Orange 63–4, 78, 103,
  105, 153, 210
Anne of Austria, queen mother
  of France 85, 95, 119,
  136, 141, 156, 157, 163,
  167
Anne, daughter of Charles I,
  birth and death of 70
Anne, daughter of James II,
  Queen of England 193,
  202, 211, 218, 243
  birth 164
  eye trouble 184
  early years and education 194
  appears in court masque 196
  has smallpox 203
  visits Brussels 207–8
  appearance and marriage
    211–12
  firm in her religion 216
  death of her children 216
  sceptical about the queen's
    pregnancy 219–21
  fears attempt to convert her
    225
  attachment to 'Mrs Freeman'
    226
  flees from Whitehall 227
  waives right to succeed her
    sister 229
  relations with king and
    queen 232–4

birth of her son 234
  her 26th birthday 235
  refuses to dismiss Lady
    Marlborough 236–7
  urged to declare for her
    father 237
  subjected to royal displeasure
    239–40
  return to favour 242–3
  accession, medical history
    and character of 244–5
  death 245
Anne of Denmark, wife of
  James VI and I 1, 6, 7,
  18–19, 22, 23, 26, 27,
  28, 30
  death of 38
Apsley, Elizabeth 37
Apsley, Frances (Aurelia), later
  Lady Bathurst 195, 196,
  202, 204, 207, 209, 211,
  215
Argyll, Archibald Campbell,
  Marquis of 99
Arlington, Henry Bennet, Earl
  of 175, 177
Arundell, Henry, Baron
  Arundell of Wardour 175,
  176

Baden-Durlach, Margrave of
  54–5
Bagnall, Dr 102

Balcarres, Lady 120, 139
Balcarres, Lord 120
Bamfield, Colonel Joseph 91
Beaumont, M. de 8
Bedford, Francis Russell, Earl of
    2
Bedford, Lucy Russell (née
    Harrington), Countess of
    6, 53, 63
Bellefonds, Maréchal de 192
Bentinck, William 202, 214,
    217, 244
Berkeley, Sir John 84, 86
Bethlen Gabor, King of
    Hungary 57
Betterton, Mrs 211
Boileau, Nicolas 168
Bossuet, Abbé 189, 190, 193
Boswell, Sir William 69
Bouillon, Henri de la Tour
    d'Auvergne 20, 40, 55
Bourdon, Daniel de 214
Bowes, Robert of Aske 2
Bradshaw, John 101
Brandenburg, Friedrich, Elector
    of 228
Brandenburg, Friedrich
    Wilhelm, Elector of 48–9,
    50, 57, 58, 105
Brandenburg, Sophia Charlotte,
    Electress of 228
Bruce, Marjorie 245
Buckingham, George Villiers,
    1st Duke of 39, 42, 57–8,
    62
    assassination of 65
Buckingham, George Villiers,
    2nd Duke of 140, 176,
    193

Burnet, Gilbert 217, 226, 241,
    242
Bussy, Comte de 168

Carey, Elizabeth 13
Carey, Sir Robert 5
Carleton, Alice 27
Carleton, Mr Dudley 63, 64
Carleton, Sir Dudley 23, 37,
    49, 50, 51, 53, 54, 56,
    63
Catesby, Robert 12, 13, 14, 15
Catesby, Sir William 12
Catherine of Braganza, wife of
    Charles II 148, 158, 164,
    184, 196, 203, 204
Cecil, Robert see Salisbury, Earl
    of
Chamberlain, John 23, 24, 25,
    27, 28, 29, 45
Charles I, King of England 6,
    13, 18, 22, 23, 25, 26,
    28, 30, 41, 46, 57, 60,
    62, 65, 67–8, 69, 70, 71,
    73, 74–5, 77, 79, 82, 85,
    90, 94, 95, 96, 102
    birth of 4
    accession and marriage 61
    makes peace with Spain
        66–7
    and the Five Members 75–6
    standard raised at
        Nottingham 81
    at Oxford 84
    surrenders to the Scots 88
    at Hampton Court 89–90
    trial of 91–2
    says goodbye to children
        92–3

Charles II, King of England 73,
79, 85, 87, 93, 96, 99,
104, 113, 117, 119, 120,
135, 136, 139, 144, 146,
147, 148, 149, 153, 154,
161, 162, 164, 165, 166,
167, 169, 170, 173, 179,
180, 181, 183, 185, 194,
195, 198, 199, 200, 201,
204, 207, 211, 233
  birth of 66
  lands in Scotland 101
  escape after battle of
    Worcester 107–8
  on holiday with Mary
    110–11
  anger at attempted
    conversion of Gloucester
    112
  relations with Mary 121–3,
    124, 126, 127
  captivated by Minette 128–9
  restoration of 130–2
  plans to use Minette as
    intermediary 158
  and the Triple Alliance 172
  and the Secret Treaty 174–6
  signs Treaty of Dover 184
  grief at Minette's death
    191–2
  jocularity at niece's wedding
    202
  death of 212
Charles II, King of Spain 172,
  207
Charles Louis, Elector Palatine,
  2nd son of Elizabeth of
  Bohemia 42, 45, 58, 65,
  73, 81, 97, 99, 104, 114,
  123, 125, 144, 147, 148,
  149, 222
  birth of 37
  restored to Lower Palatinate
    95–6
  invites his mother to
    Heidelberg 115–16
  separates from his wife 122
  death of 151
Choisy, Abbé de 141
Christian of Anhalt Bernburg
  21, 40
Christian of Brunswick (the
  Mad Brunswicker) 53, 54,
  56, 57, 62
Christian IV, King of Denmark
  16, 36, 57, 62, 80
Christian V, King of Denmark
  212
Christina, Queen of Sweden
  117
Churchill, John see
  Marlborough, Earl of
Churchill, Sarah see
  Marlborough, Countess of
Clifford, Lady Anne 8
Clifford, Sir Thomas 175
Cobham, Henry Brooke, 8th
  Baron 9
Compton, Henry, Bishop of
  London 202, 216, 220,
  227, 228
Condé, Louis de Bourbon,
  Prince de 168, 191
Conway, Sir Edward, later
  Viscount Conway 47, 60,
  65
Cosin, Dr 111
Cosnac, Daniel de, Bishop of

Valence 168, 169, 170, 171–2, 178, 179, 180, 193
Covell, Dr 214, 215
Craven, William, 1st Earl 89, 98, 115, 138, 139, 145, 146–7, 148
Croissy, Charles Colbert, Marquis de 173, 176, 180, 181, 194
Cromwell, Oliver, Lord Protector 89, 92, 99, 101, 107, 110, 111, 113, 117, 124, 133
   death of 123
Cromwell, Richard (Tumbledown Dick) 124, 127
Cyprien, Father see Gamache

Dalkeith, Lady (née Anne Villiers) see Morton, Countess of
Danby, Thomas Osborne, Earl of 199, 220, 229
Danvers, John 84
Dawson, Mrs 221
Derby, Countess of 154
Desbordes, Madame 188
Descartes, René 98
Devonshire, William Cavendish, 3rd Earl of 220, 227, 233
Digby, John, Baron of Sherborne 53
Digby, Sir Everard 14
Dohna, Frederick, Count, Governor of Orange 105, 133
Doncaster, James Hay, Viscount, later Earl of Carlisle 39, 41, 66
Dorset, Countess of 83, 87
Downing, Sir George 123
Dudley Sutton, Anne 10, 19, 26, 30, 35

Edmondes, Sir Thomas 15, 20
Edward Palatine, 6th son of Elizabeth of Bohemia 97, 107, 187
Edward VI, King of England 9
Effiat, Marquis d' 192
Elizabeth Charlotte (Liselotte), daughter of Charles Louis, later Duchesse d'Orleans 126, 145, 151–2, 163, 222
Elizabeth, daughter of Charles I 71, 82, 84, 87, 88, 89, 103, 109
   birth of 70
   appeals to House of Lords 83
   at Hampton Court 90
   says goodbye to her father 92–3
   asks to go to Holland 99
   at Penshurst 101
   taken to Isle of Wight, dies there and is buried in Newport parish church 102
Elizabeth, daughter of James I, later Electress Palatine and Queen of Bohemia 39, 55–6, 57, 61, 62, 71, 79, 106, 111, 113, 123, 127, 134, 135, 138, 152, 153, 243, 244, 246

birth, christening and early childhood 1–4
journey to England 6–8
education at Combe Abbey and visit to Coventry 9–11
and the Gunpowder Plot 13–16
at Court and appearance of 16–19
suitors and courtship of 20–3
distress at brother's death 24–5
betrothal and marriage 25–9
leaves England 30–1
arrives at Heidelberg 32–3
birth of first child and early married life 34–6
reaction to offer of Bohemian throne 40–2
arrives Prague, crowned queen 42–4
birth of 4th child 44
offends citizens of Prague 44–5
urged to leave Prague 45–7
forced to flee 48–9
finds sanctuary at the Hague 50–1
nicknamed 'Queen of Hearts' 52
6th child born 54
short of money and disappointed at failure to recover the Palatinate 58–60
unwell and in debt 63–5
grief at Frederick's death 69–70
welcomes Henrietta Maria 77
relations with Parliament 80–1
fury at Charles's execution 95–6
and de l'Epinay 97
can no longer afford to ride 98
supports her 'poore neece' 103–6
financial problems 114–16
sitting up to see dancing 117
distress at Princess Louise's unhandsome behaviour 121–2
wedding ring in pawn 125
visits Brussels 125
takes 'violent fancy' to Liselotte 126–7
and the Restoration 130–2
sorrow at Mary's death 139
prepares to leave the Hague 144–6
returns to London 146–7
quarrels with Charles Louis 147–8
receives Genoese envoy at Drury House and falls ill 149
death of and funeral 151
Elizabeth I, Queen of England 1, 2, 4–5, 6, 9, 17
Elizabeth, 'La Grecque', eldest daughter of Elizabeth of Bohemia 42, 45, 58, 65–6, 80, 98, 104, 151
birth of 38
Epinay, Jacques de l' 97

Ernest Augustus of Brunswick
    Luneberg, later Duke of
    Hanover 119, 145
  marries Princess Sophie
    Palatine 122–3
Essex, Robert Devereux, 2nd
    Earl of 4–5
Essex, Robert Devereux, 3rd
    Earl of 85
Evelyn, John 132, 151, 213,
    231

Fairfax, Sir Thomas 85, 88, 89,
    90
Fare, Marquis de la 194
Fauconbridge, Lord 182
Fawkes, Guy 12, 14
Ferdinand of Styria, Holy
    Roman Emperor 38, 39,
    48, 49, 50, 54, 56
Feuillet, Nicolas 189, 190
Fiennes, Mademoiselle de 171,
    178
Finet, Sir John 24
Fitzharding, Lady (née Barbara
    Villiers) 240–1
Frederick Henry, Count of
    Nassau, later Prince of
    Orange 28, 63–4, 68, 72,
    78, 80, 106
  death of 103
Frederick Henry, eldest son of
    Elizabeth of Bohemia 37,
    42, 46, 58
  birth of 34
  death of 65
Frederick V, Elector Palatine,
    later King of Bohemia 20,
    21, 32, 33, 34, 37, 38,
    46, 47, 51–2, 58, 59, 62,
    65, 70, 72, 95, 96, 150,
    152
  arrival in England 22–4
  betrothal 25–6
  marriage to Princess
    Elizabeth 28–9
  leaves England 30–1
  melancholy mood 34–6
  offered throne of Bohemia
    39–40
  leaves for Prague and
    crowned king 42–3
  nicknamed 'Winter King' 44
  defeated at Battle of the
    White Mountain 47–8
  loses Palatinate 49
  ridiculed by the enemy 50
  submits to Emperor 53–4
  attempts to recover
    Palatinate 55–6
  builds house at Rhenen 64–5
  anger over peace with Spain
    67
  joins Gustavus Adolphus 68
  revisits Rhineland and death
    of 69
Friesland, William, Prince of
    117

Gamache, Father Cyprien de
    95, 109, 128, 138, 140
Gaston, Duc d'Orleans 118,
    136
George III, King of England 25
George Louis, Duke of Hanover,
    later George I, King of
    England
  birth 132

visits England 211
accession 245
George, Prince of Denmark
225–6, 232, 235, 239
marries Princess Anne 212
joins William of Orange
226–7
death of 245
Gondomar, Count 39
Gonzague, Anne de 187
Goring, George, later Earl of
Norwich 63
Gramont, Maréchal de 156,
162, 163
Grant, John, of Norbrook 13, 15
Grey de Wilton, Thomas 9
Grey, Lady Jane 88
Griffin, Sir Thomas 7
Guiche, Armand, Comte de
144, 158, 159, 160, 161,
162, 163, 167
pursuit of Madame 154–7
Gustavus Adolphus, King of
Sweden 68, 69, 117

Hamilton, James, Marquis of
68
Harington, Anne 6, 8, 9, 10,
19, 20, 26, 28, 30, 33,
36, 44
Harington of Exton, John, 1st
Baron 6, 8, 10, 11, 13,
15, 16, 17, 18, 19, 20,
26, 28, 30, 33
Harington, Sir John 9, 16
Hay, Alison 3
Hay, Elizabeth 3
Hay, Lady Eleanor 3
Heenvliet, Baron 78

Henri IV, King of France 1, 20,
169
Henrietta Anne (Minette),
daughter of Charles I,
later Duchesse d'Orleans
and Madame de France
95, 132, 166, 169, 173,
175, 212, 245
birth at Exeter 84
smuggled over to France
86–7
brought up a Catholic 108–9
court debut 118
growing up a beauty 127–8
affection for Charles II 128
in England 135–6
engaged to Philippe
d'Orleans 136–7
appearance of 137
returns to France 139–40
marriage and descriptions of
141–2
relations with Louis XIV 143
illness of 144
social success 154
'affair of gallantry' with de
Guiche 155–6
deceived by de Vardes 156–7
has 'explanation' with
Monsieur 157–8
breaks with de Guiche 161
discovers de Vardes'
treachery 160
is reconciled with de Guiche
161
demands satisfaction from
Louis 162
final parting with de Guiche
163

anxiety over Anglo-Dutch war 164–5
is seriously ill 170
fears and loathes Chevalier de Lorraine 171–2
channel of communication between Charles and Louis 176–7
asks Mme de la Fayette to write her story 178
believes Lorraine means to drive all her friends away 179–80
projected visit to England 181–3
at Dover 184
returns to France 185
at Versailles 186
illness and death 187–90
suspicion of poison 191–3
funeral of 193
Henrietta Maria, wife of Charles I 61, 63, 65, 66, 70, 71, 73, 74–5, 79, 80, 82, 86, 87, 103, 108, 109, 110, 122, 123, 127, 134, 137, 140, 141, 143, 154, 158, 161, 166, 167, 175, 184, 185
leaves for the Hague 76–7
lands at Bridlington Bay 84
escapes to France 85
hears of King's execution 94, 95
attempts to convert Duke of Gloucester 111–12
receives Louise Hollandine at Chaillot 122
returns to England 135–6
death of 177
Henriette (Nennie), daughter of Elizabeth of Bohemia 98, 126
birth of 63
death of 104
Henriette of Orange 124
Henry, Duke of Gloucester 82, 84, 87, 89, 91, 92–3, 99, 100, 101, 111, 117, 119, 120, 124, 127, 138, 139
birth of 70
in Paris 109–10
joins Charles at Cologne 112
dies of smallpox 134
Henry Frederick, Prince of Wales 2, 6–7, 7, 8, 9, 13, 17, 18, 22, 23, 30, 40, 150, 192
appearance and character of 19
death of 24–5
Henry VII, King of England 5
Henry VIII, King of England 6
Herbert, Admiral Arthur 230
Herbert, Lady 147
Herbert, Sir Thomas 91, 93
Hesse, Landgrave of 111
Hohenlohe, Sophie, Countess of 66
Holles, Denzil, 1st Baron 161, 162, 165, 166
Holles, John 24
Honthorst, Gerard van 98
Hopkins, Mr 15
Hopton, Ralph 49
Hudson, Geoffrey 74
Huntingdon, Henry Hastings, Earl of 7

Hyde, Anne, later Duchess of
York 113, 119, 126, 146,
158, 164, 184, 211
pregnancy and marriage 135
dies of cancer 194
Hyde, Sir Edward, later Earl of
Clarendon 85, 108, 111,
113, 124, 135

Ireton, Henry 89
Isabella, Archduchess, Regent
of Flanders 54
Isabella of Bourbon, Queen of
Spain 57
Isabella, daughter of James II
207
death of 218

James, Duke of York, later
James II, King of England
73, 75, 88, 89, 90, 93,
101, 107, 117, 118, 124,
131, 137, 146, 158, 165,
175, 184, 185, 194, 199,
202, 203, 204, 207, 208,
211, 219, 220, 221, 225,
230, 231, 234, 235, 236,
237
birth of 70
escapes from St James's 91
serving in French army 110
romance with Anne Hyde 119
secret marriage 135
marries again 195
dislike of William of Orange
200–1
accession of 212
and Monmouth Rebellion 213
Catholic zeal 216–18
reproaches his daughter 222
retreats to London 227
goes into exile 228
death of 243
James Edward (the Old
Pretender), son of James II
220, 222, 243
James IV, King of Scotland 3
James V, King of Scotland 25,
245
James VI and I, King of
England 1, 2, 4, 5, 6, 8,
9, 11, 12, 13, 17, 18, 19,
20, 21, 23, 25, 26, 27,
28, 29, 30, 34, 35, 36,
38, 39, 40, 41, 45, 46,
50, 51, 53, 54, 57, 58
death of 59, 63
Jennings, Sarah see
Marlborough, Countess of
Jermyn, Harry 120–1, 124
Jermyn, Henry, Lord, later Earl
of St Albans 117, 167,
176, 193
John, Count of Nassau 21
Jones, Inigo 17

Katherine Howard, queen 88
Kelway, Sir Robert 9
Kildare, Frances Fitzgerald (née
Howard), Countess of,
later Lady Cobham 7, 8, 9

La Fayette, Marie Madeleine de
la Vergne, Marquise de
155, 157, 158–9, 160,
161, 162, 163, 168, 170,
178, 185, 187, 188, 189,
190, 193

La Fontaine, Jean de 141, 168
La Rochefoucauld, Duc de 158, 168
La Vallière, Louise de 144, 155, 156, 163
Lake, Dr Edward 200, 203, 210
Lake, Sir Thomas 26
Lane, Jane 113
Langford, Mrs Mary 214–15
Laud, William, Archbishop of Canterbury 70, 71
Leicester, Dorothy, Countess of 100, 101
Leicester, Robert Sidney, 2nd Earl of 100, 101, 147, 149, 150
Lenthall, William (Mr Speaker) 81, 82, 102
Lionne, M. de 192
Liselotte see Elizabeth Charlotte
Livingstone, Alexander, 7th Baron 3
Lorraine, Philippe, Chevalier de 161, 170, 173, 177, 179–80, 182, 186, 187, 192
    evil influence of 171–2
    is disgraced 180–1
Louis, 5th son of Elizabeth of Bohemia
    birth of 57
    death in infancy 58
Louis XIV, King of France 94, 118, 119, 127, 133, 136, 137, 142, 143, 144, 146, 153–4, 156, 158, 159, 160, 161, 162, 164–5, 166, 167, 169, 170, 171, 172, 173, 174, 175, 177, 178, 179, 180–1, 182, 183, 184, 185, 186, 187, 189, 190, 192, 193, 194, 210, 214, 215, 222, 234, 243, 245
    claims Spanish Netherlands 166
    sheds tears for Madame 191
    and attack on United Provinces 198
Louisa Juliana of Nassau 20, 35, 37, 40, 42, 44, 45, 58
Louise Hollandine, daughter of Elizabeth of Bohemia 58, 80, 98, 104, 151
    birth of 54
    runs away from home 121–2
Lovell, Richard 110
Lully, Jean Baptiste 173
Lumley, Richard 220

Madame see Henrietta Anne
Mademoiselle see de Montpensier
Manchester, Edward Montagu, 2nd Earl of 83
Mansfeld, Ernest, Count 54, 59, 62
Mar, John Erskine, Earl of 6
Margaret, daughter of James I 4
Margaret Tudor, Queen of Scotland 3
Marie Louise de Valois, daughter of Madame 156, 186, 187, 193
Marie Therese, wife of Louis XIV 136, 142, 143, 161,

166, 170, 172, 183, 186, 189, 193

Marlborough, John Churchill, Earl of, later 1st Duke 226, 233, 236, 238, 240, 243, 245

Marlborough, Sarah Churchill, Countess of, later Duchess 195, 226, 227, 229, 231, 232, 233, 234, 235, 236, 237, 238, 239, 240, 242, 244, 245

Marsillac, Prince de 158, 159

Mary Beatrice d'Este of Modena, Duchess of York, later queen consort 196, 202, 203, 207, 208, 211, 221, 223, 225, 243
marries James 195
said to be pregnant 218
birth of son 219
leaves for France 228

Mary, daughter of Charles I, later Princess of Orange 74, 88, 100, 110, 153, 158
birth of 70
betrothal and marriage to Prince William of Orange 71–4
leaves England 76–7
early married life 78–9
birth of son 103
disputes over guardianship 105–6
devoted to her family's interests 106
with Charles II in Germany 111–12

illness of 113
visits Paris 117–19
joins brothers in Flanders 120, 121
quarrels with Charles 124
supervises son's education 125–6
has a red nose 126
and the Restoration 130–2
prepares to visit England 133–4
grief at Gloucester's death 134–5
falls ill and dies of smallpox 138–9

Mary, daughter of James II, later Princess of Orange and Mary II, Queen of England 164, 215, 216, 218, 225, 226, 228, 230, 235, 238–9, 244
birth of 158
education and friendship with 'Aurelia' 195–6
as Calisto and Mary Clorine letters 195–6
marriage considered 196–7
appearance 199
betrothal and marriage 200–3
distress at leaving England 203–4
welcomed in Holland 205
miscarries 206
second miscarriage and illness 207–8
Betty Villiers affair and life in Holland 209–10
worries about sister's

reputation 211
learns to skate 213
jealousy of Betty Villiers 214
is advised by Burnet 217
doubts over 'supposed Prince
    of Wales' 220–1
parting with William 223–4
refuses to occupy throne by
    herself 229
reunion with William at
    Greenwich 231
coronation 232
relations with Anne 232–4
on bad terms with Anne
    236–7
faces national crisis alone
    237
feud with Anne continues
    239–40
illness and death from
    smallpox 241–2
funeral of 242
Mary I, Queen of England 27
Mary, Queen of Scots 2, 3, 5,
    25, 41, 150
Matthias, Archduke of Austria,
    Holy Roman Emperor 38
Maurice of Nassau, Prince of
    Orange 21, 40, 49, 51,
    52, 53, 54, 56, 59, 152
death of 63
Maurice, Prince of Nassau 117
Maurice, Prince Palatine, 4th
    son of Elizabeth of
    Bohemia 58, 66, 77, 81
birth of 49
death of 96
Maximilian, Duke of Bavaria
    45, 56, 95

Mayerne, Sir Theodore 64, 84,
    102
Mazarin, Cardinal Jules 94,
    110, 118, 120, 123, 135,
    140, 142
Meauty, Sir John 69
Melville, Sir James 2
Mildmay, Anthony, Governor of
    Carisbrooke Castle 101,
    102
Minette see Henrietta Anne
Mirzcovinus, Georgius Dicastus,
    Administrator of the
    Bishopric of Prague 43
Moliere (Jean Baptiste Poquelin)
    168, 173
Monk, General George 127,
    129–30, 132
Monmouth, Anne, Duchess of
    203, 204
Monmouth, James Scott, Duke
    of, son of Charles II 120,
    173, 184, 186, 212–13
visits Paris 171
execution of 213
Monsieur see Philippe d'Orleans
Montagu, Ralph 176, 177,
    180, 186, 189, 190, 191,
    192
Montague, Admiral Lord (later
    Earl of Sandwich) 131
Montalais, Anne Marie de 155,
    156, 157, 158, 159
Montespan, Madam de 173,
    183
Montpensier, Anne Marie de
    (La Grande Mademoiselle)
    118, 136, 142, 186, 189,
    193

Montrose, James Graham, Marquis of 99

Moray, James Stewart, Earl of 3

Morton, Countess of 85, 86, 87, 109

Motteville, Madame de 141, 142, 143, 163

Mounteagle, Lord 14

Mulgrave, John Sheffield, Earl of 211

Murray, Will 79

Nassau Dietz, Sophie Hedwig of 66

Nethersole, Sir Francis 46, 47, 54

Neuburg, Duke and Duchess of 111

Nicholas, Sir Edward 108–9, 117

Northampton, George Compton, 4th Earl of 227, 228

Northampton, Henry Howard, Earl of 28

Northumberland, Algernon Percy, 10th Earl of 83, 87, 88, 89, 90, 91, 99, 150

Northumberland, Henry Percy, 9th Earl of (the Wizard Earl) 12

Nottingham, Charles Howard, Earl of (Lord Admiral) 30

Orange-Nassau, family of 71, 72, 105–6, 133

Ormonde, James Butler, Duke of 112, 145, 147

Pembroke, Philip Herbert, 4th Earl of 83

Pepys, Samuel 131, 132, 137, 140, 195

Percy, Thomas 12, 13, 14, 15

Petre, Father Edward 218

Philip II, King of Spain 1, 4, 27, 106

Philip III, King of Spain 20, 39, 66

Philip IV, King of Spain 120, 165, 166

Philip, Prince Palatine, 7th son of Elizabeth of Bohemia 97
   death of 98

Philippe Charles, Duc de Valois 160, 168–9

Philippe, Duc d'Orleans (Monsieur) 136, 139, 141, 144, 151–2, 156, 157, 158, 161, 166, 168, 169, 173, 177, 178, 185, 186, 187, 191, 192, 193
   appearance of 136–7
   early married life 142
   jealousy of 154
   renews friendship with Chevalier de Lorraine 170
   quarrels with Louis XIV 180–1
   his unkindness to Madame 182–3

Pilkington, Mr, of Leicester 7

Plessen, Madame de 58

Pomponne, M. de 184

Portsmouth, Duchess of 233

Puisars, Katherine de 215

Pym, John 74, 75

Racine, Jean 168
Rakoczy, Prince Siegmond 104
Raleigh, Sir Walter 9
Retz, Cardinal de 95
Rochester, Laurence Hyde, Earl
    of 220, 240
Roe, Sir Thomas 55, 57, 58,
    60, 70, 79, 80, 81–2
Rookwood, Ambrose 14, 15
Roxburgh, Countess of 82
Rumph, Dr Christian 69, 135
Rupert of the Rhine, 3rd son of
    Elizabeth of Bohemia 48,
    51, 58, 77, 81, 82, 96,
    146, 149, 150, 151, 158,
    184
  birth of 44
Russell, Edward 220, 237
Russell, Rachel 230
Russell, Lord William 230
Ruvigny, Marquis de 165
Ruyter, Michiel de 169

Sabran, M. de 84
St Chaumont, Madame de 178,
    179, 182, 186
Sainte Catherine, M. de 34
Salisbury, Robert Cecil, 1st Earl
    of 4–5, 6, 13, 14, 15, 17,
    18
Salisbury, William Cecil, 2nd
    Earl of 83
Savoy, Duke of see Victor
    Amadeus
Saxony, John George, Elector of
    57
Saye and Sele, William Fiennes,
    1st Viscount 82
Schomberg (von Schönberg),

Colonel Meinhard 22, 33,
    35–6, 40, 58, 150
Sevigné, Madame de 168
Seymour, William (Earl of
    Hertford) 19
Shrewsbury, Charles Talbot,
    12th Earl of 220, 233
Shrewsbury, Countess of (Bess
    of Hardwick) 5
Shrewsbury, Gilbert Talbot, 7th
    Earl of 7
Sidney, Henry 220
Skelton, Bevil 214
Soissons, Olympe, Comtesse de
    159, 162
Somerset, Charles Seymour, 6th
    Duke of 237
Sophie, yougest daughter of
    Elizabeth of Bohemia,
    later Duchess of Hanover
    77, 98, 104, 125, 145,
    151, 152, 211, 232, 243
  birth of 66
  marries Ernest Augustus of
    Brunswick Luneberg
    122–3
  visits the Hague 125–6
  birth of son 132
Southcote, Lady 83
Spencer, Sir Robert, of Althorp
    8
Spinola, Ambrogio 45, 46, 49
Stanhope, Catherine 78
Stanhope, Henry 78
Strafford, Thomas Wentworth,
    Earl of 72, 74
Stuart, Lady Arabella 5, 6, 18,
    19
Swift, Jonathan 245

Sydenham, Colonel, Governor
   of the Isle of Wight 101

Temple, Sir William 197, 198,
   199, 200
Thurloe, John 111, 120
Tillotson, Dr 230
Tilly, Johann, Count von 55,
   56, 62
Trelawny, Anne 214–15
Tresham, Francis 14
Trumbull, William 32
Turenne, Maréchal de 118,
   168, 181

Vallot, Antoine 191–2
Vane, Sir Henry 66–7, 68
Vardes, Marquis de 156–7,
   158–60, 161–2
Vendôme, Duchesse de 95
Vere, Sir Horace 47, 54, 56
Vernon, Francis 179, 193
Victor Amadeus, Prince of
   Piedmont, later Duke of
   Savoy 20, 38, 119
Victoria, Queen of England 102
Villiers, Colonel Edward 194–5
Villiers, Elizabeth 208, 209,
   214, 215
Villiers, Lady Frances 195, 197,
   203
Villiers, Mary 62

Wallenstein, Albrecht von 62,
   69
Waller, Edmund 185
Walter, Lucy 104, 120, 213
Weston, Sir Richard 47
Whalley, Colonel 90

Wilkins, Ernest 102
William, Duke of Gloucester
   240, 243
  birth 234
  death of 243
William I, Prince of Orange
   (the Silent) 20, 72, 103,
   198
William II, Prince of Orange
   64, 77, 78, 105
  marriage 71–4
  death of 103
William III, Prince of Orange,
   later King of England
   117, 130, 134, 153, 197,
   203, 204, 205, 206, 207,
   208, 213, 214, 215, 217,
   230, 231, 233, 236, 239,
   240, 241
  birth 103
  christening and disputes over
   his guardianship 105–6
  early childhood 125
  plays with Liselotte 126
  grief at his mother's death
   139
  emerges as war leader 198
  comes to England 199
  marriage to Princess Mary
   200–3
  discretion of 209
  troubled with 'bussiness' 210
  invited to come to England
   220
  prepares for invasion 221–2
  says goodbye to Mary 223
  sails for England 223
  lands at Brixham 225
  enters London 228

will not be his wife's
    'gentleman usher' 229
crowned jointly with Mary
    232
goes to Ireland 234
dislikes Princess Anne 235
campaigning in Flanders
    237
grief for Mary 242
death of 243–4
character of 244–5
Winter, Robert, of Huddington
    14

Winter, Thomas 12, 14, 15
Winwood, Sir Ralph 32, 34
Witt, John de, Grand
        Pensionary 133, 153, 198
Wotton, Sir Henry 52, 152
Wright, Christopher 14, 15
Wright, John 12, 14, 15
Würtemberg, John Frederick,
    Duke of 45

Zizka the Hussite 43
Zuylestein, Frederick 221